Crosby, Stills,
Nash and Young's
50-Year Quest

Crosby, Stills, Nash and Young's 50-Year Quest

Music to Change the World

ROBERT MCPARLAND

McFarland & Company, Inc., Publishers

Jefferson, North Carolina

LIBRARY OF CONGRESS CATALOGUING-IN-PUBLICATION DATA

Names: McParland, Robert, author.
Title: Crosby, Stills, Nash and Young : music to change the world /
    Robert McParland.
Description: Jefferson, North Carolina : McFarland & Company,
    2019. | Includes bibliographical references and index.
Identifiers: LCCN 2019003398 | ISBN 9781476674896 (paperback :
    acid free paper) ∞
Subjects: LCSH: Crosby, Stills, Nash & Young. | Rock musicians—
    United States—Biography.
Classification: LCC ML421.C76 M36 2019 | DDC 782.42166092/2
    [B] —dc23
LC record available at https://lccn.loc.gov/2019003398

BRITISH LIBRARY CATALOGUING DATA ARE AVAILABLE

ISBN (print) 978-1-4766-7489-6
ISBN (ebook) 978-1-4766-3600-9

Front cover: *left to right* Graham Nash, David Crosby, Neil Young
and Stephen Stills (Atlantic Records/Photofest)

Printed in the United States of America

*McFarland & Company, Inc., Publishers
    Box 611, Jefferson, North Carolina 28640
    www.mcfarlandpub.com*

Table of Contents

Preface

This book brings together pieces from various sources to provide an overview of Crosby, Stills, Nash and Young. The 50th anniversary of Woodstock in 2019 provides a symbolic marker of a time when rock music came together with a feeling of community and a sense of possibility. Woodstock was the place of the second concert by CSN&Y. Representative of a generation, Woodstock suggested harmony, a space apart from contemporary violence. Crosby, Stills, Nash and Young, of course, were so much more than Woodstock. They represented the hope of that moment. They became a voice with a claim to being heard. In poignant songs, in vocal harmonies, in their concern for human rights, they entranced their listeners and became an important fixture in the rock music firmament. This they accomplished despite—or perhaps because of—their fierce independence and sensitive artistry.

This book is written in appreciation of these four uniquely talented musicians who first joined together about fifty years ago during a tempestuous time of social ferment and change. While drawing upon published sources, this volume rests upon questions: What became of the idealism of the generation that once sought community, peace, freedom, and human rights as they joined together at events like the first Woodstock festival? What are our American dreams today? And where has America come to now? As an appreciation and overview of Crosby, Stills, Nash and Young, this survey of their work is for general readers. It presents an overview of their work; it does not present an academic argument. Given the extensive catalog of each of these musicians, this text does not attempt to be comprehensive. Rather, it looks at more than fifty years of accomplishment with gratitude and seeks to provide an introduction and encouragement to people to listen to their work.

Preface

Of course, a book is only words: interpretations, gestures, hand signals pointing to the music and public expression of Crosby, Stills, Nash and Young. As you explore these pages, I hope that you will explore their music. The almost staggering creative output of these four men has contributed something lasting. Crosby, Stills, Nash and Young represent a hopeful cultural voice still underscoring the quest for human rights while making music that is memorable, inspiring, and affecting. In 1988 they recorded *American Dream*. Today some people ask, what has become of American dreams? In this broad, pluralistic democracy, what has become of kindness and care, unity, dialogue, and integrity? Graham Nash, in the final phrases of his song "Chicago," once held the hope that we can change the world. It is clearly an ideal and a visionary faith to believe that we have that capacity. For each life can change a bit of the world. Certainly, music alone cannot change things. Yet, it can inspire us; it can do fine things to move our emotions, to stir our hearts, and awaken our minds. That inspiration that resides within the music and the earnest commitment of Crosby, Stills, Nash and Young is what this book is dedicated to.

On a personal note, I also dedicate this book to Walter G. Smith, for his friendship and irrepressible love of music. Across the years he has traveled with me as soundman, home recording guru, fellow CSN&Y concertgoer, and folk coffeehouse companion. This is for all the times we've sung "Teach Your Children" and the music we've shared. It hasn't exactly been the Marrakesh Express but it's been an interesting journey.

Introduction

Music to Change the World

Crosby, Stills, Nash and Young are one of the most enduring and creative music acts who emerged during a pivotal time in recent American life and culture, from 1968 into the 1970s. Their distinctive vocal harmonies, characteristic blend of folk, blues, rock, and jazz-inflected music, and social and political stance have persisted across more than four decades. They have become a familiar part of the lives of thousands of people. Crosby, Stills, Nash and Young are rock music icons. Highly influential in the early 1970s, their work has remained vital to the present day and thousands of fans buy their recordings, buy their autobiographies, and attend their concerts.

This volume might be called "Crosby, Stills, Nash and Young: An Appreciation." It gathers material about them from a wide variety of sources. David Crosby, Graham Nash, and Neil Young have written memoirs and their recollections are illuminating. Yet, these fascinating stories alone do not tell us why Crosby, Stills, Nash and Young have become a lasting voice for the culture. *Crosby, Stills, Nash and Young's 50-Year Quest: Music to Change the World* examines the songs and themes of Crosby Stills, Nash and Young that continue to resonate among us. Several of these themes are anchored in the hopes of the generation of which they remain representative: the social and political climate of the late 1960s and early to mid–1970s. For some listeners, the voices of David Crosby, Stephen Stills, Graham Nash and Neil Young recall a time when they were young and were also experiencing those social currents. For others, they are "classic rock," legendary voices recalling the richness of rock music's history. Or they are an interesting, influential folk-rock sound, a cultural and musical experience. They remain voices for now. The musicianship of Stephen Stills, the rich singing voice and social concern of the now gray haired and thin Graham Nash, the voluble expressiveness and musicality of David Crosby are a present experience as well as evocative of memories. Their popularity, their themes, and their influence, while recalling the sixties and seventies, persist beyond it. They are part of the present voice of America.

Crosby, Stills, Nash, and Young have been part of our cultural life since the 1960s. Since you've picked up this book, chances are that you've heard them. You're familiar with their music. You've probably heard of the soap opera of their interpersonal feuds. That is, you've heard stories of the conflict that brews when four strong-willed personalities mix like chemicals in different variations that can be life enhancing or simply volatile and combustible. Yet, if you're like me, you might stand in a kind of near-overwhelmed respect for their popular music artistry and how much there is to explore in the ideas, messages, and emotions they have conveyed. The variety of recordings by these singer-songwriters can feel overwhelming. By listening to their solo albums and duo recordings one can begin to trace some of the phases of their creativity.

We can get to know Crosby, Stills, Nash and Young individually a little better through a plentiful array of videos of interviews that are available on YouTube. There are numerous other interviews with David Crosby, Stephen Stills, Graham Nash, and Neil Young that have appeared in print. These range across the fifty years from 1968–69 to the present. In the interviews they tell us some things about their songs, their lives, and their commitments to humanity, environmental and political awareness, and social justice. Their music is available for streaming, or on CD.

The period of the 1960s and the early 1970s is "a powerful memory shaping contemporary discussion," observes Alexander Bloom.[1] Music embodied the underlying themes of the sixties generation, he points out. In the music was "the same sense of creating something new and something better" as there was in political and social reform movements.[2] Having emerged during this time, Crosby, Stills, Nash and Young and the humanistic values they represent are part of the broader story of contemporary American culture, part of a history that threads through present

American experience. An examination of the songs and themes of Crosby, Stills, Nash and Young is important to us because they are part of our story, and the mysterious force of music and the call of stories is deeply important to the imagined community which is America. To recall the story of Crosby, Stills, Nash and Young is to ask again what the labels folk-rock, or "classic" rock, or "the sixties" might mean. It is also to ask what American means. Crosby, Stills, Nash and Young, as icons of the sixties and seventies, reflect idealism, commitment, a belief in the possibility of changing the world. They represent the romantic, utopian hope that led to the liberalizing of American culture and to turning points in race and gender and rights. Because they still sing and create and speak out, they remain controversial and relevant.

Every listener has a unique sensibility and experience of life. We may approach music and interpret lyrics differently. This book is an invitation to listening to Crosby, Stills, Nash and Young. It intends to be a gathering that is best extended by your participation as a listener and your exploration of their autobiographies and of articles written about them in a variety of publications. This volume, which includes some commentary and retrospective, is indebted to the writers and critics who have interviewed Crosby, Stills, Nash and Young or seen them up close. The book is written in appreciation of each of these musicians and their contribution.

Crosby, Stills, Nash and Young are arguably one of the most representative music groups of the 1968–1974 years during which there was considerable social-political tension in American life. In the first chapter, we learn who they are, how they joined together, and why they are significant, as representatives of the emerging "sixties" generation and beyond. The meeting of Crosby, Stills, Nash and Young was fortunate, like an alignment of the stars. Yet, the new group was also forged by music businessmen with commercial instincts. Their work on their first album began with the rich blending of their voices and musical talents as they worked to create their defining sound. Graham Nash's song "Marrakesh Express" reflected an entire generation's desire for a journey toward new possibilities. "Marrakesh Express" was a journey to an exotic, new geography that broke with Western conventions and norms. It suggested the quest of a generation. That train offered the idea of motion and change, the possibility of newness and the hope for transformation that the sixties were about. It brought listeners on a bright, sensual journey—not only to Morocco but to all of those inner and outer places worth exploring. One could image the air filled with the richness of smoke and spices and dreams. With this song, Crosby, Stills, and Nash reflected their audience of the sixties, who sought new sensations, a sense of freedom, and a new vision or model for experience. The seven-and-a-half-minute "Suite: Judy Blue Eyes" by Stephen Stills characterized Crosby, Stills, and Nash's musical range and sound. "Teach Your Children" by Graham Nash was another single, characterized by smooth harmonies and Jerry Garcia's pedal steel guitar. The song called for dialogue and mutual understanding. It announced Crosby, Stills and Nash's hope and confidence youth and in future generations.

While continuing the story chronologically, there are reflections on the albums *Déjà Vu*, *Crosby Stills and Nash*, and *4 Way Street*. These albums comprise some of their strongest and most memorable work together. This section investigates the music, the themes and ideas within their songs. Elements of material culture of this period enable readers to identify the band's orientation: Crosby's boat *The Mayan*, blue jeans, the peace sign, hair, "the garden," "our house," images from their album covers. Stills' musical instruments convey the meeting of different musical styles. With Woodstock, in summer 1969, a fourth member, Neil Young, joined this entourage. Young was fiercely independent, ever following his own star, and he practiced a loose affiliation with the others. Yet, he contributed considerably to the dynamics of this group's most productive and memorable years. When National Guardsmen fired upon student protesters at Kent State four students died. Appalled by this, Neil Young wrote "Ohio," recording the horror. The lyric immediately offers us the image of "tin soldiers," associating them with "Nixon coming." The vocal identified with the fallen. The singer asked his audience: "what if you knew her?" Shock filled the lyric with vowels that exclaimed "uh": "coming," "summer," "drumming," "gunning," "us," "done," "run." These sounds alternated with other tight short vowels and the open "oh" of "on our own" and "Ohio." Crosby, Stills, Nash, and Young recorded "Ohio" within twenty-four hours of the event in an aggressive and scathing indictment of grinding guitars in D minor, a stomping rhythmic march, and plaintive vocals.

Neil Young has had an extensive and productive music career. He has been so influential and so prolific that a book on CSN&Y one can hardly give him his just due. However, he has been a necessary part of the CSN&Y sound and story. A chapter is devoted to an overview of Neil Young's work with reference to Crosby, Stills, Nash and Young.

"Going Solo" presents the solo albums and duos. This chapter provides a closer analysis of the Crosby, Stills, and Nash (and sometimes Young) albums and singles from their first releases through the mid–1970s. This includes an analysis of lyrical concepts, songwriting craft, arrangements and production, and the critical response to each record. The chapters will be focused on their key albums together. Their solo work is mentioned in passing but is not emphasized. Rather, the albums *Déjà vu* and *Crosby, Stills and Nash* are treated in detail, song by song. *So Far* is a compilation recording and *4 Way Street*, similarly, is a live album primarily of previously recorded songs. These are noted but are given less detailed attention.

Crosby, Stills, and Nash—and sometimes Youn—have been an on and off again phenomenon and it is important to recognize the solo work by each of them. This chapter recognizes the diversity and individuality of each of these musicians. There is a detailed examination of the music and themes of their early solo albums and duo efforts to encourage the reader to listen to them. Neil Young's work, at this point, is addressed only where necessary. As Stephen Stills wrote in "Helplessly Hoping," they are one, they are two together, and they are for (four) each other. Their solo work and duo combinations are an essential part of their creative contribution. However, it is as a group that they gain the most strength and are most popular. It is their combination of talents as CSN&Y that is the focus here. Their recent solo work is discussed in the final section.

Central to this book is a cultural analysis of "the sixties" and the 1970s and their meaning for us today. "Almost Cut My Hair: Lifestyle, Social Concerns and the Sixties" takes its title from David Crosby's song and explores the mind-set and dream of getting back to the garden, to something natural, to consciousness and community. Through attention to the popular music of Crosby, Stills, Nash and Young and to the themes addressed by them, we will look at their commitment to social issues and reform connects with American culture and experience in the late sixties into the seventies. The "sixties" generation, the fusion of folk and rock music, and the rise of the singer-songwriter in the 1960s and 1970s are all central to the Crosby, Stills, Nash and Young story. Placing them and their work in historical and cultural context is the focus of this chapter. Fifty years after Woodstock, we might consider the strengths and weaknesses of popular cultural analyses of that period.

We move on to consider the music making of Crosby, Stills, Nash and Young since 1976. The guitar-based romanticism of the singer songwriter seventies dissolved, in part, into punk, or other forms, as commercial disco took the airwaves in the mid- to late 1970s. David Crosby's "long time gone" into drug addiction and Graham Nash's role, as a friend, in his recovery is part of the story here. The key albums are the 1977 *CSN* album and the 1988 *American Dream* album, for which they joined with Neil Young.

In 1988, Crosby, Stills, Nash and Young released *American Dream*, their first studio album in 18 years. They sang "Night Song," Crosby's "Compass," which was a song of redemption, and Nash's "Soldiers of Peace." This section covers their work through the 1980s and 1990s beyond the year 2000. A very strong fan base emerged at this time, as a Gallup Poll indicated in the 1990s. This section examines that revival and the growth of their fan base among new audiences, while continuing the analysis of their songs across this period of more than two decades.

The final section of this book observes that Crosby, Stills, Nash and Young today are continuing to perform actively as individual acts. This chapter focuses upon developments in their work. They performed several concerts in the first years of the twenty-first century, first spurred on by 9/11 to tour again. Neil Young became part of these tours and the concerts were financially very successful. This chapter explains what they are doing creatively today as solo artists, where they are performing, and why they remain iconic and popular. This final section explores their most recent solo albums and considers their disputes and their political and social concerns. It shows you where you can find Crosby, Stills, Nash and Young on YouTube videos. The bibliography will point you to further reading and resources. This appreciation of their craft and musical contribution intends to reaffirm why Crosby, Stills, Nash and Young are important for us culturally and to suggest what we can continue to gain by listening to them.

1

Beginnings

Becoming Crosby, Stills, Nash and Young

Often by night they are on a stage, visiting some restless city under the stars. From a shadowy region beyond the stage an audience flickers like stars of their own, restless, anticipating, wearing green and blue and other colors, moving, almost dancing, then becoming still, falling into an expectant hush as the recorded music is turned down. With the first notes of the band the lights come up. The audience breaks into applause. Crosby, Stills, Nash and Young songs burst into public spaces every day with their distinctive harmonies. Their vocal harmonies, characteristic blend of folk, blues, rock, and jazz-inflected music, and social and political stance have graced the airwaves across more than five decades. Their creative and enduring music has become a familiar part of thousands of people's lives. Crosby, Stills, Nash and Young are icons of what are sometimes called "the sixties," although their off and on again work as a group began at the very end of that decade. They have been influential voices in popular music ever since. Because the songs and themes of Crosby, Stills, Nash and Young continue to resonate among us, we need to think about what their songs, their sound, and their ideas mean to people. Today a Crosby, Stills, Nash and Young song might burst out on the speakers of a shopping center, blending with the background sounds of mainstream life. The song may rise over the rumble of voices in a bar, or it may be streamed by satellite radio across car speakers as one drives. For example, you might hear Stephen Stills' guitar breaking into that first musical phrase of "Wooden Ships," and the rich blend of harmonies following it. Some listeners recall the radical edge to their songs, the countercultural voice in them. For others it is a pleasant sound, as they simply go about their business. The music of Crosby, Stills, Nash and Young has become a soundtrack that people recognize and carry with them.

While CSN&Y continue evolving as individual artists, they remain representative of a time in contemporary history, a way of life. They are readily associated with the social and political climate of the late 1960s and early to mid 1970s. For older listeners, the voices of David Crosby, Stephen Stills, Graham Nash and Neil Young recall a time when they were young and were experiencing those social currents. For thousands of younger listeners who were not yet born when CSN&Y made their mark upon popular consciousness, they are legendary voices recalling the richness of rock music's history. They offer an interesting, influential folkrock sound, a cultural and musical experience that is now part of our collective memory. The musicianship of Stephen Stills, the rich singing voice and social concern of the now gray haired and thin Graham Nash, the voluble expressiveness and musicality of David Crosby, and the edginess and creativity of Neil Young, who has remained remarkably current, are a present experience as well evocative of memories. Their popularity, their themes, and their influence persist. They are part of the present voice of America.

Crosby, Stills, Nash and Young are also part of the story of American culture, part of a history that threads through American experience. That is something we might begin to explore here. Some years ago, Todd Gitlin wrote: "the genies that the sixties loosed are still abroad in the land, inspiring and unsettling, making trouble and offending."[1] Crosby, Stills, Nash and Young remain part of this spirit. Their story is important to us because it is part of our story. It is a story in which the mysterious force of music and the call of stories is deeply important to our world. For Crosby, Stills, Nash and Young are dreamers of a new world, musical storytellers in a nation in which stories connect families, cross generations, and enrich communities. They are rock bards engaged in story-making and songwriting with a message: one that calls us to confront problems, to transform them, and to sustain life.

To recall the story of Crosby, Stills, Nash and Young is to ask again what the labels folk-rock, or "classic" rock, or "the sixties" might mean. It is also to ask what America means. America in 2019 is still struggling for self-definition. It is a house divided politically in need of a dialogue about race, immigration, health care, economic fairness, and the environment. It is a dream that urges renewed moral grounding. Crosby, Stills, Nash and Young, as icons of the sixties and seventies reflect idealism, commitment, and a belief in the possibility of changing the world. Emerging during a period of disastrous war, civil rights strife, and a loss of faith in government, Crosby, Stills, Nash and Young represented the romantic, utopian hope that led to the liberalizing of American culture and turning points in race and gender and civil rights. As representatives of a counterculture that some conservatives believed was better off left behind, they prompted neo-conservative criticisms of excess. Now, years later, they continue to sing and create and speak out and they remain relevant.

The root of CSN&Y is undeniably in the sixties: David Crosby with the Byrds, Stephen Stills and Neil Young with the Buffalo Springfield, Graham Nash with the Hollies. Together they became one of the quintessential early 1970s groups who anchored the radicalism of their cultural vision in folk-rock music. Philip Jenkins, in *Decade of Nightmares*, recognizes the importance of peace and changing authoritarian structures that emerged in what we call "the sixties." He believes that "a marked change of the national mood occurred in the mid–1970s" and lets us wonder if this was a change of fading idealism, or a return to stability. Stephen Paul Miller reflects upon the "transition … the sixties put into play." He suggests that America in the decade of the 1970s was "incorporating the sixties mores." Perhaps, it was trying to overcome them, as well as to integrate them. Miller notes that "we still debate the Vietnam war," and although we have now moved to "a different cultural mindset," clearly "the sixties is not quite over" and "the sixties shape our ontological horizon." Perhaps the sixties also left us with some unfinished business, he adds. If this is so, we may agree with Alexander Bloom when he concludes: "The decade maintains a unique place in contemporary life, unlike that of any previous era." And something else he says rings true: "Music seemed central to the entire 60s experience, not the narrowly defined cultural role it plays today."[2] Crosby, Stills, Nash and Young were at the very center of this phenomenon.

So, listening to Crosby, Stills, Nash and Young today continues to evoke an important time in recent American history and cultural memory.

They continue to inspire us and to remind us of issues that we are still dealing with. References to CSN&Y come from many places. For example, Brenda Laurel, a Silicon Valley computer media expert, comments about the humanistic values she drew from a period when "Laura Nyro, and Crosby, Stills and Nash was woven into the fabric of my identity." Mark Massa, points to Graham Nash's song "Chicago" as he refers to America's youth and the state of the church today. Diane Snyder Cowin reports in *Music Therapy Perspectives* that a therapist had suggested their music, along with some "new age" music, to patients to reduce their anxiety before surgery.[3]

Crosby, Stills, Nash, and Young remain important because these musicians collectively and individually reflected an era. They became an influential part of people's awareness and they continue to be engaged in social concerns and creating new music. When the grinding D minor chords of "Ohio" burn across the radio from Neil Young's guitar, one may recall how Richard Nixon appeared to promise an end to war and shifted tactics with air strikes and incursion into Cambodia. Some may recall this as a strategic move in the war effort, while others who were appalled remember the student protests of Spring 1970 and the tragic deaths and injuries at Kent State that brought sorrow, horror, and seemed to break some people's idealism. Crosby, Stills, Nash and Young, in this sense, represent a vision and a hope, the meaning of alternative lifestyles that permeated American society, the impact of a style and a voice of protest that spread across North America, Europe, and elsewhere in the world.

When Lloyd Jansen reviewed Don Zimmer's *4 Way Street: The Crosby, Stills, Nash, and Young Reader* for *Library Journal* (February 15, 2004) he began by critiquing what he called "their quaint hippie earnestness" but went on to acknowledge that "their impact on pop music is undeniable." That book, he noted, "assumes that the reader already knows why Crosby, Stills, Nash and Young is important."[4] This one, which does not make that assumption, will give you the Crosby, Stills, Nash and Young story and a sense of their music in relation to American culture. It will provide you with an overview of their history, brief descriptions of their recordings, listings of online sources, videos, and books so that you can explore their substantial output further.

The names of Crosby, Stills, Nash and Young are forever linked interpersonally, as they are in their music. However, the rock press has often revealed stories of disharmony between these talented songwriter-musicians. Part of their remarkable story is how they have consistently created compelling music despite these disagreements. Vocalists have to listen to each other to sing harmony and they need to feel connected with each other to sense each other's timing. Crosby, Stills, Nash and Young have done this well. Stills remains a strong instrumentalist, gritty and bluesy. Nash's vocal is like the thread that winds through the music like a choir tenor's bell-like tone. Crosby's tenor is like crystal, a voice David Fricke in *Rolling Stone* once compared with a cello. Young remains a force to be reckoned in the rock music industry. Now, a bit heavier, a bit grayer, and a bit wiser, they stand alone. For years they stood side by side on stages across the world.

Among the remarkable aspects of the long musical life of Crosby, Stills, Nash and Young is their audience. This includes fans across several generations, many of whom first encountered the group in the 1980s or the 1990s, or after 2000. It is this audience that affirms that Crosby, Stills, Nash and Young remain engaging and relevant and that their musical relationship with each other is expressive of an ongoing artwork that is ever creative and not merely nostalgic. In recent years, the prolific Neil Young continues to create cutting edge music. Stephen Stills has joined with Judy Collins to both recall the past and to create something new. Graham Nash has explored photography, found new life after a divorce, and has given us *This Path Tonight* and a career retrospective. David Crosby found some happiness with family and has entered an extraordinary songwriting streak, recording and performing songs on *Croz, Lighthouse, Sky Trails* and *Here If You Listen*. Yet, as beautiful as their work can be, these sensitive, ego-strong, and sometimes quirky personalities once tossed together can be combustible.

The creativity and tension that make up Crosby, Stills, Nash, and Young can be attributed to the fact that each of them is a uniquely talented individual. David Crosby is the son Floyd and Aliph Crosby. They named their first son Floyd and he would be known as Chip. David was born August 14, 1941. David Crosby's father was a cinematographer for *Talu* and *High Noon*. He played some mandolin. His mother had a classical music collection of 78 rpm records. The family played and sang the *Fireside Book of Folk Songs*. Chip liked jazz and David came to know the work of Dave Brubeck, Chet Baker, Gerry Mulligan and others. The jazz influences are plentiful in David Crosby's music and lend an almost scat singing quality to "Déjà Vu" and other cuts. More recently, songs like "She's Got to Be Somewhere," by James Raymond, suggest a bit of Steely Dan. The Crosby family moved from Los Angeles to Santa Barbara and David Crosby tried out acting. He sang blues and folk at the Unicorn Club and Sunset Boulevard. In 1963, he met with the musicians with whom he would form the Byrds.

Stephen Stills has southern roots. He was raised in the Midwest in Indiana and Southern Illinois by his parents, William and Talitha Stills. Before Stephen was born, his father booked bands in the Champaign, Illinois, area and did engineering work for Westinghouse. The family then moved to Dallas, Texas, where Stephen was born. The family moved to Illinois and then to Louisiana, as William Stills worked a variety of jobs in construction and engineering, including construction and the molasses industry. Stephen heard everything on the family phonograph from Leadbelly blues to the jazz of Bix Beiderbecke, Cole Porter, and the Dorseys. He started playing the drums at the age of eight. The family moved again, to Florida. He attended a military academy in St. Petersburg for a time. He picked up the guitar and began to play. He especially played blues on his guitar.

Graham Nash is the one with the British accent. William and Mary Nash raised him several thousand miles and an ocean away in northern England. Graham Nash's father had experience in the British army and worked at a foundry. The family knew some English folk songs but there was not a great deal of music in the home. Mostly the atmosphere was that of working class labor and a father who returned home after working long hours. Graham Nash met Allan Clarke in school, where they sang in a school chorus, and they remained friends. It could be expected that Graham Nash would enter that English Midlands tradition of becoming an apprentice in a trade. He worked in a factory, an engineering firm, post offices, and at a tailor shop. However, he also sang and made music with Allen Clarke. In 1961, he and Allen were "Ricky and Dave." They listened to rhythm and blues records, to Chuck Berry, the Coasters, and the Zodiacs. In 1962, Nash, Clarke, Eric Haydock, Don Rathbone, and Tony Hicks became the Hollies. They derived their name from their interest in Buddy

1. Beginnings

Holly and soon were developing an audience in the north of England. They soon played the Cavern Club in Liverpool. The band would break into the pop mainstream, following the Beatles' success with their rich harmonies.

Neil Young is a Canadian. He made the trip to the United States with other Canadian musicians and landed in the Los Angeles area when the time was ripe for the convergence of folk and rock. His father Scott was a journalist and sportswriter who also wrote fiction. His mother Edna hailed from the Daughters of the American Revolution. Neil Young contracted polio as a child in Ontario. He lived in a small town there and later in Winnipeg and in Toronto. He was drawn to popular music he heard on the radio.

Crosby, Stills, Nash and Young converged in 1968. Crosby came from the Byrds (1964–1967), Nash from the Hollies (1962–1968), and Stills from Buffalo Springfield (1966–1968). Their sometime collaborator Neil Young, who had worked with Stills in Buffalo Springfield, came along for the ride in 1969 and joined Crosby, Stills and Nash intermittently thereafter. Together, they appeared at Woodstock, their second public concert, and they soon had an extraordinary impact on the pop music charts. The "sixties" generation they emerged from, the fusion of folk and rock music, and the rise of the singer-songwriter in the 1960s and 1970s are all central to the CSN&Y story. The period saw the intersection of the Byrds and Buffalo Springfield members, the emerging West coast sound of the Eagles, Linda Ronstadt, Jackson Browne, Warren Zevon and others, the connection of J.D. Souther, Chris Hillman, and Richie Furay. There was a fusion of rock, blues, and country filled with vocal harmonies. Their close relationship with Canadian folk singer Joni Mitchell and their at times contentious interactions with Neil Young and with each other were crucial to their development.

The first songs that Crosby, Stills and Nash sang together were in the summer of 1968. Their mutual discovery of the richness of their vocal harmonies may have occurred at Joni Mitchell's home, as Nash and Crosby recall, or at Cass Elliott's home, as Stills contends. After singing together in the living room, they then turned to the stage at the Troubadour in Los Angeles. One might call this a key moment in popular music. Three distinct individuals, with rather headstrong egos, would have to find the flexibility to make room for each other. They would sing solos, duos, and all three would sing together, sometimes linking with a fourth member, Neil Young and his shaky tenor vocals. They would become the most fluid of groups: appearing together, vanishing into their own lives and their own projects, and then reuniting. They would adopt and blend a variety of musical forms: blues, jazz, folk, pop, soul, and country. Through it all, their richly harmonized songs would carry notions of peace, protest, social responsibility, democracy, and high ideals.

In the summer months of 1968 they began singing at Joni Mitchell's house on Lookout Mountain Road and/or at Mama Cass's house. You might imagine a Volkswagen turning around a corner in Laurel Canyon and a musician with wild hair and a looping mustache driving it. The car did not sound like a Volkswagen because David Crosby, that musician, had just had a Porsche engine installed in it. It was a compact vehicle and it had a round hood and that VW was shifting gears and so was Crosby. He was heading out to visit Mama Cass Elliott. Crosby preferred the San Francisco sound and Jefferson Airplane to what the Byrds were doing at the time. He received a buyout from the band for about $10,000 and he had gotten that Volkswagen and a new boat. Crosby was now free of his commitment to the Byrds and their record company and had signed on with Elliott Roberts as his manager. Now new plans awaited and not far around the bend, on the road up ahead, there would be a new combination of personalities—Stephen Stills and Graham Nash—and new sounds to join Crosby's dreamy, jazz-inflected music.

That VW bug buzzing out to Laurel Canyon was one of the stars of summer 1968. It came in bright primary colors. Sometimes a peace sign appeared on the side of a Volkswagen. The car even found its way into a movie: *The Love Bug*. David Crosby's VW pulled up and parked outside the home of Mama Cass, by birth Naomi Cohen of Baltimore. She had transformed her home into a place of welcome, an artistic salon that might be likened to the nineteenth century artistic salons of Madame de Stahl. One might say it also reflected today's house concerts. Here the gathering was informal, a community in the making, and it was graced by some extraordinary talent.

The merging of the four musicians in Los Angeles was facilitated in some respects by Cass Elliott. Crosby brought Nash to a gathering at the home of Peter Tork of the Monkees and introduced him to Stephen Stills.

---

1. *Beginnings*

At that time, Stills' band Buffalo Springfield was near the point of dissolving. Neil Young had become increasingly distant from the group's activities. Ever the individualist, Neil Young had moved apart and in his own direction. He had avoided a television appearance on the *Tonight Show* and the group's performance at Monterey Pop. Buffalo Springfield was unraveling and both Stephen Stills and Neil Young had begun seeking other possibilities. Crosby and Stills were innovative and competitive but stifled in their bands. They were seeking something new.

David Crosby had been writing ethereal songs that did not match the Byrds' musical direction. He could be as irascible as he was creative, and tensions arose in the band. In August 1967 there was a parting of the ways between Crosby and McGuinn, Hillman, and Gene Clark and Michael Clarke. Crosby was experimenting musically. He was also experimenting with drugs, unlocking mind and body in a hedonistic lifestyle.

Graham Nash was still under contract with the Hollies in 1968. He performed with the Hollies when they went on tour. In Ottawa, he met Joni Mitchell and felt attracted to her even before she began to play her songs. Then the artistry of her songs overwhelmed him. He recalls that he was "awestruck."[5] Nash, meanwhile, was increasingly dissatisfied with the pop song shallowness he was churning out with the Hollies. Change had begun to blow away the familiar cords of his marriage and his connection with the band. Nash was drawn in new directions: toward expressionist art, toward Los Angeles, and more deeply into his photography. He had also begun to sing with Stephen Stills and David Crosby. A rich and surprising sound came when they harmonized, a rare alchemy, with Nash's voice riding above that of Stills and Crosby's vocal textures filling in the middle.

Stills, who had written Buffalo Springfield's biggest hit, "For What It's Worth," brought to the informal session with Crosby and Nash his new songs, like "Helplessly Hoping," and his dazzling musicianship. Stills was watching his band Buffalo Springfield dissolving. Richie Furay had begun assembling Poco with Jim Messina. Neil Young, drifting away from Buffalo Springfield, had worked out a record deal with Reprise Records, a subsidiary of Warner Bros.

For several months, the new connection between Crosby, Stills, and Nash was undefined. They were three people hanging out together, singing the songs that they were creating. Crosby had put his experiences with the Byrds behind him. He brought to their sessions his songs "Guinevere" and "Long Time Gone." Nash had written "Teach Your Children" and "Marrakesh Express," which would later be CSN's first hit singles. A trip to Morocco inspired Nash's "Marrakesh Express" and art, photography, and a concern for the world lay behind his song "Teach Your Children." In his autobiography, Nash recalls that he was moved by a photograph by Diane Arbus of a boy in Central Park holding a plastic grenade. It was a warning that a vulnerable and innocent world could be overtaken, that the future held the prospect of violence. The human future depended upon teaching children about love, peace, and respect. These themes would remain at the core of Crosby, Stills and Nash and their recordings. Nash says that the pace of "Teach Your Children" was, at first, slow and its atmosphere was "eerie."[6] It was unlike the folk-country sounding song with which we are familiar: a song filled with harmonies and Jerry Garcia's distinctive steel pedal guitar hook that has become a radio classic. Songs like this have changed as they have passed from creation to performance, but the social and political concern of Crosby, Stills, and Nash has remained constant across the years.

The adventure began in 1968. On November 1 of that year Crosby, Stills and Nash boarded a plane to London. Ahmet Ertegun, the president of Atlantic Records, had given Stills money to finance their journey. This became a focused incubation period for them, as they blended into a group. The experience each of them had with harmonizing formed their sound. Their vocals merged spontaneously; they worked through this intuitively, supported by a knowledge based upon previous years of harmonizing. They sang Stills' "Helplessly Hoping," "49 Reasons," "You Don't Have to Cry," and Crosby's "Almost Cut My Hair," "Wooden Ships," "Guinevere," and "Long Time Gone." They breathed new life into Nash's "King Midas in Reverse" and "Lady of the Island" and sang "Teach Your Children" and "Marrakesh Express." Nash had a new team, new musical partners with whom to sing the songs that the Hollies would never record. It was a new beginning. Three unique individuals—Crosby, Stills, and Nash— were formulating a musical partnership and interdependence.

It has been said by many cultural critics that community is achieved through tension, as well as cooperation. Crosby, Stills, and Nash have had their share of both. Their squabbles with each other have been legendary. One may wonder at how such brilliant vocal harmony could arise from three individuals who were so often pulling apart in interpersonal disharmony. Yet, like a dysfunctional family, they have continued in their music. The rub of voice against voice, parallel vocals and the pull of dissonance, have made their creations different from harmonies that more simply make use of the parts of a chord. The common way to achieve a strong harmony is to sing a triad: to start with the tonic or root, the base of a chord, the key it is in. Above this comes the third, a middle tone, sung by the second voice. The third voice may climb a whole octave, singing the same note as the first vocalist, eight tones higher. Crosby, Stills, and Nash sometimes do this. However, they often engage in more complex harmonies.

In the record grooves of rock music history, there are several harmony-sounds that are quite memorable. The vocal magic of the Everly Brothers deeply influenced the Hollies, the Beatles, and other groups of the 1960s. The mid to late 1960s was filled with vocal delights: from the Mamas and Papas, the Turtles, and the Beach Boys, to the Byrds and Buffalo Springfield. In the 1970s we heard from Poco, the Eagles, Alabama, the Doobie Brothers, Orleans, the Little River Band and many others who featured male vocal harmonies. However, in some respects, Crosby, Stills, and Nash rose up the charts with something exquisite and unmatched.

Musical harmony is something different from interpersonal harmony, however. It is difficult to keep a band together. A traveling musician is pulled away from home, from life's anchors and grounding. Headstrong, sensitive artists are forced to live with each other and to deal with each other's personalities. Along with public adulation comes criticism, the highs and lows of a career; there are personal issues, creative issues, sometimes drug addiction. Yet, these people are compelled to sing and make music. In part, they do it for the financial profits that come from such work. Yet, they are sustained by the sheer love of the music and the sound they can produce when together. After the many years and miles, the tensions and their differences, they still recognize that there is wonder in it.

When Crosby, Stills, and Nash first joined forces, David Crosby's relationship with Christine Hinton was developing. She had started a Crosby fan club with her friend Debbie Donovan and the relationship with Crosby became intimate. Joni Mitchell, who had spent time with Crosby, became closer to Graham Nash. As they became increasingly serious about the music they were making together, Crosby, Stills, and Nash sought a space away from Laurel Canyon. In Nash's view, it was "too social."[7] So, they left the West Coast for the East Coast, upon the suggestion of John Sebastian of the Lovin' Spoonful, who pointed them toward a quiet retreat in Long Island. Sag Harbor in the Hamptons, in winter, was isolated. From there they could travel into Manhattan to the Record Plant, where Paul Rothchild recorded some demos with them. He was aiming for precision and they found his working methods too rigid. So, they aimed at finding a good engineer and producing a record themselves.

David Geffen now entered the picture. He was a brash entrepreneur, who Nash has described as "fast-talking, intimidating, fearless, a punk."[8] Those qualities added up to a sharp, ambitious businessman who could take them places. Geffen had managed songwriter Laura Nyro's recording career. An aggressive fighter, he now teamed up with Elliot Roberts, who was managing Joni Mitchell and Neil Young at the time. Geffen pursued a record contract for CSN with Ahmet Ertegun, the president of Atlantic Records.

Existing contracts precluded the new connection between Crosby, Stills, and Nash. Stills remained signed to Atco Records and he was tied by his Buffalo Springfield commitment. Crosby had been released from his connection with the Byrds. Nash was still a member of the Hollies, on Epic Records. Deals had to be made so that they could work together for another record label. Poco and Richie Furay agreed to sign with Epic and Nash left the Hollies, to be free to record on Atlantic Records. Buffalo Springfield dissolved. Stills was now free to work with Nash and Crosby. They each signed with Atlantic Records. The names Crosby, Stills, and Nash became linked formally, but, since each of their names was involved, no individual could lay claim to the band. In the 1990s, Gene Clark toured with a group of musicians who called themselves the Byrds. The group did not include Roger McGuinn or Chris Hillman. That kind of use of a band name, or brand name, for the commercial purposes of some band members exclusive of the other band members, would never happen with Crosby, Stills, and Nash.

---

1. Beginnings

What would the first album sound like? Initially, they sat together with acoustic guitars and joined their voices on their songs. There was a strong folk and blues dimension to their acoustic work. Yet, they were also folk rockers; each of their bands had been among the premier folk-rock groups of the 1960s, whose electric guitars and harmony vocals created some of the distinctive sounds of that era. Stephen Stills was a particularly versatile musician; he played guitar, piano, bass, and banjo all well. He was a talented arranger with a very good ear and he could lay down a strong musical foundation for every song on his own. However, to play their music live, they needed other musicians. They needed a drummer, a bass guitar player, and someone to play keyboards, while Stills was playing lead guitar. So, Crosby, Stills, and Nash turned to Dallas Taylor for the drumming and they added Harvey Brooks on bass and Paul Harris on keyboards. They began to rehearse, in December, at Sag Harbor, fueled by pot and cocaine, experimenting musically and shaping their songs. By the end of January, they decided to move on. They were now Crosby, Stills, and Nash: three names grouped by sound. If you think of it metrically, that sequence of names has a rhythm to it. Crosby: two syllables, snap-snap, with that forceful consonant C, and the "b" and "ee" springing toward Stills, whose very name anchors the group in that still middle. There is the hiss and slide of that "s," the short vowel "i" and soft l's in a name rounded with two "s" sounds. Those "s" sounds pick up the "s" in Crosby also. Then comes a conjunction—the "and" that is followed by Nash's name, reversing the "n" and the "a" of "and," with a strong, one syllable, "Nash": a definitive final sound. Yes, this sounds right. It is only when one adds the name of their sometime collaborator Neil Young that they begin to sound like a law firm, as some people have said. This "Y" seems like a slingshot, a propulsion device that is ready to shoot and fly off in his own direction. Young adds an inimitable edge that yanks them toward other musical dimensions.

Crosby, Stills, and Nash began to record at Wally Heider's studio on a 16-track reel-to-reel. Stills selected Bill Halverson as their recording engineer. Stills also wrote the song that would open their first album: the long overture of "Suite: Judy Blue Eyes." It was a remarkable blending of pieces. Still's song was a series of four song fragments, each like a beautiful crystal, coming together into a sparkling creation. The opening song

---

reflected the qualities of Stills' relationship with vocalist Judy Collins. Strung together, these melodies and movements became a 7½ minute song: the stunning beginning of the first CSN album. The vocal begins with an ascending line (G, B, quarter notes of E F#) and descends to the word "lonely." It is the final movement of "Suite: Judy Blue Eyes" that people seem to remember most. Words dissolve into festive, rhythmic harmonizing (dit-dit-dit-dit-dit-dit-dit-dit-dit-dit-dit), punctuated by broken Spanish interjected amid jubilant yells, like an ecstatic dancing at a festival after consuming too much sangria.

Nash had begun living with Joni Mitchell in the residence he memorialized in "Our House." Her art and musical innovation—open tunings and folk music drifting toward jazz— fascinated him.[9] He began to write more songs and to do some painting. Crosby has said that they were all trying out things and inventing.[10] Each was quite different in personality and style. Crosby's "Long Time Gone" was reworked into an arrangement by Stills that highlighted the musical textures of Crosby's song. He had previously made a demo of this song with Crosby.[11] Now Stills put his talents to work on it while Crosby and Nash were away from the studio. His arrangement provided an atmosphere for Crosby to sing.

"Long Time Gone" is one of the first of many CSN songs that focused upon politics and social awareness. Crosby had been bothered by the assassination of Robert Kennedy in early June 1968. Unable to sleep, he tossed and turned a lyric over in his mind about speaking out against the madness. Crosby has never stopped doing this. Although waylaid by periods of addiction or of illness, he has thought and spoken out about politics and greed, issues of war and peace, and problems of the environment. Crosby has addressed the wrongs he sees and the hopes he has for humanity. Nash, who expresses a similar commitment to social justice, has said that "Long Time Gone" was difficult to record and it was an effort to achieve the right balance and feel for the song. Stills built the track, playing organ, bass and guitar, while Dallas Taylor provided the drums. Meanwhile, in the same sessions, Crosby's "Guinevere" received a richly layered vocal treatment, an atmosphere that seemed to have been created by ethereal minstrels.

"Guinevere" provides an example of the feeling that intervals approached in harmony singing have upon a listener. Rather than singing

only the parts of the major chord, Crosby has said
some interval shifts and movement "to non-parallel
and non-parallel movement may owe something
advances in harmony introduced by Beethoven, the
of the nineteenth century, or later by Wagner, Liszt
which stretched the harmonic possibilities of clas
music often has a spacious, ethereal quality and h
sure middle part that solidifies the group's harmoɪ
"on" his vocals fill the CSN sound like honey sweet
voice is the rich middle of a frosted layer cake: so
the senses.

As Side Two opens CSN gives us the powerful
rying along their rock-edge. Energy ripples out fro
minor chords, resting into the quieter opening ve
out. The song was written with Paul Kantner, who
son Starship the idea of a spaceship taking off for a
features some strong guitar work from Stills.

Following a divorce, Nash had traveled to C
down into Africa. From this came his song "Marra
Stills, and Nash's first hit single.

"Marrakesh Express" was a journey to an exot
broke with Western conventions and norms. That
and change, the possibility of newness and the hɩ
that the sixties was about. It brought listeners on
ney- not only to Morocco but to all of those inner
exploring. One could imagine the air filled with thɩ
spices and dreams. With this song, Crosby, Stills, ɛ
audience of the sixties, who sought new sensatio
and a new vision or model for experience.

"Marrakesh Express" by Graham Nash reacl
Blue Eyes" reached #18 on the *Billboard* charts
Nash's album appeared in June 1969. The recɩ
of folk-rock. Greg Reeves played bass and Dalla
Crosby, Stills, and Nash sought precise harmo
Stills was especially focused on this effort. Nash
ness.

bee
forɪ

beeɩ
higl
banɩ
Spri
kneɯ
a pe
a ch
and
gero
lone
and
dishɛ
thesɩ
Youɪ
achiɩ
had
playɪ

ham
for a
wres
descɪ
tal."[13]
both
Howɩ
from

Peter
drix ɛ
ming
glimɸ
tosseɩ

Crosby, Stills, Nash and Young's 50-Year Quest

In July 1969, Neil Young was invited to participate. Woodstock had
planned for August. The concert at Woodstock began their two-set
at: one acoustic and one electric.

The addition of Young for the group's first concert tour is said to have
Atlantic Record Company president Ahmet Ertegun's idea. Young's
pitched wail and aggressive guitar playing would add a fiery edge to the
Stills resisted the suggestion. He had worked with Neil Young in Buffalo
gfield and knew the vicissitudes of Young's personality as much as he
of his formidable talent. There would always be a professional tension,
sonality clash, a wave of potential disruption between them. It was like
mist tossing together two volatile elements. Each element was dynamic
o bring them together- two strong egos blasting guitar runs- was a dan-
s mixture. Neil Young brought a fierce creativity and a hair-trigger
personality to Crosby, Stills, and Nash. Mix this with the sensitivities
trong will of Crosby, and the result is something as interpersonally
rmonious as their vocal harmonies are stunning. We may wonder that
individualists managed to work together at all. Nash has said that Neil
g brought a "dark edge" to the group. The merger with Neil Young was
ved because Elliot Roberts also managed Neil Young. The first record
een a creation of Crosby, Stills, and Nash. Now they were CSN&Y, and
g their songs live, they were creating something new.

The high, reedy voice of Neil Young began to find a place atop Gra-
Nash's vocal, creating a four-part harmony. When they plugged in
electric set, Young's ragged guitar lines entered into a competitive
ling match with Stephen Stills' lead guitar work. Graham Nash has
bed Neil Young as immensely talented, while "brash, temperamen-
When such a personality is placed alongside that of Stills or Crosby,
f whom are equally strong willed, there is bound to be some conflict.
ver, the respect they had for each other's musicianship was clear
he first days of their work together.

ogether they rehearsed at Shady Oak, a place that Stills rented from
ork of the Monkees. The Studio City place was visited by Jimi Hen-
d Eric Clapton, those guitar magicians that Stephen Stills was jam-
with. In their memoirs both Nash and Crosby give us an anecdotal
e into their time there, as they recall the day that David Geffen was
fully clothed, into the pool.

Woodstock

In the summer of 1969 and CSN&Y were unveiled for a 3½-hour concert on August 17 in Chicago, the day before the greatly anticipated festival at Woodstock. Their recording was already in the top five on the *Billboard* chart. But their inaugural concert for their peers in the industry awaited. They had heard it would be a big outdoor festival, attended by more than 20,000 people. Before they arrived in the New York City area to make their trip upstate, the number had begun to grow. There would be many more thousands of people in the rain and the mud. CSN&Y took two helicopters from Teterboro Airport, near Hackensack, New Jersey. They flew upstate in New York along the Hudson River to where the vast tribe of Woodstock stretched out in all directions from the brightly lit stage.

As the helicopter descended they saw the crowd below. Nash recalls exiting the helicopter and being greeted by John Sebastian and having a muddy party in his tent.[14] Crosby recalls nervousness about what the response of the music business people would be to Crosby, Stills, Nash and Young. "Everybody was curious about us," he said.[15] Festival producer Michael Lang says that "Suite: Judy Blue Eyes" led to the Woodstock booking. Greil Marcus wrote: "Their performance was scary, brilliant, proof of the magnificence of music."[16] New York disc jockey Pete Fornatale wrote that CSN&Y went to Woodstock "for a coronation." He compared their formation to "a baseball trade."[17] In brief interviews with Fornatale, comments come from Ahmet Ertegun of Atlantic Records and from Stills, Crosby, Sebastian and others.[18] Fornatale points out that the Woodstock film made much use of CSN&Y. (Less of Y, who did not want to be shown.) Michael Wadleigh says that this film was "about community" and a generation gathering. The Crosby, Stills, Nash and Young vocals reflected group feeling.

Crosby, Stills, Nash and Young were eagerly anticipated by a curious crowd. Many had heard their record but none had not seen them perform together. That included the members of the bands they also listened to and whose work they admired. Artists, writers, and thinkers often find that it is toughest to present something to a jury of one's peers. David Crosby and Stephen Stills have let it be known that this experience generated a bit of anxiety for them. They were surrounded by members of the Jefferson Airplane, the Band, Jimi Hendrix, Janis Joplin, and dozens of people from the industry who were checking them out for the first time. The real challenge was to just play the songs well, in spite of the muddled sound equipment and creaky monitors. Rain chilled the air. Guitar strings slipped out of tune. "Suite: Judy Blue Eyes" gave them more than seven minutes to adjust. Then they followed with "Helplessly Hoping," "Guinevere," "Marrakesh Express," "Long Time Gone," and Neil Young songs. (Those were songs he did not want recorded, so they appear on no Woodstock compilation.)

Joni Mitchell wrote their signature song "Woodstock" in an apartment room in New York City. Stephen Stills took her ballad and rocked it up. Harmonies were forcefully brought to bear and Neil Young contributed a searing guitar line. Stills ripped into the lead vocal and all of their voices lifted the recording into a powerful tribute to an experience of a generational hope. Joni Mitchell had only observed Woodstock from a distance, on television, but her imagination had been deeply connected with it. Stills reworked the arrangement of her song and with the vocals of Crosby, Stills, Nash, and Young it burst onto the airwaves. CSN&Y Woodstock footage only came together with David Geffen's provision that the song "Woodstock" be used for the film in 1970.

On Monday, after the Woodstock festival, they visited the *Dick Cavett Show*. Crosby told Cavett and the viewing audience that from the helicopter the crowd looked "like an encampment of the Macedonian army on the Greek hills."[19] Graham Nash comments that the legend and myth of Woodstock "became greater than the actual reality."[20] He adds: "I think that the time when music could change the world is past."[21]

Neil Young refused to appear on any of the Woodstock footage for the Woodstock film. A similar denial for use of Creedence Clearwater Revival's performance footage came from John Fogerty. CCR flew in by plane from Los Angeles following a television appearance there. They arrived at Woodstock, two at a time, on a small helicopter. CCR was scheduled for a 9 p.m. show, but they were delayed and went on after 2 a.m., following the Grateful Dead. By then much of the audience had fallen asleep. Fogerty did not sign the release for the performance. Consequently, CCR did not appear in the film and some of the wider potential audience did not realize that the band was at Woodstock at all.[22]

Déjà Vu

Not long after Woodstock, Crosby, Stills, Nash and Young began to pull together their first album, *Déjà Vu*. Beginning their work in Los Angeles, they soon moved to the San Francisco area. David Crosby and Christine Hinton had moved in nearby. Graham Nash stayed in a city motel near Wally Heider's studio while moving to a house in the area. When Neil Young joined them, they all went to Novato, California, to work on a record. The image that we get from those years is one of the band as an extended family.

At the end of September tragedy struck. Christine Hinton got into Crosby's VW van with her friend Barbara Lang and their cats, which they were bringing to the veterinarian. In town, one of the cats leaped into Christine Hinton's lap while she was driving. The car went into the opposite lane, where it was hit by an oncoming school bus. She died that day and the loss crushed David Crosby. He was emotionally broken and never quite the same. Where there had been this lively spirit, this lover in his life, now there was emptiness and tears.

Following an invitation to Crosby from Jerry Garcia of the Grateful Dead, CSN arranged to play at the infamous concert at the Altamont Speedway on December 6. Even today, it is remembered as the concert that ended in disaster. The crowd that day heard Crosby, Stills and Nash, Santana, the Jefferson Airplane, the Flying Burrito Brothers, and the Rolling Stones. The hired security of the Hell's Angels drank beer and became rowdy amid a crowd pumped up by the music, and by amphetamines, LSD, and other drugs of choice. The Grateful Dead had declined to play when the Jefferson Airplane's singer Marty Balin was hit in the head. When the Stones went onstage the crowd became more unruly and a Hell's Angels member fatally stabbed a fan in front of the stage.

After Altamont, the album *Déjà Vu* remained before Crosby, Stills, Nash and Young. Graham Nash has said that the record reflects some of the darkness they were going through.[23] There were shifts in their relationships with the women in their lives. Tensions arose between Stills and Young. Crosby was in mourning. For many weeks the album seemed to contain no single. The title song "Déjà Vu" was a drifting, airy song that seemed sent into space by an oracle. "Almost Cut My Hair" had energy but was too disparate and was not structured like a pop song. So "Teach

Your Children," with its new country arrangement, and the reflective "Our House," coming from Nash's relationship with Joni Mitchell, were chosen as A and B sides for a single. Then Stills brought in the blockbuster "Carry On." The song ripples with energy and is elevated by harmonies that still burst with life on the recording. The voices of Crosby, Stills, Nash and Young join a cappella, pushing the top of the treble clef staff, rising powerfully together to say that love is coming to us all.

"Carry On" emerged as a single with high rhythmic harmony. The album included Stills' "4 +20" and Neil Young's "Helpless." Graham Nash contributed "Teach Your Children," his country-folk reflection on the generation gap, on which Jerry Garcia played steel guitar. There was Crosby's mystically drifting, jazz-influenced title track and "Almost Cut My Hair," representing his countercultural stance. *Déjà Vu* brought some tensions in the studio, where they spent about eighty hours recording. The imagery for the recording included the Diane Arbus photograph of a child holding a grenade in Central Park. "Woodstock," which Joni Mitchell had begun writing in a New York hotel room, was included, too.

They did complete the record, despite those many emotions. The *Déjà Vu* recording was completed before the year and the decade came to a close. Stills repeatedly remixed the tracks they had done. They battled about the sound. Young was in; Young was out. He did not play on Nash's "Teach Your Children" or on "Our House." With the mix of the recording almost completed, Crosby and Nash decided that it was time for them to travel. David Crosby was like a raw nerve of sorrow and he needed some help from his friend. They went to New York and to London, on "a binge" before returning to finish the album and play some concert dates. Stills soon left for England, where he bought an estate. The group played shows in Stockholm and Copenhagen and vented their distaste for the war in Vietnam. Once back in the United States, Crosby and Nash went sailing on Crosby's boat, the *Mayan*, to the Caribbean and Panama for seven weeks. Neil Young was now recording *After the Gold Rush*.

Déjà Vu appeared on March 23, 1970, following two million advance orders for the album. By this time, LP albums had become every bit as important as the commercial single. Bands were creating "concept albums" with songs that were thematically connected. Record buyers were getting an entire package. Album covers carried photos of the recording artists, or cleverly designed artwork. Not expecting CSN&Y to perform together at that time, Stills created another band and recorded with them. He went to England and Stills played music with Eric Clapton and Jack Bruce, Buddy Miles, and Jimmy Page for a film called *Supershow*. He sat in on sessions with Jimi Hendrix and Eric Clapton and played on Ringo Starr's "It Don't Come Easy." On *Déjà Vu* there were only three songs, including "Woodstock," that were performed by Crosby, Stills, Nash, and Young together.

Plans were being made for a CSN&Y arena tour. It was expected that they would travel with their own stage set and crew. Stephen Stills arrived from England, where he had been working with his own band and was now tending to horses and riding them at his place in Colorado. On July 9, 1970, Crosby, Stills, and Nash performed their last show of this first incarnation of the group. They would not perform again as a unit until four years later. In September 1970, while in Colorado, Stills was shaken by learning of the death of Jimi Hendrix. He dedicated his solo album to him. The song "Love the One You're With" from the album was a hit.

David Crosby and Neil Young were at a cabin in Pescadero in northern California when the news came that four students had been shot at Kent State by members of the National Guard. Steve Cohen, who owned the cabin, brought home the magazine that showed the disturbing photograph by John Filo of a girl kneeling near the body of one of the dead students. She looked up with a puzzled look of horror on her face and the image seared into the conscience of a nation. Appalled by this, Neil Young took his guitar outside and wrote the scathing song "Ohio." Like that photo, the song, recorded quickly, would burn itself into the awareness of America. It joined "Teach Your Children" on the charts. Perhaps someone might be taught something about violence and the need for a remedy after all.

The lyric immediately offers us the image of "tin soldiers," the vocal identifies with the fallen; the soldiers are "gunning *us* down." Shock fills the lyric with vowels that exclaimed "uh": "coming," "summer," "drumming," "gunning," "us," "done," "run." These sounds alternate with other tight short vowels and the open "oh" of "on our own" and "Ohio." They recorded "Ohio" within twenty-four hours of the event in an aggressive and scathing indictment of grinding guitars in D minor, a stomping rhythmic march, and plaintive vocals.

Crosby, Stills, Nash, and Young remained a loose affiliation after this. Drummer Johnny Barbata, who had played with the Turtles, joined them for rehearsals. When they rehearsed, Neil Young tended to face off against Stephen Stills in a battle of guitars. Young was mixing *After the Gold Rush*. Stills had resurrected his song "Love the One You're With" for his own solo album. David Crosby had begun his solo album *If I Could Only Remember My Name* and worked with Paul Kantner on *Blows Against the Empire*. Graham Nash began writing the songs he would collect on his album *Songs for Beginners*. He would include Crosby on the record, with Rita Coolidge, who he recalls, composed the piano tag part for Clapton's song "Layla," that was played by Jim Gordon. Nash assembled a group of musicians for his record that also included Dave Mason, Phil Lesh, Jerry Garcia, Barbata, and several fine female background singers. Nash says that Crosby, Stills, Nash, and Young never disbanded; they just drifted toward their own projects. They remained under contract with Atlantic Records but had the freedom to pursue their own solo work.

This was a time when CSN&Y had some cultural influence as well as commercial strength. Recognizing this, their record company, Atlantic, released a live album, *4 Way Street*, on February 1, 1971. Bill Halverson had a role in getting the album out, whereas Crosby, Stills, and Nash would have liked to have done some overdubs and maintained the live feel of the album. This reflected Stills' concern about live recording sound versus Crosby's concern about being pure and true in their sound. The recording is a bit more raw than polished. Yet, the album reflected their 1970 tours. It includes "Triad," "Lee Shore," and "Love the One You're With" from Stills and "Right Between the Eyes" from Nash. "Southern Man" by Young appeared on this record also, as did "Ohio."

In 1971, Crosby and Nash lived near San Francisco. Crosby was in Mill Valley and anchored the *Mayan* in Sausalito harbor. Sometimes he stayed upstairs at Nash's house. They went on the road as a duo that year. An incident while on tour in Vancouver prompted Nash's "Immigration Man Song." He was delayed and questioned by immigration officials and the experience set him to work on a lyric. He wrote it on the inside cover of a paperback of a Ray Bradbury novel he was reading, *The Silver Locusts*. Upon hearing Tom Rush's version of Joni Mitchell's song "Urge for Going," Graham Nash also considered adapting the song.[24]

---

1. Beginnings

By this time, Crosby, Stills, and Nash could look back at their beginnings, as they approached their solo projects. They had met, fortuitously, in a context formed by choice and coincidence. In the mid to late 1960s, on the West coast, some of the best of the counterculture pop-rock music creators lived in Laurel Canyon: the Turtles, Frank Zappa, Joni Mitchell, Mama Cass, John Mayall, members of the band Love and others. "California Dreaming" by the Mamas and the Papas was released in 1965. The Turtles recorded Bob Dylan's "It Ain't Me Babe" in 1965. "Happy Together" was released in 1967 and appeared on the Turtles' third album. Frank Zappa's *Freak Out* (1966) was a double album.

In January 1967 there had been a "happening" in Haight-Ashbury, a community be-in of folk and blues and rock and LSD and Timothy Leary. San Francisco was now a rock music center with the Jefferson Airplane, the Grateful Dead, Quicksilver Messenger Service, Moby Grape and other bands. The scene became permeated with drug use, sometimes viewed as a means to higher creativity, sometimes dedicated to just getting higher. There was harmony and music and brilliance and potentially damaging indulgence.

Some wondered if the growing anti-war movement could stay connected. Were people only there for the entertainment and music and not for causes? The Beatles had taken rock beyond pop-love songs through *Revolver* and *Rubber Soul* to *Sergeant Pepper*. The Rolling Stones had broken new ground. Blues rock extended from Britain from the Yardbirds to the West coast of the U.S. with the Doors. Blues rock guitar announced its tones from humbucking pickups from John Mayall to Jimi Hendrix, on to the southern rock of the Allman Brothers. Eric Clapton stirred audiences with Cream and joined forces with Stevie Winwood in Blind Faith. Other bands like Deep Purple and Grand Funk would also take this combination of blues and hard rock into the 1970s.

There was interaction between Crosby, Stills, and Nash with the members of the Grateful Dead and the Jefferson Airplane. When "Wooden Ships" emerged from Paul Kantner and David Crosby in 1968, their lyric painted a scenario of escape from calamity. The song announced that they were leaving as the world was devastated by a nuclear war. From Jefferson Airplane emerged Paul Kanter and Grace Slick's *Blows Against the Empire*, with contributions from David Crosby and Graham Nash, who mixed the second side of the record. Many years later, Crosby discussed "Wooden Ships" with Paul Zollo as a collaboration. According to Crosby, Paul Kantner's name was left off the credits for the song because of entanglements with Jefferson Airplane's management at the time. However, Crosby and Kantner met in their mutual love of science fiction.

The Grateful Dead, friends with Crosby, Stills, and Nash, became one of the most substantial rock concert acts. Their audience would follow them from show to show, in a ritualistic manner, and were known as Deadheads. Yet, aside from "Truckin'" there were no singles that became hits with extensive radio airplay. In 1988, *Relix* magazine pointed out how many of those fans (about 91 percent) traveled some distance to see and hear the band. Many would see several shows along their journey.[25]

Joni Mitchell was another friend. In an interview with Eric Alterman, Graham Nash recalled meeting Joni Mitchell in Ottawa in 1967 after a Hollies show. David Crosby produced Joni Mitchell's *Song to a Seagull* (1968). Another Canadian was the most lasting and perhaps most curious addition to their work: Neil Young.

2

Enter Neil Young

Neil Young is central to any discussion of Crosby, Stills, and Nash. He is a powerful creative force, a prolific songwriter, and an engaging performer who merits a book-length review of his music and influence. Neil Young played at Woodstock with Crosby, Stills, and Nash, and then at Big Sur at the Esalen Institute, on the California coast off Route 1, two weeks later. To Crosby, Stills, and Nash, Neil Young brought an "intensity," observes Robert Gottlieb.[1] He brought vision and prolific songwriting creativity, a confident and unique personality, and high tenor vocals and piercing guitar lines that seemed to enter a collaborative duel with the guitar work of Stephen Stills.

You might call Young an illegal immigrant arriving from Canada to Los Angeles. He traveled with bass player Bruce Palmer and joined Stephen Stills and Richie Furay to form the Buffalo Springfield, adding Dewey Martin on drums. Young added his voice to "For What It's Worth," which was not an expected hit. When Young was with the Buffalo Springfield his song "Expecting to Fly" was recorded in studio across a month. The composition, with Jack Nitzsche, appeared on the second album by the band, *Buffalo Springfield Again*. Young teamed up with Nitzsche for his first solo effort. Young discovered a group of people who played music who called themselves the Rockets. Their playing was by all accounts loose, ragged, and far less precise than the musicians he would work with in Nashville on *Harvest*. They would become his band, Crazy Horse. *Everybody Knows This Is Nowhere* would be his second album. It was more back to basics than his work with Nitzsche. It was around this time that Crosby, Stills, and Nash were beginning. Soon Neil Young was part of that circle. Neil Young moved to his ranch in August 1970. Young's *After the Gold Rush* was musically diverse. When it came time for Crosby, Stills, and

Nash to perform live there was an obvious problem. While Stephen Stills could play many instruments well, he couldn't play them all at once. David Crosby and Stephen Stills talked with Ahmet Ertegun about this and Neil Young was suggested. According to Nash, Stills was resistant. He had spent enough time with Neil Young in Buffalo Springfield to feel uncomfortable with that proposition. They had already worked out their harmonies and their sound. Yet, Neil Young brought strengths of songwriting and a guitar playing edge that was indisputable.

The most distinctive feature of Crosby, Stills, Nash and Young are their richly layered vocal harmonies. This is abundantly clear on *Déjà Vu*. "Carry On" bursts out with their vocals, in thirds and fifths. We are awakened with the narrative to a new way of hearing as well as seeing. The ideal that love comes to us all rings out in the lyric. We have the vocals forming chords: D, F, and a high B. With Graham Nash's "Teach Your Children" the familiar line of Jerry Garcia's steel guitar playing joins Nash's vocal and the group's harmonies. The song has been considered a reflection on generational conflict and preserving life and values for the future. One's dreams can be passed along, and the generations can learn from each other. The song is easily played on guitar (D-G-D-A) opening on B minor on a "sigh."

On "Helpless," Neil Young's high tenor trembles across a similarly simple chord structure of D A G, repeating the word three times in the song's bridge. We are invited to imagine north Ontario and the moon, the stars, and the shadows of bird wings. The melody moves within that key of D. David Crosby declares his freedom and independence from constraint with "Almost Cut My Hair." He leaves aside any jazz inflections and treats this as a straightforward statement. "Déjà Vu," on the other hand, ripples through a 6/8 time signature in vigorous motion, opening into triplets. An epiphany, an awakening, is signaled by the long held B note that extends on the word "feel." The swirling motion of the song's beginning with voices in tandem gives way to the dreamy ethereal drift of this next section. As that rapid harmony-laced opening gives way to this slower, dreamy recollection of the title, words melt away, dissolving into something like scat singing. There is a shift to E minor-C-G and D suspended and jazz-like harmony. To wonder what is going on might be taken as open-ended curiosity toward the experience, or as a reflection on the social and political environment of the time. The harmonies, resting on the D chord, jump to a high A and climb higher, declaring that we have been here before and are re-experiencing this moment. In a 2008 interview with Andy Greene, Crosby called it a very unusual song with "strange tunings and strange time signatures."[2] Crosby's song reflects interesting musical thinking: something innovative, right-brained, and artistic. (Anyone playing the song should recognize the alternate tuning, or some passages might be a bit difficult to play.)

"Our House" begins with a gently climbing melody. The song brings us Nash in ballad mode and his song seems to carry a bit of joy and reverie. The lyric paints a picture of contentment: two lazy cats sunning in the back yard. The melody and rhythm skip along cheerily, like children in a pleasant circle game. The song emerges from Nash's association with Joni Mitchell and has a folk-like simplicity. Singing voices blend into liquid morning coffee on the patio, flowers in a vase, and fiery gems in the evening fire, their la-la-la's blending into sunny brightness. One feels connection, an affirmation of life in simple actions like placing new-bought flowers into a vase.

"Helplessly Hoping" combines generous harmonies with alliterative excess. "Long Time Gone" gives us another side of Crosby. "Lady of the Island" evokes romance, sensuous relationship, a caring closeness. There is a satisfying fullness to the album.[3] The re-release adds Neil Young's acoustic "Down by the River." There is the live concert at the Forum in Los Angeles. C. Michael Bailey speaks of the recording resting on "the turbulent sixties." He notes release with Stills' "Black Queen," Nash's "King Midas in Reverse." Dave Marsh once called the CSNY *4 Way Street* record "One of the worst live albums of all time." C. Michael Bailey believes that *4 Way Street* captures the spirit of time and calls it the "sound track of a generation." It is a record capable of "capturing all the drama and rage of the period."[4] The album is half acoustic, half electric. A vein of protest runs through it. Graham Nash solos on piano on "Chicago." Stills improvises on "49 Bye-Byes." "Ohio" burns with power on the other side, as does "Southern Man." Crosby's "Long Time Gone" recalls a troubled time of Robert Kennedy's assassination. "Carry On" comes alive with strong vocals.

Déjà Vu (1969) was followed by Neil Young's *After the Gold Rush* (1970), the live Crosby, Stills, Nash, and Young record *4 Way Street* (1971), and Neil Young's *Harvest* (1972). Young followed this with his film and soundtrack *Journey Through the Past* (1972) and *Time Fades Away* (1973). "Sea of Madness" appeared on the Woodstock soundtrack album but not in the film. (The song starts on an F chord but moves out also in D and runs D-A-G-F.)

Young liked to record at home, to create the studio long before that became thoroughly possible for most musicians. He would create a recording in the basement in Topanga Canyon or out on the ranch.

After the Gold Rush is a strong musical statement. Neil Young's "Only Love Can Break Your Heart" unfolds in 3/4 time and comes to us in D major, with two sharps, and chords chiming a steady pattern: A-D-G-A-D-G-A-D. "After the Gold Rush" is a medieval dream of knights, peasants, drummers, and archers. In the midst of the 1970s, Mother Nature is on the run and that high voice is singing of a dream of spaceships, getting high, and freedom. With the second verse we see images of sun and moon. "Tell Me Why" brings an elliptical lyric vaguely saying something about heart ships and dark horses. It starts out on the C chord and runs B minor, E minor, C, D with that plaintive vocal landing on the note of E on "sell." "Southern Man" aches out an appeal, a criticism, a warning. It begins in D minor, which offers a different tone for this song. A reference to the good book of the Bible urges some grounding in a moral focus that faces the contradiction in burning crosses. With an urgent insistence come harsh images of plantation homes, black workers, screams, and bull whips. The D minor, B flat, G minor chords pound out the song. "Heart of Gold" is fairly simple and it is catchy. With a few strummed E minor chords and a D a musical hook rings out and repeats. There are acoustic guitars on the left channel and on the right. We hear of a quest for love as time goes by. How anyone is growing old at 24 or 25 is anyone's guess. But a song becomes everyone's—part of the audience—once it is recorded and performed. A singer can adopt a narrative persona. Ben Keith's pedal steel whines at it. We all do get a little older every day. To travel from Hollywood to Redwood, of course, sounds like it comes from the singer's life experience. The song sounds personal but becomes a song for everyone. It doesn't hurt that Linda Ronstadt and James Taylor sang on the song. Meanwhile, it is obvious that Neil Young moved on to something else.

2. Enter Neil Young

Music occurs in time, and Young seemed to reflect about time as he wrote songs for *Harvest*. "Old Man" from *Harvest* received much radio airplay. (There are reflections on time in *Journey to the Past* and *Time Fades Away*.) The narrator of "Old Man" identifies with the old man. The Nashville sessions would be at the center of Young's album *Harvest*. Bob Dylan had gone to Nashville to record *Nashville Skyline*. Young chose to record some of his *Harvest* album in Nashville also. Young preferred less studio manipulation and a more direct approach. Those strengths of disciplined creativity he brought occasionally to Crosby, Stills, and Nash and (sometimes) Young. Of course, we might have heard less of Crosby, Stills, and Nash together across the years without the intervention, connections, and leadership of Neil Young, who has developed a towering rock music solo career.

Some rock musicians could hardly ignore Neil Young's impact. Lynyrd Skynyrd's "Sweet Home Alabama," for example, is a response song that underscores Neil Young's influence. It has appeared to many listeners that "Sweet Home Alabama," which mentions him, directly confronts Neil Young's "Southern Man." (Also one might think of "Alabama" on *Harvest*.) Neil Young criticizes southern racism in "Southern Man" and Lynyrd Skynyrd reacted fiercely. Was this interpreted correctly? Perhaps it meant— "okay, you have your view, now go away. We don't need you!" There is ambiguity in the line concerning how people love the gov.

Harvest was a studio creation both in the Nashville studio and at the barn on Neil Young's ranch. This is a collection of songs with no central theme. It is not really a country album. *Harvest* was a diverse album. The cover art, pedal steel guitar, and a song "Are You Ready for the County" suggested country. Even so, this was a folk album, not Merle Haggard or Willie Nelson. It was also something different from later Neil Young intensity and gutsiness. In *Rolling Stone*, John Mendelsohn reviewed *Harvest* harshly. Yet, *Harvest* was a fine collection of songs. It was a clear, well-crafted record of diverse performances with good musicians and songwriting.[5]

On acoustic guitars all across the U.S. and Canada and in Europe and elsewhere, one can hear the easy, familiar run of "The Needle and the Damage Done." On the recording we hear Young's chords, Kenny Buttrey's hi-hat rhythm, and Ben Keith's pedal steel guitar.

"Heart of Gold" is fairly simple. Of course, it is catchy. A few E minor chords and a D. It speaks of a quest for love as time goes by. Acoustic guitars are on the left and the right channels. Young plays one guitar. Teddy Irwin, uncredited, plays the other. Keith's pedal steel whines. As for "Old Man," how anyone is growing old at twenty-four is anyone's guess. But a song becomes everyone's, part of the audience once it is recorded and released. A singer can adopt a persona. As noted earlier, to travel from Hollywood to Redwood was part of Young's own experience.

Upon creating *Harvest,* Neil Young turned to his interest in filmmaking, an interest that has persisted across his career. He created *Journey Through the Past.* In 1972 *Harvest* was on the charts. Young assembled a band at the ranch with Jack Nitzsche, Danny Whitten, Ben Keith, and Tim Drummond. The busy drummer Kenney Buttrey was replaced by Johnny Barbata. The drug-addicted Danny Whitten fell apart and died of a drug overdose. This musical collective produced *Times Fades Away,* an album that was uneven and not particularly well-crafted in comparison with other Neil Young efforts.

Neil Young held folk, rock, and a touch of a country sound together in his work. He was performing "Don't Let It Bring You Down," "I Believe in You," "Tell Me Why" and rock songs like "Down by the River" and "When You Dance." The "Old Man" guitar part and "Sugar Mountain" are folk.

"Are You Ready for the Country" gives us eighth notes, across G-F-D, a simple chord pattern on guitar or piano. "A Man Needs a Maid" comes to us in B flat with a lyric that seems to ask how to make a positive change happen. The singer feels things changing and recognizes that maybe he needs some help. It sounds like this would be a relationship without commitments. Maybe a man needs a helper. This need not be hired help or someone subservient; although the title may sound to some ears like this is some male chauvinist who wants a servile female to pick up his dirty laundry. Feminists and proponents of the #MeToo movement might cringe but the song welcomes a variety of interpretations. "Out on the Weekend" declares a desire to start new, to take a pickup out on the road. (Maybe the brass bed reference recalls Bob Dylan's "Lay Lady Lay." Maybe not.) "There's a World" reminds us that every individual is part of a wide world. Whether they live in a city or on a mountaintop they are all God's children.

"Alabama" reminds us that some of those children are in social contexts that affect them. "Alabama" evokes images of a Gothic South with banjo music coming from behind a broken window. There is a heavy weight of history on one's shoulders and the car is immobile, stuck in a ditch. "The Needle and the Damage Done" tells of loss and a broken life and Young plays its familiar riff coming off the D chord. "Words" brings images of ponds, fields, windows, and a road, soil and stars, a junkman and a castle king and aging lines. Some songs were recorded in a barn which is pictured with a high ceiling, a mix of sunlight and shadow, a window and music equipment.

Later, soundtrack completed, *Time Fades Away* makes references to Canada, winter rain, travel, drifting restlessly. We hear "Soldier," "Yonder Stands the Sinner," "Love in Mind," with its question of where has nature gone. "Don't Be Denied" recalls Winnipeg. Emotive and simple, with its half-time 3/8 feel, there is "The Bridge," reminding us that there is a connection that we can build.

Young remained open, listening, always writing songs, like a natural force available to the change of seasons. *Rust Never Sleeps* (1979) closed the decade with a movement from folk to punk/new wave influences. After 1980, Young left Warner Bros. and signed with Geffen. The market had changed toward more record company insistence on hit singles from albums. Even so, a well-established artist like Neil Young still has the freedom to explore new terrain. With *Trans* he moved across styles, from folk to electric, from rockabilly to bluesy, curiously techno. Then he swung back to country Nashville Neil with Tim Drummond and Ben Keith. Acoustic Neil did not work well for Geffen Records at that time. Young released *Old Ways* (1985), embracing the country sound. Folk rock followed on *Freedom* (1989) with Crazy Horse and then came his burst of rock noise and grunge on *Ragged Glory*. Young's *Harvest Moon* was a sequel that was not a Nashville record. It was recorded with the Stray Gators. It was moody and melancholy, politics and the environment, although perhaps not cutting as deeply as some other Neil Young records. Beyond this, Neil Young has repeatedly been a creative energy and an influence on other musicians.

Of course, Neil Young was always simply Neil Young: innovative, edgy, thoughtful, and determined to go his own way into great performances and into personal expression. *Tonight's the Night* was released rather than a planned recording of acoustic-rendered songs. "Homegrown" recordings may have connected *Harvest* with the later *Harvest Moon*. *Rust Never Sleeps* (1979) moved from folk to side two's punk influence. After 1980, Young left Warner Bros. and signed with Geffen Records. The market had changed towards more insistence on hit singles from each album.

Young released *Old Ways* (1985) connecting these recordings with new ones. This time he had embraced more of the country sound than he had years before on *Harvest*. Folk and folk rock followed on *Freedom* (1989) with Crazy Horse and then came his burst of rock sound, noise, grunge grind on *Ragged Glory*. *Harvest Moon* was a sequel that was not a Nashville record. There was melody and melancholy, politics and the environment.

In an interview with Paul Zollo on songwriting, Neil Young observed that he has written several songs in minor keys (E minor, A minor) and "D with no thirds." Zollo recognizes the "striking imagery" of some of Neil Young's songs. There is a suggestion that, along with creating images, Neil Young likes to leave space in his songs.[6]

Young's politics appear flexible, more anarchist and libertarian than committed to any agenda. "Resist the Powers That Be" is vague, suggesting all powers. While affirming democracy and encouraging resistance, it seems to target only a shadowy Big Brother of power and privilege. Neil Young responded to the National Rifle Association's spokesperson Dana Loesch's dislike of his music. She compared Young's voice to that of a dying cow. "Well, she's one of the gang over there," he told *The Daily Beast*. Loesch's uncle likes Neil Young's music and she was familiar with *Mirror Ball*. She calls "Downtown," recorded with Pearl Jam, "dumb." If she began hearing Neil Young in 1995, it seems like she has missed more than twenty-five years of his music.[7] *The Calgary Herald*'s Peter Glenn pointed out (January 18, 2014) that while Neil Young is a libertarian his political stance is hard to determine.[8] He is among those who protest war and the establishment. However, he appears to pick and choose what appears workable or not. With Buffalo Springfield, he opposed American involvement in Vietnam. With Crosby, Stills, and Nash, he wrote and sang "Ohio." He rejected racism and violence in "Southern Man." His appreciation for some of Ronald Reagan's ideas is on record but he was not ever an all-out Reagan supporter. He joined with John Mellencamp for Farm Aid in 1985, with concern about the loss of family farms. Political Neil Young spoke out with "Welfare Mothers" (1991). In 2001, he wrote the rallying cry "Let's Roll" against the evils of terrorism, recalling the brave souls who responded to the plane hijacking over Pennsylvania on 9/11. After that incident he appeared to turn neo-conservative in the fight to oppose terrorists and he supported the Patriot Act to confront that evil. It was a fight of "going against Satan on the wings of a dove," he told reporters. Freedom has been a constant theme. "Homegrown" expressed support for marijuana smoking as a personal freedom. Progressive Neil Young called for "Freedom" and included lines that opposed the first Bush administration's actions in "Rockin' in the Free World." His move to support environmentalism connected with *Living with War* (2006). He told the *Calgary Herald* reporter that his statements in song have to do with "a bigger way of looking at what we're doing here."

There are several other Neil Young songs that carry a political edge or voice a protest against the impacts of war, racism, or corporate environmental degradation. "The Monsanto Years" (2017–18) directly confronts the agribusiness giant Monsanto for its agrochemical exploitation and poisoning of the land. Neil Young, of course, is a Canadian who has turned his attention to issues across North America. In 2013 there were climate change concerns. He expressed his view about oil sands and his support for the Athabasca Chippewa First Nation's opposition to Shell's Jackpine oil sands mining. It was all about money, not integrity, he told the *Calgary Herald*. *USA Today* reported: "Review: Neil Young Is as Political as Ever On 'Peace Trail.'" (December 8, 2016). *Forbes* (January 19, 2017) reported that Neil Young expected "a rise in activism" after the Trump inauguration.

Creativity intersects with Neil Young's voicing of human concerns. He continues to participate in a benefit for autism awareness each year. Heartstrings are somehow attached to the guitar strings. If this humanistic impulse can be called spiritually motivated it is not tied to any religion. Young tends toward pantheism. He told one interviewer that he recognizes "a higher source of creation" and sees religions as expressions of the same thing.[9]

Neil Young's 2015 tour with Promise of the Real was captured on *Earth* (2017), a live album. In 2018, Neil Young again joined with Promise of the Real. Miles away one thinks of Neil Young and a ranch: an open landscape swept by sun, a sparse population living close to the land. We see again those photos of Young the individualist in a country dream: long hair, flannel shirt, letting the Muse play in his mind, filled with more music than an iPod. Is Neil Young writing a science fiction novel? Several news outlets have reported that he is. Evidently, he let the news slip in an interview with *Rolling Stone*. So, the rumor went around. On March 19, 2018, one outlet announced that the story would be called *Canary*. There was a new film, *Paradox*, directed by Daryl Hannah. Neil Young has produced some 34 studio albums across 40 years, with the Buffalo Springfield, Crosby, Stills, Nash and Young, and Crazy Horse and other collaborations. The fires of creativity have not dimmed.

If one goes back more than fifty years, Neil Young is a musician in his twenties setting out on a solo path, breaking free of the Buffalo Springfield. In California he begins his self-titled first album. Stephen Stills is finding his own way, trading the acoustic guitar for the electric and back again. Now solo, they are a little more folk-based. Graham Nash has come to the West coast also and David Crosby, no longer with the Byrds, is in Los Angeles. In L.A. clubs like the Troubadour, Linda Ronstadt is working with a band that includes Andrew Gold. Future members of the Eagles Don Henley and Glenn Frey enter the picture. Cass Elliott and John and Michelle Phillips are singing, and the young Jackson Browne and Warren Zevon are writing songs. Elliot Roberts is managing the careers of Joni Mitchell and Neil Young. This is the context of new beginnings. It is a seething ocean of creative ferment.[10]

In 1970, in the distance, on the periphery, folk music endured. Pete Seeger persisted. Peter, Paul, and Mary gravitated further from pop to activism. The era of the singer-songwriter had emerged from the likes of Tom Paxton, Tom Rush, Buffy St. Marie, and Eric Andersen. In the wake of Bob Dylan, Dave Van Ronk, or Richie Havens, New York City folksingers came to the Bitter End, to Folk City, walking by West 4th and Mac Dougal and crossed Father Demo Square. (Was it really named after the patron saint of demo records as one folksinger, Steve Key, has quipped?) They gathered at places like the Kerrville Folk Festival in Texas, or the Mariposa

2. *Enter Neil Young*

Festival in Toronto. Some were, as the Australian folksinger Eric Bogle sings, still willin' to listen to Dylan. After releasing *Blonde on Blonde* in June 1966, Bob Dylan had gone to Woodstock, joining with musicians who began calling themselves The Band. The press reported he had had a motorcycle accident on July 29. With The Band, he recorded in 1967 what has come to be known as *The Basement Tapes* (1975 release). Dylan's *John Wesley Harding* (1967), a folk and country inflected album, followed. The Band released *Music from the Big Pink* in 1968. Dylan recorded *Nashville Skyline* (1969). Some critics suggest that that paved a path for Neil Young's *Harvest* (1972) album.

Sometimes folk music got dumped into the same bins as country music in the record stores. There were some connections: those three chord patterns on acoustic guitars, the collaboration with banjos, harmonica, and fiddles. Folk could embrace bluegrass. It emphasized song lyrics and was inclined toward storytelling. It participated in the communal sense of common folks sitting at home, sharing their music. When folk entered the world of popular music, there was the confessional song that seemed to be at the center of James Taylor's craft. James Taylor recorded his introspective and melodic album *Sweet Baby James* in the weeks before Christmas 1969. *Sweet Baby James* reached the top 100 on the *Billboard* charts on March 14, 1970. It went to #4 by May 23. In late July the lives of James Taylor and Joni Mitchell intersected at the Mariposa Folk Festival. He wrote "You Can Close Your Eyes." Folksinger Harry Chapin called the personal, atmospheric folksong the "attitudinal" song, to distinguish it from his lengthy story-songs, like "Taxi." Jackson Browne wrote "attitudinal" songs. Neil Young would write them too, emphasizing a songwriter's art that was idiosyncratic, authentic, and distinctly personal.[11]

Rock began to experience its casualties and loss of talent. The Rolling Stones lost Brian Jones in 1969. In 1970, rock music lost Jimi Hendrix and Janis Joplin. Jim Morrison vanished and died in France in 1971. Mama Cass died in 1974. Elsewhere, the sad story of Badfinger unfolded. The band scored four international hits, including productions by Paul McCartney and George Harrison, between 1970 and 1972. They encountered disaster and contractual hell in 1974. By 1975 singer Pete Ham was dead. The losses would continue.

43

Crosby, Stills, Nash and Young's 50-Year Quest

From 1969 through 1970, Crosby, Stills, Nash and Young had become a pop music phenomenon. By 1971, the audience for Crosby, Stills, Nash, and Young anticipated another tour, or a follow up to *Déjà Vu*. However, Crosby, Stills, Nash, and Young had to split to go down those four streets on solo projects. Representing hippie peace ideals and embracing those ideals, they had been writing songs of social commentary and songs of romantic idealism, or disenchantment and disillusion. They sought to speak individually.

3

Going Solo

After *Déjà Vu* Crosby, Stills, Nash and Young split. Each released a solo album. Crosby created *If I Could Only Remember My Name*. Stills simply called his album *Stills*. Graham Nash developed a recording he called *Songs for Beginners*. Neil Young, with two albums already behind him, set to work on *After the Gold Rush* and on the songs that would appear on his *Harvest* album. The solo projects of Crosby, Stills, Nash, and Young were timely. The early 1970s brought a rich cluster of singer-songwriters: James Taylor, Joni Mitchell, Jackson Browne, Laura Nyro, Cat Stevens, Harry Chapin, John Denver, Jesse Winchester, Jimmy Webb, Don McLean, Elliot Murphy, Neil Diamond, Carole King, Tom Rush, Dan Fogelberg, and Bruce Springsteen among them. Crosby, Stills, Nash and Young had the freedom to go solo. They had used their personal names to maintain their independence as singer-songwriters, even as they entered into their collaboration as a band. As Anthony Lane wrote in *The New Yorker* (June 18, 2018): "Writing, like dying, is one of those things that should be done alone or not at all."[1] Most Crosby, Stills, Nash and Young songs were written individually. Although they performed together, they wrote separately, contributing their songs to the group.

David Crosby, Stephen Stills, Graham Nash, and Neil Young each fit comfortably into this singer-songwriter period of the early 1970s. They brought the expression of their distinctive talents and styles to their solo work. In 1971, David Crosby released *If I Could Only Remember My Name* (Atlantic). On this record he set forth his voice and personal vision with his own compositions, recalling his relationship with Christine Hinton and featuring "Song Without Words." There would be no further solo albums from Crosby for the next eighteen years. The year 1971 also saw Neil Young create his album *After the Gold Rush* with his band Crazy Horse.

Rolling Stone placed David Crosby's *If I Could Only Remember My Name* as #37 in their list of Greatest Stoner Albums (June 7, 2013). The first song is described as "like a stoned-out campfire jam" which sounds to the reviewer as if much of it was "made up on the spot."[2] David Crosby's first solo album begins with the sound of an acoustic guitar and a four-note pattern that is repeated three times. The final line reverses this, three notes down to the root note. A rhythmic pattern becomes clear. The word "everybody" is repeated, Crosby's vocal jumps higher, and "Music Is Love" becomes a ragged chant from a chorus of singers that sound like they have kicked off their shoes on a beach or joined in a circle in a field at a picnic. The guitar takes on a sitar-like sound as the chorus of voices stumble over each other a bit in communal connection. "Cowboy Movie" immediately chimes out with an electric guitar sound that listeners can hear on "Wooden Ships" and other CSN&Y tunes. To a slow, steady 4/4 Crosby's voice drops from the upper register of the previous song to a strong tenor with a rougher, throatier edge. It is an evocative vocal that sometimes borders on speech and declaration. Drums clearly hold the bottom and punctuate this. The recording has a live sound. Some guitar leads have a high-pitched sound with some gain and sustain but no overdrive, as if they were emerging from a hollow body guitar through a small Ampex or Peavy amplifier. "Tamalpais High" follows with "Déjà Vu"-like harmonized vocals. These vocal intricacies move into an instrumental of guitars, bass, and drums, as Jorma Kaukonen, Jerry Garcia, and others join in. By now Crosby has indicated that this will be a listenable journey in which he will leave a good deal of instrumental space. Clearly, Crosby loves to sing and to play and harmonize with vocal lines. "Laughing" opens with acoustic guitar chords. A solo voice says, "I thought..." and comments on a man who said he knew what was going on. This melts into rich harmonies. It's butter on sweetened pancakes. We hear a mellow and reflective, almost meditative track. Crosby's clear vocal comes through amid touches of pedal steel guitar or slide and vocals that sound very CSN&Y. There is a pause, some space—not John Cage silence, but a moment. There is some guitar noodling. At about 1:40 drums enter and a repeating pattern is established. We have a song "What Are Their Names" which challenges the men that Dylan called the "Masters of War" to step out of their anonymity and identify themselves. Who really runs this land, asks Crosby.

This now becomes a big vocal chorus that sounds like a Jefferson Airplane song, with Grace Slick and Paul Kantner among those who are calling for a peace that is not a lot to ask for. Then the music fades. When music returns it drifts into gentleness and dreaminess with "Traction in the Rain." The strings sound like a hammer dulcimer. (Crosby creates a pattern that is similar to the third cut on his recent *Lighthouse* album, "Drive Out to the Desert.") "Song with No Words" performs vocal gymnastics. It begins with guitar arpeggios and begins to move in harmonized vocals. Voices caress a melody that proceeds in a kind of circular motion. A jazzlike vocal pattern emerges and carries through the song. Crosby begins the next song, "Orleans," a cappella. Chorus vocals join Crosby's, thick like in a Gregorian chant. Crosby's vocal joined by acoustic guitar comes to us in French. A picked pattern on the guitar ends the song with harmonics. A sense of chant and reverie follows in the playful wordless vocals that conclude the album.

Crosby's recording brings together Joni Mitchell, Neil Young, Graham Nash, photographer/folk musician Henry Diltz, and members of Jefferson Airplane (Grace Slick, Paul Kantner, Jorma Kaukonen, and Jack Casady) and the Grateful Dead (Phil Lesh, Jerry Garcia, Bill Kreutzman, Mickey Hart). It was dedicated to Christine Hinton and recorded at Wally Heider's studio with Bill Halverson.

Graham Nash's *Song for Beginners* has a minstrel quality. Recorded at Wally Heider's studio in San Francisco, Nash's first solo album is song-driven. It is folk music based and tends to be more lyric-centered than Crosby's record. The liner notes quip "All Artists Appear Courtesy of Themselves." And guest artists there are: Rita Coolidge, Jerry Garcia, Dave Mason, Joe Yankee, Phil Lesh, saxophonist Dorian Rudnitsky, and Seemon Posthuma. Nash appears on the cover in a self-portrait, as if in a mirror in a garden, holding a camera. The album sleeve insert is a sharp black and white photo by Joel Bernstein that shows Nash intently perusing reports on the state of the world in an open newspaper. Bill Halverson was the recording engineer for this album, along with Larry Cox and Russ Gary. Nathaniel Kunkel remixed the tracks in Kauai. Nash begins the album with "Military Madness" and concludes with "Chicago."

"Military Madness" is about his father in wartime Britain in the 1940s. Nash traces a bit of his own autobiography and reflects upon how his father's experience of war and his own intersected with how the war affected the country. The song sounds the keynote of social concern about war and peace and the note of nostalgia or memory that winds through this album, along with its wistful romantic feelings. "Military Madness" opens on a full strum of the acoustic guitar and moves along with a bounce. A wah-wah pedal adds its distinctive color and later becomes the sound of a guitar lead. "Better Days," which follows, is in one sense a hopeful recollection and a meditation on love that has gone away. In the lyric the speaker recognizes a search for love and truth in a strange land. Nash's vocal is front and center and very present above a piano that is then joined by guitar, bass, and a gated drum sound heightened with a touch of reverb. Nash's vocal jumps an octave over a slow march rhythm. There is a tempo change introduced by a piano and this is accompanied by Beatles-like background harmonies. A beautiful saxophone solo breaks in melodically and the song fades on a drum pattern, sax, and background vocals. "Wounded Bird" brings an acoustic guitar and a quiet, intimate vocal and an ABAB rhyme scheme. The song is addressed to someone who has gone through difficulties. It counsels that a person has to love himself and balance humility with pride. A minstrel image of a wandering hobo or knight who faces danger for the sake of the lady enters the song. The wounded bird could be Crosby but the personal tone of this song also gives it a universal quality embracing anyone who has been wounded in some way. "I Used to Be King" may be a self-critique. One can have big dreams and feel like a king but if one builds on sand those illusions can all be swept away. The sand shifts and the dream disintegrates. This is also a love song that asks questions, considers overcoming loss and hurt, and vows to not be heartbroken again. It begins in 3/4 time and then jumps to double-time only to slow back to a steady 3/4. Nash doubles his vocal. Jerry Garcia adds the steel pedal guitar that CSN&Y listeners would also hear on Nash's song "Teach Your Children." The song "Be Yourself" has a chorus "comprised of everyone loose there," say the liner notes. With the strummed acoustic-guitar the folk music quality of Nash's album continues. This song is not the quite the spontaneous sounding hippie fest of Crosby's "Music Is Love" but it is similar in its communal spirit. The singer begins by asking what it feels like when drifting aimlessly. There may be a trace of the biblical in references to a lost savior and the prodigal son's return.

The song seems to be about self-awareness and authenticity. It argues against computers or mechanisms that may shut off true vision, or TV broadcasts that may teach lies. There is a call to be true to oneself and set oneself free. With "Simple Man" he speaks of singing songs and playing tunes and addresses someone in a sincere-sounding love song. He recognizes a need for her companionship and realizes that alone he might not "make it." There is a simple chord-based piano part. Rita Coolidge adds a nice vocal that complements Nash's. Dorian Rudnitsky contributes stirring lines on a fiddle. "Man in the Mirror" beginning in 3/4 time is almost country-sounding. The mirror seems to be a through-line on this album: an image of self-reflection, like the album sleeve cover image. In this song, the singer is walking on a wire, as if he is a performer in a circus. Even living at this height—in a tree, or in the air—does not mean that one is free. The tempo increases and we hear Hollies or Beatles-like harmonies. The title is appropriate: this is a song of self-reflection. "There's Only One" favors a locked end rhyme. It begins by moving from "-all" to "-ool" (five times each). This is broken up by three short lines that end "on," "one," "in." The song continues with the end rhyme of "-ace" three times followed by the matching off-rhyme "waste" and "taste." A saxophone solo returns and is joined by "ooo" background vocals as the song plays out to the end. "Sleep Song" begins with a simple strum of the guitar and a quiet, intimate vocal that sounds almost like a lullaby. The lyric speaks of the exchange of a kiss and a couple's arms placed around each other. The singer asks if it was all a dream and watches the lover leave, seeing a trace of her disappearing through a doorway. It is as if he has captured the moment in a camera frame and then the image has evaporated. Yet, as the lover vanishes he makes a promise of a return to that intimacy they knew together. The song slips into a beautiful vocal round. "Chicago" is the song that declares that we can change the world by attending to the call of justice, by being uniquely individual yet joining in solidarity. (Nash slips in a caustic reference to the "silent majority" of the Nixon years.) "Chicago" opens on drums and organ and moves into an insistent march. Nash's assertive doubled-vocal rises over the top on the chorus. His vocal and the five female backing vocalists singing in unison lift the song to further insistence and an almost jubilant declaration of purpose. People need freedom beyond regulation and freedom is a possibility. We can create that change.[3]

Stephen Stills alternated styles on his rough edged first album with his acoustic guitar in the snow outside Gold Hill in the Colorado mountains. He opened with "Love the One You're With." This was followed by "Do for the Others," "Sit Yourself Down," "Black Queen," and "Cherokee." The record included appearances by Jimi Hendrix, Eric Clapton, Ringo Starr, John Sebastian, Rita Coolidge, Cass Elliott, and Crosby and Nash.

Stills' second album (1971) included "Change Partners," "Sugar Babe," and "Marianne." The year 1972 brought along Chris Hillman and Al Perkins, as Stills created Manassas and recorded a live double album. Hillman adds much musically with mandolin and his vocal and instrumental skills. However, it is primarily Stills' band and album. CSN was reviewed at the same time as Stills' *Manassas* (May 25, 1972) by Bud Scoppa.[4]

In 1972, audiences were again clamoring for a reunion tour of Crosby, Stills, Nash, and Young. Stephen Stills was busy with Manassas. Crosby and Nash were performing concert dates together. They had joined as a duo and ABC Records had signed them. The *Graham Nash and David Crosby* album appeared in 1972. In Boston, Neil Young arrived on stage one night with them. Crosby and Nash continued to work together as duo. *Wind on the Water* was produced in 1975 and *Whistling Down the Wire* emerged in 1976. *Crosby and Nash Live* (1977) was cobbled from live performances on their tour. Material from their autumn 1971 tour was later released as *Another Stoney Evening* (1998).

Atlantic Records, meanwhile, had released the CSNY live album *4 Way Street*. In November, Crosby and Nash went into Heider's studio to record. They brought in a stellar group of musicians with them: Russ Kunkel on drums, Leland Sklar on bass, Craig Doerge on piano, Danny Korchmar on guitar, and the versatile David Lindley on just about everything else. Jackson Browne, Joni Mitchell, and James Taylor contributed background vocals.

During this time, Crosby and Nash's contact continued with Joni Mitchell and with the emerging talent of Jackson Browne. Joni Mitchell released *Blue* (1971), one of her finest albums, and followed it with *For the Roses* (1972). Soon she was exploring jazz tones and textures which appeared on *Court and Spark* (1974). The album included "Help Me" and "Free Man in Paris." She began the movement toward the jazz exploration of her late 1970s work with Charles Mingus, Jaco Pastorius, and Herbie Hancock.

---

3. *Going Solo*

Jackson Browne's first album, released in January 1972, was self-titled. However, it appeared in a brown sleeve with a canvas bag with the words "Saturate Before Using" stamped on it and most of the record buying public decided that that must be the name of the album. The record was mostly filled with the kind of introspective, lyric-laden mellow folk-rock you'd expect from early Jackson Browne records. There was "Doctor My Eyes" though. That was the song Graham Nash recognized was a sure single. Asylum Records, established with David Geffen's energy, was on its first trial run with that album. After Jackson Browne's album, the Eagles joined the Asylum roster, recording and releasing their songs. Jackson Browne's second album, *For Everyman* (1973), was recorded across nine months.[5]

The song "For Everyman" was written with David Crosby in mind. Crosby contributed vocal harmonies to the recording. Anthony DeCurtis connected it with "Wooden Ships" and "that escapist thing" about "human possibility," as Crosby once called it in speaking with *Rolling Stone*.[6] Sixties utopian dreams were affected by social and political tensions in America in the early 1970s. David Crosby and Paul Kantner were science fiction readers and created the daydream of escaping on a spaceship to freedom. Jackson Browne wasn't leaving. He was affirming everyman (and woman) in his song.

Jackson Browne's *Late for the Sky* (1974) appeared to offer a recording of songs that were linked together as a cohesive album project concept. His use of his touring band may have had much to do with this (David Lindley, Doug Haywood, Jai Winding, Larry Zach). Bruce Springsteen called the album Browne's "masterpiece" when Browne was inducted into the Rock Hall of Fame. (Springsteen would begin to record his *Born to Run* album in May 1974.) *Late for the Sky* included background vocals from Dan Fogelberg, J.D. Souther, and Don Henley.[7]

During this time, Stephen Stills seemed to be spinning out of control, personally and commercially. His album with Manassas, *Down the Road* (1972), did not have the verve and focus of their first recording and went nowhere commercially. As David Crosby was watching his mother become ill and die, Neil Young was experiencing some troubles of his own. Danny Whitten, the guitar player in his band, Crazy Horse, was enmeshed in a heroin habit that soon took his life. Whitten overdosed and died. Young went into semi-seclusion.

Crosby, Stills, Nash and Young's 50-Year Quest

In 1972, Neil Young re-emerged with *Harvest,* one of folk-rock music's classic recordings. During this time Young turned to Crosby and Nash for solace and musical collaboration. Meanwhile, Graham Nash was going through his own sorrow. His girlfriend Amy Gossage had been killed by her brother and Nash was deeply affected. Crosby's own loss of his girlfriend Christine stayed heavily on his mind and now his mother was struggling with cancer. Despite CSN's rousing popular success, this was a difficult time. Crosby and Nash joined Neil Young on his tour for nineteen shows, providing vocal harmonies. Stephen Stills, at this time, continued working with Manassas. He had gotten married to Veronique Sanson and had taken some time off. But when Crosby, Nash, and Young decided to go to Hawaii to record, months later Stills joined them.

This was their first reunion attempt. In the summer of 1973, Neil Young, with his girlfriend Carrie, rented a house in Maui, in Hawaii. Stephen Stills and Veronique joined him there. Elliot Roberts and his girlfriend soon followed, as did David Crosby with Debbie Donovan. Graham Nash, who went unaccompanied, fell everlastingly in love with Hawaii, where he lived for many years. They planned to record an album they intended to call *Human Highway,* starting with their sessions in Maui. Could they make a fresh start? Their songs suggested that they had the means to do so. David Crosby's boat and the Pacific breeze inspired more images of "wooden ships on the water." "Human Highway" was a Neil Young song. Graham Nash's "And So It Goes" and "Prison Song" were recorded with bass player Tim Drummond and drummer Johnny Barbata. That wide array of songs and their talents should have coalesced into an album, "Human Highway." However, that is not what happened. Instead, the album project dissolved. They would tour together but the recording was not completed. Nash says that the energy just fell out of the project.[8] Again, they went their separate ways.

Critics got word that tensions had arisen between Crosby, Stills, Nash, and Young. There was really no surprise in that. Collaboration can be difficult. The hearts and minds of artists become invested in their work. Sometimes collaborators are sensitive to each other's criticism or else they may be insistent upon their vision. It can be rewarding when the unique musical abilities of others stretch one's own. However, there is always a need for mutual respect and communication and the volatility of fiercely

---

independent creators can be a difficult mix. Further dismay would come in 1973, when equipment manager Bruce Berry overdosed. Again, Neil Young was close and cut by that loss. He went off to work with his band Crazy Horse and decided to go his own way—again.

In autumn 1973, Nash began assembling material for *Wild Tales*, his second solo album. A CSN&Y tour was suggested for 1974 by promoter Bill Graham. This would be among the first of the arena tours that have become a feature of rock music for many years. They opened many shows with Stills' "Love the One You're With." Whatever was happening between them offstage seemed to disappear when they got into the music. The tour was wildly successful but that summer, on July 29, news came that their friend Cass Elliott had died. Cass Elliott was unforgettable. She had been such an energetic presence in their lives in the early days of Crosby, Stills, and Nash.

Meanwhile, Stills returned to Colorado. He attempted to revive Manassas, although Dallas Taylor was caught up in an addiction to heroin. Stills turned to bassist Kenny Passarelli, who had been working with Joe Walsh. Walsh opened on Manassas's East coast tour. Passarelli played both sets, with Walsh and with Stills. Passarelli would play bass on Dan Fogelberg's *Souvenirs* album, produced by Walsh. Graham Nash sang background vocals on Fogelberg's first hit songs, "Part of the Plan" and "The Long Way," while the Eagles' Don Henley and Glenn Frey joined him on another song. Soon the popular Eagles country harmonies sound would go through some changes with the addition of Joe Walsh's guitar and Don Felder's guitar. The band would journey further from the country inflected Jackson Browne-Glenn Frey song "Take It Easy," Frey's "Lyin' Eyes" and J.D. Souther's contributions, to "One of These Nights," on to "Hotel California" and "Life in the Fast Lane," as Joe Walsh joined the band. Henley would begin writing his lyrics of scathing satirical social commentary that would be featured in the Eagles' later work and would become characteristic of his solo career. Crosby, Stills, Nash and Young may also best be followed as four solo careers during this time.

In the midst of this blossoming age of the singer-songwriter, the work of Joni Mitchell, Jackson Browne, and others continued to prosper. Neil Young increasingly became a star in his own right. Stephen Stills produced a wide range of music with Manassas and on his own. Former Buffalo

Springfield member Richie Furay turned his heart over to Jesus and Christian faith and produced several sincere sounding records, like *I've Got a Reason*. His bandmate from Poco, Jim Messina, began producing Kenny Loggins and soon joined him in recording and performing as a duo. J.D. Souther wrote for the Eagles and Chris Hillman embraced bluegrass with the Desert Rose Band. Graham Nash and David Crosby each recorded solo albums, as Crosby sunk deeper into drug addiction. Nash was supportive throughout and the friends later recorded together.

Crosby and Nash, after the Hawaii sessions, put together an electric rock band. Usually they had worked as an acoustic duo, or in acoustic group arrangements. Tim Drummond played bass and Crosby and Nash sang and David Lindley joined them on guitar. Lindley caught the flu and could not continue on the tour. They were able to substitute Don Felder, who would soon be working with the Eagles.

Late in 1973, as Stephen Stills performed an acoustic set on stage he was joined by Nash and Crosby. Neil Young joined them on stage. This was a brief reconnection—like a flicker of light. In fall 1973, Graham Nash worked on his own project in San Francisco. (The studio was called Rudy Records after a Doberman.) He was working through the loss of Amy Gossage. This became a solo album, *Wild Tales* (December 1973). Joel Bernstein and David Crosby provided harmonies. Atlantic did not strongly support the record, although Ahmet Ertegun claims the public did not react to it.[9] The front cover showed a bearded Graham Nash and suggested a tone of life matched by the album's cover, drained of color.

The end of that year brought Neil Young back in contact with Crosby and Nash. During their rock set in San Francisco before Christmas 1973, Young walked onstage and mixed his songs with theirs. This generated some excitement among their fans and suggested possibilities of a reunion. Yet, creative interests and personal dispositions seemed to take them in other directions. In early 1974, Stephen Stills had a solo album in the works, "As I Come of Age." Stills concert cuts became *Stephen Stills Live*, which Jan David engineered and mixed. Young was also recording his solo album *On the Beach*. Nash thought of doing further solo work and a tour. However, there would be a CSN&Y summer tour. Bill Graham discussed possible venues. Crosby, Stills, Nash, and Young would include their acoustic sets in big arena spaces. It looked like a promising deal. So, they began to bring their music together again. Neil Young's ranch in the Santa Cruz Mountains was a free and open rehearsal space where they gathered. In May 1974, they were playing outdoors to the hills. Then they would go into Neil Young's studio, Broken Arrow, with Tom Drummond on bass, Russ Kunkel on drums, and Joe Lala playing percussion.

In summer 1974, they began their tour of stadiums and other large venues. Fans wondered if there would be a new record. Atlantic Records capitalized on the tour with the release of *So Far*, a greatest hits album for a group that had only released two previous studio recordings. *Déjà Vu* and *Crosby Stills and Nash* had all of these songs on them, except for the searing and quickly recorded "Ohio" and their cappella dirge-lament "Find the Cost of Freedom." The songs were masterful but they did not represent an entire career, as some greatest hits albums do. Rather than *So Far*, the record might have been called So Few. (Or maybe So Fa, with a nod to Rodgers and Hammerstein.) A Joni Mitchell watercolor sketch graced the cover, outlining their images in colors against a white background. It became their bestselling album to date. In 1974, *Rolling Stone* carried Ben Fong Torres' article that held that America, Bread, the early Eagles, Poco, Seals and Crofts, Loggins and Messina, and Souther, Hillman, Furay paled in comparison to Crosby, Stills and Nash. Yet, by listing those acts he suggested a category of folk-rock, if not a similarity of sound. *Human Highway* was to be a studio album, one begun on Hawaii. Again, this title suggested motion and life on the road. *Human Highway* turned out to be a dead end. The recording was held back rather than released.

July 13–14 at the Oakland Coliseum was the first stadium venue. The Band, Jesse Colin Young, and Joe Walsh were also on the bill. A 6 p.m. show began in the sunshine. Out they came: Crosby with fluffy long hair, Nash with a little chin beard, Stills with his Firebird electric guitar. Crosby was the talker, the emcee. Neil Young joined them on "Wooden Ships," a white Gretsch guitar in his hands and shades over his eyes. There was, as expected, an acoustic set and a plugged-in rock set. They sang Crosby's "Carry Me," Nash's "Grave Concern," Stills' "First Things First," Young's "Pushed It Over the End." There was also Paul McCartney's song "Blackbird" and Neil Young's "Long May You Run" and "Only Love Can Break a Heart." Neil Young traveled from show to show in his Winnebago, while the others flew by plane to their gigs.

CSN&Y remained political. The political themes have been everywhere in their songs: from Stephen Stills' "For What It's Worth" to Crosby's "Long Time Gone" and from Nash's "Military Madness" and "Chicago" to Neil Young's "Ohio" and "Southern Man." These songs have appeared on CSN albums, CSN&Y albums, Neil Young albums, and on Crosby-Nash recordings. Crosby, Stills, Nash, and Young were opposed to the war in Vietnam and rejected the approach of the Nixon administration to that overseas conflict. In 1974 they were virtually glued to their television sets, watching the proceedings of the congressional Watergate hearings. During their concert at Roosevelt Raceway August 8, 1974, backstage they tuned in to Nixon's resignation and they then announced it to the crowd. Later, Nash's song "Grave Concern" would include overdubs of the statements of Nixon's staff, denying knowledge of the Watergate break-in. The tour ended at Wembley Stadium in England.

After the tour they went in different directions. Young and Nash went to Europe and drove together to Holland. Stills went to Paris. Crosby went back to the United States where his daughter Donovan Ann was born. Later they all met for sessions in Sausalito for the album that never materialized. They tossed around the *Human Highway* album idea again. However, that was not to be. Conflict resumed and Stephen Stills sliced up a master tape.[10] Nash, who was furious at this, sought distance from CSN&Y issues. Social conscience was tugging at Nash, who was clearly seeing the disparity between the income and material acquisition that was evident at David Geffen's gatherings and the poor farm workers who were not far away. He knew that there was a need to balance privilege with being a strong voice and an advocate for social causes. Social justice themes entered more of his songs, like "Field Worker" and "Take the Money and Run." He wrote "Cowboy of Dreams," reflecting on the difficulties CSN were having with Neil Young, coupled with his admiration for him as an artist. Crosby, Stills, and Nash were going through yet another period of change and transition.

4

Almost Cut My Hair

Lifestyle, Social Concern and the Sixties

There was a synergy of broad-based protest that emerged in the late 1960s: anti-war protest, civil rights concern, a call for reform, a new assertion of the rights of women, an awakening of environmental concern. Within the context of U.S. history, the sixties were not entirely unique in emphasizing change. There were precedents. However, there was a significant energy, a spark of ideals. Rock music was its soundtrack.

Crosby, Stills, Nash and Young represent a generation's earnest concern for peace, civil rights, environmental stewardship, women's rights, and social justice. Yet, the generation has also been faulted for excess, for a swing toward hedonism, or for unreconciled inner violence. Was this the tribe of tribulation: one that saw a broken world and wanted to remedy it, or one that sought to escape from it? How are we to reconcile the near-ethereal beauties of Crosby, Stills, Nash and Young music with the dissonance of personal struggles, the combustible emotion, the valuable pronouncements, and the edginess of conflict?

The counterculture critiqued the establishment and proposed responses of inclusion, youth, lifestyle, activism. "The passion for change ranged widely," say the historians who have edited the academic journal *The Sixties*. In "Time Is an Ocean: The Past and Future of the Sixties" Jeremy Varon, M.S. Foley and J. McMillan consider concerns about race, culture, the distribution of wealth, legal and political rights, power, class, and ethnicity. They call the sixties transformative. Born between 1964 and 1970, they were just a bit too young to be "in" the sixties and yet have been affected by it and have seen its "best values and impulses." In the sixties there was concern, a dream of community, a new social energy, they observe. It was "by turns dignified, militant, utopian, and delusional."[1] David Farber contributes an article in the journal in which he underscores the energy of civil rights, feminism, youth protest, and shifting social mores.[2]

We may think about American cultural history in terms of decades for the sake of convenience. However, no period is contained in this way. Some historians and sociologists divide what we call the sixties into two periods. The first ranges from John F. Kennedy's run for the presidency and his inaugural (1960–61) to the middle of the decade. The second period begins around 1967, including the tumultuous year of 1968, and extends to about 1974. Other cultural critics mark the era as the long sixties, extending from about 1955–56 to about 1974. They see a youth culture and an oppositional stance that appeared in the 1950s with the Beats, greasers, the James Dean image, and John Osborne's angry young man onstage in London. Rock and roll was a rebellious partner. Rock music developed with youth culture from the days of Elvis Presley, Chuck Berry, Little Richard, and Jerry Lee Lewis into the early 1960s. It appropriated the blues and was an amalgamation of the ballad traditions of the British Isles and their transformations in Appalachia, the Delta blues and Chicago blues, country and western, and rhythm and blues. It was earthy. It was passionate. It had an infectious backbeat.

From the mid–1960s, rock culture developed alongside social consciousness and calls for reform in politics and in lifestyle. When Crosby, Stills, Nash, and Young began to create music with the Byrds, the Hollies, and the Buffalo Springfield, they began to participate in the ritual, experiential, philosophical, and social dimensions of rock music culture.[3] Crosby, Stills, Nash and Young reflected the pop/rock music of the British Invasion (Nash, the Hollies), the emerging California sound (Crosby), southern roots, blues and country (Stills), and a folk/rock voice from Canada (Young).

We use the sixties to signify. The seeds of our present political and cultural separations were sown in the sixties and the period still resonates among us. The positions of the sixties have been used politically since the Reagan and the Clinton years, as Bernard von Bothmer points out in *Fram-*

ing the Sixties (2010). For some people whose politics align on the right, the sixties brought the curse of political correctness; it is the bogeyman who lurks behind the curtain. Those sixties fostered permissiveness, is their claim. Others recall a hope that came from the best in that era and hope that what emerged in terms of human rights, racial equality, gender equality, and ecological concern would not be thrown away by what they consider regressive politics. That sixties is recalled as an era of dreams. As Alan Wolfe wrote in the *New Republic* (June 2018), "The world that 1968 ushered in is a far cry from the one activists imagined." The year 1968 was tempestuous. In the year 2018 books were written to try to make sense of it.[4]

In *Imagine Nation*, Peter Braunstein and Michael Doyle examined the conservative criticism that the sixties left in its wake consumerism and individualism. They observed that neither of these trends can bind a nation. These writers did not regard the sixties as a movement but as "an inherently unstable collection of attitudes, tendencies, postures, gestures, lifestyles, visions, hedonistic pleasures, moralisms, negations and affirmations."[5]

There are conservative positions that approach the sixties more harshly. In *Newsweek* (August 21, 1995) George F. Will argued with "the myth that there is something inherently noble about adopting an adversarial stance toward bourgeois or middle-class values." He insisted that "society's success depends on these values." Will's opinion piece appeared one year and one week after the 25th anniversary of Woodstock and soon after the passing of Jerry Garcia.[6] He cited the irresponsibility of one young couple who abandoned their baby and claimed to be Deadheads, as if they characterized all of the Grateful Dead's listeners. Will called the spirit of the sixties "infantile" and asserted that the period promoted "disdain for inhibitions on recreational drugs and sex" and "shattered lives and devastated cities." His rhetoric appears hyperbolic. However, his acerbic comment that the graying sixties cohort "seeks derivative vitality from aging rock stars" may bear a grain of truth. Many rock acts today live on nostalgia and are sustained through nostalgia tours. However, his conclusion that it means nothing to say that a rock band "epitomizes freedom" is too dismissive. Artists from CSN&Y to U2, Bruce Springsteen, Tom Morello, to others continually express the call for freedom.

In contrast to George Will's conservative assessment, President Bill Clinton told *Rolling Stone* (September 17, 1992): "The postwar generation was raised with a sense of unlimited possibility." He acknowledged, "It didn't all work out but we did a lot of good." Jann Wenner shared with Clinton and his readers his perception that Clinton-Gore was a "generational ticket" singing the words to Fleetwood Mac's "Don't Stop" at the Democratic National Convention.[7]

By the time that Clinton became the American president in 1993 the rise and fall narrative of the sixties was prevalent. It held that the idealism generated by JFK's New Frontier and the optimism of Martin Luther King's "I Have a Dream" speech began to wane as the war in Vietnam escalated. It suggested that the counterculture's Summer of Love disintegrated with assassinations, race riots, Kent State, and a decline that culminated in Watergate. However, assessments since the 1990s have contested this view. New historians have emphasized the conservative movement in America. Historians have discussed the global context of post-colonialism and sixties revolutionary movements and the student movement in France and throughout Europe. Others have considered the long sixties, the cultural influences that extend across more than a decade.

In *The Road to Character* (2015), David Brooks suggests that "both capitalism and Woodstock were about the liberation of the self, the expression of self." They were able to merge in this generation because both of them "encouraged people to measure their lives by how they were able to achieve gratification."[8] That makes some sense, but surely there is something more: something that has to do with the kind of virtues and character the *New York Times* columnist discusses in his book.

The counterculture movement of the sixties was a response to postwar America. It was a quest for the liberation of the human spirit and a resistance to technocratic structures that restricted or dehumanized the individual. Science and technology advanced after the Second World War. There was government funding for research and development and an emphasis on "knowledge industries." The Second World War had consumed the energies of people across the world. It launched further scientific and technology development and an upsurge of the economy in the United States. Science made many contributions and people believed in the prospects made possible by science. However, scientism and technique had a down-side. President Dwight Eisenhower designated the intersections of business, government, and technology "the military-industrial complex." Meanwhile, the world of popular culture was spreading out, along with film, public relations, and advertising. The presence of the atom bomb cast a shadow of concern about the fate of the earth.

Public consciousness and critical discourse was changing. There were social movements, transformations, a quest for peace, a growth of feminism and environmental consciousness. There was dissent. However, family often took precedence for Americans from the 1950s through the 1960s. The troubles of Vietnam beamed in over the television. For many Americans, politics, war, urban conflict seemed far away. Even so, it was a time when war did appear within public vision on television. In 1970, "Ohio" sounded on radios across North America with an appalled urgency and fury-driven insistence.

Intellectual Precursors

The intellectual ground for the sixties was prepared by a variety of thinkers. A political perspective and critique of totalitarianism came from Hannah Arendt. Arendt's *The Origins of Totalitarianism* countered the totalitarian threat she saw emerging in the 1930s and during Second World War. Arendt rejected tyranny. She explored issues of control and hegemony and rejected totalitarianism as rule of the mob. In her view, people ought not to be led into a reckless venture that was antithetical to democracy. In a spirit of ethical concern, she critiqued "the banality of evil" in the figure of Adolph Eichmann. Arendt recognized that the collapse of the European class structure in the nineteenth century occurred under the influence of modernity and nationalism. She proposed that when institutions and structures dissolved there was a void that was filled by totalitarianism.[9] European intellectual voices arrived in the United States, such as Theodor Adorno of the Frankfurt School, Albert Einstein, the novelist Thomas Mann, and Erich Fromm, who brought together thought from Freud and Marx in *Escape from Freedom* and *The Sane Society*. Postwar existentialism had an impact upon some thinkers in the 1950s. Jean-Paul Sartre rose to prominence in France and Simone de Beauvoir wrote

The Second Sex. These were some of the intellectual forbears of critique and resistance.

In the 1950s, C. Wright Mills developed a sociological investigation of *The Power Elite* (1956). William Whyte explored post-war conformity in *The Organization Man* (1956). Vance Packard critiqued advertising in *The Hidden Persuaders* (1957), the social climbers of *The Status Seekers* (1959), and the disposable society of planned obsolescence in *The Waste Makers* (1960). Herbert Marcuse wrote *One Dimensional Man* (1964). He opposed what he viewed as the intrusiveness of techno-society and he addressed the repression of Eros. He saw no Marxist revolution in the making. What he asserted was a declaration of human potentiality in *An Essay on Liberation.* Rachel Carson's *Silent Spring* (1962) helped to initiate the environmental movement. Feminists like Kate Millett, who wrote *Sexual Politics* (1970), and Germaine Greer, who wrote *The Female Eunuch* (1970), would foster a women's liberation movement. John Kenneth Galbraith and Robert Heilbroner called attention to economic issues and the new industrial society. Critical voices entered the media via periodicals like *Esquire, The New Yorker, Playboy, Time, The New Republic* and others that opened the way for alternative publications.

If history can be said to be cyclical and to move in a dialectical pattern, where on that pendulum are we now? How has America changed? Why? These are the big historical questions. More than 50 years later we are still close to the sixties. It may take future historians to help us to unravel it all. In the sixties people were asking meaningful questions: What is the good life, the meaningful life? What is legitimate authority? The U.S. Constitution provides the right of free speech, freedom of the press, and freedom of assembly to question authority. What is the role of the Federal government in protecting human rights and civil rights? How can we respect the dignity of all persons and create greater equality and opportunity for women, for minorities, for indigent people who are marginalized? Can the environment be respected and preserved for the sake of future generations, both human and non-human, as an integral system that sustains life?

Crosby, Stills, Nash and Young are among those who hold the notion that musical expression and political thinking matter to the future of American democracy. Obviously not everyone who has listened to Crosby,

Stills, Nash, and Young subscribes to their worldview or their activism. For more than fifty years CSN&Y have addressed themes of freedom and liberation. Their political stances are part of this. As they point out, you don't have to agree. They are going to speak anyway.

In the sixties, activists set forth challenges to conventions, institutions, and the bottom line. The civil rights struggle sought a clear voice. The anti-war resistance escalated as the casualties in Vietnam increased. A new conversation was also brewing. There were many people who sought to make America better, individuals who had humanitarian impulses to improve life. This includes people whose politics or approach is different from CSN&Y. This was also a time in which the seeds of conservativism were planted. The story to be told here, however, is the one in which CSN&Y was part of. The varied landscape that reshaped America for a time from the left projected a determined liberalism. What this generation said and did in the sixties increased freedom of expression.

The Making of the Counterculture

When Theodore Roszak wrote *The Making of the Counterculture* (1970), he positioned the counterculture as a response to a society of "technical expertise." Roszak followed this study with *Where the Wasteland Ends.* In one passage in that book he pictures a family that typifies consumerism waiting breathlessly to see the geysers spout at Yellowstone National Park. Roszak's thought then moved toward "ecopsychology." In later years, he cautioned that information could "crowd out ideas" and critical literacy. This would leave us with "disconnected facts," lost among "shapeless heaps of data."[10] In other words, Roszak was reminding us that information in itself is not knowledge. Discerning, thinking individuals are needed to make sense of the overflow of information. In Roszak's view, techno-scientific society had alienated the young who sought meaning in alternatives. This, in his view, was the alienated soul of the counterculture he sought to revive.

In 1970, R. Serge Denisoff and Mark H. Levine wrote on "Generations and Counter-Culture." Calling upon the theories of Karl Mannheim, they wrote that generations have a unique relationship to historical time and place. They are situated and develop a distinct awareness. Thus, the sixties generation, or Woodstock nation, responded to their moment. Denisoff and Levine wrote: "in periods of rapid social change, generations are likely to develop highly distinctive outlooks and aims which conflict with those of older generations, thus leading to political youth movements as groups consciously emphasizing their character as generational units."[11] Denisoff was the first editor of *Popular Music and Society*. He was a sociologist who wrote on folk music, dissent, and the record industry. He addressed popular culture and the goal of mobilizing consciousness through song. However, he pointed out that "there is little, if any, concrete or empirical evidence that songs do in fact have independent impact upon attitudes in the public arena."[12] In *The Journal of Folklore*, writing with Jens Lund, he pointed out that the rise of the political voice of this generation could be situated historically as an outgrowth of an historical-intellectual progression beginning with the "garden of Eden image of man." You could trace this to ideas of humanity in the state of nature that had been approached in different ways by the philosophers Hobbes, Locke, and Rousseau. Or, one could consider images of the untrammeled and ascetic life and faith advocated by St. Francis of Assisi. In American literature we meet James Fenimore Cooper's "hero of the wilderness," Natty Bumpo, and the transcendentalism of Emerson and Thoreau. Added to this vision of freedom and self-reliance might be the figure of "the American Adam" that has been explored by literary critics like R.W.B. Lewis. The desire to get back to a prelapsarian garden also echoes throughout American theology. The counter to apocalyptic millenarianism is salvation beyond this world, or the drive for reform and healing within it. One sees this in the Crosby-Kantner dream of escape in "Wooden Ships," or in Joni Mitchell's song of urgency of getting back to the garden. The hard realities of the nuclear age hang over the hope embodied in each of those proposals.

More recently, cultural critics and historians have reflected upon the direction in which America has gone since the 1960s. Thomas Franks has attempted to chart the path of counterculture to cyberculture. He appears to agree that the sixties remains at the center of our culture wars as he writes on business culture. Robert C. Cotrell affirms that sex, drugs, and rock and roll were "serious" and part of "a force for change."[13] He points to unresolved social conservatisms and radicalisms. A conservative critique of the sixties views it as a time of a fall from grace. For them it is a time when Adam bit the apple, an anomaly that resulted in the unraveling of America. Allan Bloom wrote *The Closing of the American Mind* (1986) from a concern about social and intellectual decline and he blamed rock music for clouding and distracting the American mind. Robert Bork asserted that we were slouching toward Gomorrah. Conservatives like Bork asserted that we were losing traditional values, succumbing to relativism, losing civility. Our moral compass was shot and we were falling into a culture of anything goes. No doubt citizens of the Western world were experiencing the social strains of modernity, the future shock that Alvin Toffler wrote of in 1970.

The counterculture offered energy in the search for peace, human understanding, and brotherhood. It called for freedom. It called for people to question authority. It embraced rock music and a sense of urgency. Yet, the counterculture was pluralistic rather than monolithic. For some, there was a transgressive break with traditional mores. There was no break with capitalism per se, but there was a challenge to reform institutions, a search for alternatives to mechanization and depersonalization. The hippies sought to break with convention, to proclaim freedom with bright colors and tie-dye against the man in the gray flannel suit, to live with hair set free beyond crew-cut conformities. This was an era disturbed by Vietnam. It rejected the abridgement of civil rights and cried out for a vision of democracy.

Twenty-five years after Woodstock, in August 1994, there was another gathering of bands in Saugerties, New York. Woodstock revisited (version II) went commercial and drew criticism.[14] Likewise, another festival five years later, in 1999, appeared to be commercialized. How would anyone ever reconstitute the original, which was so linked with the spirit of the times of the sixties? Bethel didn't exactly become Babylon but the branding and tacking on of corporate logos was a disappointment for some, even if the bands were good. Who needs replicas of the sixties, they argued. The world needs not rock imitators but originals. Save the facsimiles for bat day at the stadium. We live in an age when TV commercials play the countercultural hits of the sixties to sell product, a time when actors tote guitars they cannot play. However, to mark a fifty-year anniversary in 2019 is an act of historical memorialization. Could Michael Lang's goal of a Woodstock reunion at Bethel Woods in 2019 achieve a balance between the economics of hosting such a festival and the kind of inspiration that drove the first one in 1969?

The rock counterculture was idealistic. It held a dream of a new cultural agenda and promoted possibilities for self-expression, a hope for "peace and love," and a breakthrough of something communal. The rhetoric of the time found its way into song lyrics. The Youngbloods called upon their listeners to get together and try to love each other. "Love the One You're With" wrote Stephen Stills. Whether this was a call for intimacy and availability to whomever one was with, or a call for promiscuity, who knew? You could interpret songs in different ways.

So, amid the binaries of optimism and cynicism, community and alienation, transcendence and absorption in the mundane, Crosby, Stills, Nash and Young were vocal harmony and interpersonal friction. In *The Different Drum* (1987), M. Scott Peck affirmed that relationships can be difficult and that community is not without tension and disagreement. Yet, in the first line of his introduction to that book he stated: "In and through community lies the salvation of the world."[15] Crosby, Stills, Nash and Young are four very different individuals, strong-willed artists who, like a dysfunctional family, can fall into sharp disagreement. When that happens, gone is the incredible harmony. They become like guitarists hitting the overdrive pedal, wailing in dissonant sustained feedback from an amplifier. The work of negotiating differences and rising to a renewed harmony is difficult. It is not just Crosby, Stills, Nash and Young's problem. It is America's problem. It is the ongoing problem of human needs, domestic tensions, and a world being pushed by globalization toward a modulation into a new key.

If rock is to have a meaningful cultural voice, one that can prompt conversion of the heart and societal transformation, it must face the dissonance of economic and social challenges. It must actualize its potential to transform blues notes into soulful melodies. To affirm that rock and roll can never die is to also embrace the darkness. It is not only to proclaim with Chuck Berry that you love that "Rock and Roll Music," or to affirm with the Rolling Stones that you like it. It is to face the music, to resolutely encounter experience as muddy as Yasgur's Farm, and to believe in the redemptive possibility that rock music bears.

The Graying of America

The Greening of America by Charles Reich (1970) claimed to be an analysis of what was going on in the consciousness of this country. The book hit a nerve, received sharply critical reviews, sold several thousand copies, and then disappeared from the world of critical discussion. Why resurrect a work which has been largely dismissed by America's intellectual historians and has faded from social circles like yesterday's blue jeans? It is because today, along with books like Marilyn Ferguson's *The Aquarian Conspiracy*, Fritjof Capra's *The Turning Point*, or Theodore Roszak's *Where the Wasteland Ends*, Reich's popular analysis of corporate culture and his hopes for a libertarian future address the spirit of a changing awareness in America. We now recognize that we are indeed operating in transformed surroundings. Economically, we have moved into a post-industrial service economy. Socially and culturally, we are presented with the awareness that we live in a pluralistic, multi-ethnic society. Our lives are connected with an electronic universe of the Internet and the media. We are post-modern, perhaps post-post-modern.

In the sixties, the social critiques of Herbert Marcuse and Erich Fromm, to name only two, were far more acute than Reich's.[16] In comparison, Reich's 1972 book is popcorn—but it is good popcorn. It has the sound of hot air expanding. It rises into buttered rhetoric. Perhaps it was never a substantial diet, but it was tasty and interesting. It caught the heat of its times and made some noise.

The book, which sensed a shifting consciousness in America, has not endured, however, largely because there are difficulties with its method and its thesis. Reich deftly analyzes several aspects of corporate America, but he is vague about power and control. There is little in his book that would account for today's difficulties on the stock market or bailouts of banks or of automakers with their executives arriving in Washington in their corporate jets. Senator Bernie Sanders' claims may today seem more cogent. For the theorist Herbert Marcuse the hoped-for change was extremely formidable. For Reich it appears too easy—and it has not happened. In the days of Donald Trump some wonder what ever happened to the idealism of the sixties. Crosby, Stills, Nash and Young appear to be among them. We have thoroughly entered the age of globalization, the information age. The transformation of longstanding social and economic structures is not accomplished overnight. The shift in human consciousness may indeed be a necessary first step, but it does not follow that change in society is as simple as switching television channels with a remote control. Time has shown that the lauded sixties generation of Reich's "Consciousness III" are neither angelic saviors or notably different from the generations which preceded them. Perhaps, in all likelihood, neither are the Gen Xers and Millennials, although one can hold out hope.

Today there is greater ecological consciousness throughout the United States, Canada, and Europe and elsewhere. The voices of Rachel Carson's *Silent Spring*, Aldo Leopold's *Sand County Almanac*, or Thomas Berry's *Dream of the Earth* ring out among some of our contemporaries. Neil Young urges attention to oil sands and to Farm Aid. Graham Nash addresses the environmental issues and David Crosby declares that the climate change deniers are focused upon self-interest and not the public good. When we turn back to the pages of *The Greening of America*, however, there are few practical guidelines for ecological stewardship. For all of Reich's emphasis upon a return to naturalness, it must be noted that "natural" is not synonymous with the good and the green; it includes mold and algae as well as luxurious fields and hilltops. Today the new green world is shrewdly packaged and marketed. Everyone from publishers to Clairol Herbal Essence have climbed onto the ecological bandwagon. Our consciousness is raised by advertisers. The popular culture of young adults is saturated by advertising.

In his book, the law professor, Reich, too often tossed out reason and logic, stating his case with flourishes of rhetoric that would make Perry Mason proud. Espousing a change in consciousness, he invented a mythical prototype which would carry out this mission and vision of a new, green America. The dream was commendable. But what did it have to say about workers and women, blacks and Hispanics, the poor and the underprivileged who were not white and middle class like Reich himself? What did it really have to say about spiritual growth, or political engagement, or rock music's role in that?

The economist John Kenneth Galbraith noted that Reich had not worked out the economics of the Consciousness III lifestyle. Who, Galbraith asked, will take care of the ever-increasing consumption-oriented society? Will the rejection of the contrivances of the corporate state lead to a rejection of all serious mental and artistic pursuits? Galbraith found Reich "too vehemently critical."[17] He noted that life is a process and that today's critics who critique an earlier economic state of affairs are not necessarily wiser than those who have preceded them, only later; they critique in retrospect. That is true of us today also.

To speak in terms of economics or sociology, Reich's book appears naive. In fact, it is far more an eschatological tome of prophecy than a documented and intellectually grounded work of sociology. *Greening*, as Emile Capouya noted in *The Nation*, can be profitably approached in terms of a religious myth. Capouya wrote: "His language and images are often those of religious enthusiasm, and it is clear that the substance of his prophecy is little short of salvation in the religious sense." Capouya continues: "The myths he names ... have indeed been the dominant ideologies of the respective periods, and they have been persuasive enough as views of reality to lead us to that compound mistake, contemporary society." Greening is "designed to point up just those activities and expectations that we must abandon if we are to survive." It presents our experience to us as a metaphor.[18]

Most popular fads tend to mutate and go the way of the dinosaur. Reich, no doubt, caught a sense of the spirit which remains alive today in entrepreneurialism, new age and holistic approaches, small is beautiful, and back to nature green politics. There was in his narrative a hope that expanded consciousness and commitment would generate reform. Such thoughts are not new. They go back millennia. We may place aspects of the generation of changing consciousness alongside the Romantics. Reich's book frequently recalls the spirit of Jean-Jacques Rousseau, who said that "man is born free but is everywhere in chains." Rousseau, in *Emile*, urged an educational focus upon the nurturing of natural inclinations. His writings inspired Immanuel Kant's categorical imperative: a universal ethic of respect for the individual person as an end in himself or herself. All of this is duly noted in the critique of *Greening* that was provided by Charles Fried, a fellow law professor at Harvard. In his response to Reich in 1971, Fried called Reich's scenario sadly lacking in its analysis of labor and insight. To gain insight requires an expense of human labor and human spirit. Or, as Ringo Starr said, "It don't come easy."

The rock music infused spirit of the sixties has sometimes been likened to Romanticism.[19] The Romantics were passionate people consumed by the arduousness of their labor. Percy Bysshe Shelley called poets the unacknowledged legislators of the world. Charles Fried writes: "Their passionate and revolutionary conceptions were not born in casual, idle rap sessions." Reich's version is far "too intellectually lazy, too passive to overcome the enormous inertia of the existing system."[20] The past fifty years have borne out Fried's contention. It takes a tremendous amount of human energy and commitment to initiate change. Utopian visioning has a role to play in a process which must be backed by political action, social presence, and personal resolution. We all can be morally concerned about the national soul. But change is only fostered by personal and collective action. Crosby, Stills, Nash and Young seem to have indicated as much as their vision has matured across the years. Indicting our society and giving voice to its apparent failings is a form of deconstruction which must be followed by responsible reconstruction.

To Reich's credit, he did attempt to construct a vision of the future, a promise of salvation. To extol human potentiality is indeed a good thing. However, does personnel transformation lead to broader social change and renewal? We have been coming to our Bethel Woods reunion for some fifty years now, ever since Joni Mitchell and Crosby, Stills, and Nash sang "Woodstock" utopian dreams of getting ourselves back to the garden. The marketplace of anticipations, future prescriptions, and apocalyptic visions continues unabated.

What has become of the social revolution prophesied by Charles Reich in his *Greening of America*? If the events of the 1970s through the present are held alongside Reich's book, we may say that Consciousness III, so highly touted in his post-sixties romanticism, has revealed itself as only a limited victory. The writing of Christopher Lasch in *The Culture of Narcissism* appears more realistic and appropriate in speaking of the subsequent decades. With Lasch's theme of narcissism we come to a mirror of culture which could easily be catalogued in book form as "The Preening of America"—the age of the selfie.

The revolution of the individual and culture which Reich called for did not fully occur. Nor does it show signs of occurring "naturally" by some inevitable evolutionary process or entelechy. The inevitability of progress of humanity, however desirable, remains questionable. The powerful forces of entropy, the limitations of institutional arrangements, the patterns of economic growth and decline, the complexity of society are hardly taken into account in *The Greening of America* (or in idealistic song lyrics, although they do express hope). Reich, like Karl Marx, saw a particular group or class as the vanguard of the new society he envisioned for America. This was a group of the young, mostly college educated people who began to come into adult maturity in the late 1960s and early 1970s. These baby boomers have now taken their place among our nation's leaders in business and government, health and education. However, it is questionable whether this now older "new generation" has turned around anything. Certainly, strides have been made in terms of women's rights, but there have also been limitations and denigrations. There is also something to be said for America's progress in terms of racial equality, although much further evolution of respect and opportunity appears to be called for. People are conscious of their right to free speech. Whether America has become more tolerant it is hard to say. In his book, Reich offered a glowing and encouraging vision. But he spoke in truisms about our loss of community in America, about our loss of self in the modern age. He seldom pinned anything down in solid sociological data.

This led to some sharp criticism of Reich's writing- and of sixties countercultural dreams. One of Reich's harshest critics was Andrew Greeley, a practicing sociologist who emerged as one of America's best-selling popular novelists. "Nothing is greener than a graveyard," said Greeley in his review of the book in 1971. Greeley wrote of *Greening* that "it is at best only occasionally perceptive; as a program for social action it does not begin to exist."[21] Reich's indictments of American society are global statements, generalities, said Greeley. Reich was engaging in "rhetorical overkill" and he had better get more specific and temper his indictments with some data. Greeley asked: Is there really a loss of community in America? Is there really less freedom and selfhood than in some mythological past?

For Reich, the modern corporate state is the bad guy which has usurped human values. (That view lingers in the air of David Crosby's or Graham Nash's perceptive critiques of the limitations of the American political system.) Yet, this is a rather broad statement. It is not followed

---

up adequately by Reich with specific examples that prove his case. In other words, this law professor has written an incomplete brief. This is even more true when Reich goes on to say that the dilemmas prompted by corporate industrialism are "reversing." Are they? In what ways? Who is he kidding? We have certainly not seen much evidence of that in the past fifty years. Reich, like many others in the counterculture, dreamed of a new age but little in his vision was startlingly new. His voice was like that of a biblical prophet. His three stages of consciousness directly parallel the stages of social development portrayed by Auguste Comte in his 19th century system of positivism.

Have flowers pushed up through the concrete pavement to give us a new world transcending the wasteland of the corporate state as Reich prophesied? Are not most people still on "the escalator of success" rather than engaging in dreams of adventure and romance or in active social service? And who is to say that any of these—success, adventure, romance, service—are incompatible? Crosby, Stills, Nash and Young have been economically successful, socially concerned, and adventurous.

Greeley makes an important point about Reich's book: he says that it is essentially religious. Greeley and Capouya found *The Greening of America* to be an exercise in religious vision and eschatological prophecy. This is how this book needs to be read and indeed perhaps picked up and looked at again now, years later. America is not "irretrievably encased in metal and plastic and sterile stone": a "greening" is possible. But it is a greening that will come with the green of dollars and with reference to I-phones and computer screens. If we insist upon using the "green" metaphor, we cannot forget the green beauty of the American landscape. A "green" view confronts the politics of Scott Pruitt and the Trump Administration's decision to pull out of the Paris climate change agreement. A "green" view stands with the opposition by Neil Young, or the Sierra Club of Canada, to the oil sands issue in Canada.

The Greening of America is worth looking at again as a religious statement, an eschatological hope, as America approaches the election year of 2020. Perhaps Woodstock might be seen as an expression of this. For Reich, salvation is at hand: "There is a revolution coming. It will not be like revolutions of the past. It will originate with the individual and with culture.... It is now spreading with amazing rapidity.... It promises higher reason, more human community, and a new and liberated individual. Its ultimate creation will be a new and enduring wholeness and beauty—a renewed relationship of man to himself, to other men, to society, to nature and to the land."[22] There is good stuff there. It is the faith of the spirit of hope for a new age, an eschaton of promise.

Who would not like to live in this new green world? But where is this world? Look around at Detroit or the Bronx crumbling and sweating in the summer heat. Look at hunger in Appalachia, gun violence in South Chicago, or witness factories closing in Michigan and ask—where is this brave new world? Some hard, sharply drawn social facts may cause us to question the vision. But that does not mean there should not be the vision, for we do need the energy of its hope. We can ask of any vision, including that of CSN&Y, if it is capable of giving force to real human efforts which will make some measure of such a society possible. The difficulty with Reich's vision is that he sees the new age dawning with historical inevitability, without effortful action at reform. Serious politics are just not part of the vision. The progressive politics of Bernie Sanders or Elizabeth Warren that Crosby and Nash support, and the earnest engagement that Stills and Young each express, is tempered by realism, determination, and human concern.

The Greening of America is a hopeful dream. It cannot be construed as social science. Reich's models are incomplete and are not backed by data. The college-educated fringe of society he speaks of (people who are now in their sixties and seventies) is only a fraction of the wider society which comprises America. The indications we have seen since 1970 indicate a continuity between generations. Rather than a messianic people, the sixties and seventies generations have become ordinary people little different in character than the previous generations.

There are those who have made personal lifestyle changes or what they might refer to as spiritual changes. A transcendent revolution based upon personal self-transformation is a fine idea. It is a rock and roll idea. It is an idea which is Nietzschean: a self-overcoming. It is an idea which can be traced to the American Transcendentalists Emerson, Channing, Fuller, and Thoreau. It remains a valid theme for our time and has been heartily endorsed by progressive thinkers, New Age proponents, and self-help and human potential advocates. There is something healthy about a search for insight and wholeness. But it is questionable whether self-reliance and personal transformation alone is an adequate response to the economic, political, and social challenges of a nation of more than 200 million people.

As M. Scott Peck notes in the beginning of his classic bestseller *The Road Less Traveled*, "life is difficult." Charles Reich's 1970 book of dreams did not adequately account for the challenges of a new era which we now face. For Reich, powerlessness has happened to the American people—and nobody likes to be powerless. In his view, we must overcome the domination of our lives by technology and the market and take back our ability to choose and control our own lives. All this is very fine preaching. How are we to effectively do this? He does not say.

A song might help to change the world—at least by a fraction—by stimulating conscience and concern. However, if "the urgent need of our times in transcendence," as Reich held, how is this transcendence to be accomplished?[23] Scott Peck's book of the 1980s, with its emphasis on discipline, is perhaps closer to the mark than Reich's breathy preaching. Reich (like a good disciple of Marshall McLuhan) sees possibilities for a new culture in its electronic dimensions. Many among us still hold onto the prospect and promise of global communications and information technology. But in 1970, Reich could not see into the twenty-first century and view all the permutations of electronic culture in our time. These are not necessarily allied to a return to our natural rhythms, as Reich (qua Rousseau) once recommended. The liberal reformation Reich offered in 1970 has failed because it offered no tangible new way of life for all. Freedom, creativity, humor, and community can be allied with technology. This is a healthy vision. We can still have this hope and imagine the means for recreating the social order. We may ask: What is the role in this context of rock music, which has moved from Ampex reels and record stores to Pro Tools and digital recording and distribution? More specifically, given our focus here: What can the voices of Crosby, Stills, Nash, and Young contribute to the dialogue? What role can their music have in inspiring people?

In his 1970 book Reich suggests that we can work toward the concept of "together." By going with technology ("go with the flow") we can create the new society. Here, years later, in the new century, we may ask, is this vision tenable? In what sense can a cooperative venture with technology open up human possibilities and give us a richer and truer future? And when we speak of "together," does this mean a healthy respect for our differences? One would think that this hope resides at the heart of the music that is being created by Crosby, by Stills, by Nash, and by the ever-resilient Neil Young.

In 1970–71, the conservative writer Michael Novak called *The Greening of America* "a record of conversion," an unconscious progression from a liberal, meritocratic and pragmatic mode to something more religious, dating from Reich's experiences in the California sun in Berkeley in 1967. It is, said Novak, a "program of missionary activity." Reich sounds too much like Billy Graham, says Novak, who brings forth the conservative critique. For in Novak's estimation, the vision of *Greening* is "full of the blossoming seeds of its own corruptions." We are called to political action, Novak insists. "We are called to invent new procedures, new directions for affectivity, and striving and inquiry." However, our task is not one only of placing "supreme value on the development of consciousness, sensitivity, experience, knowledge" but using this depth and awareness for "inventing new political forms" with whatever means we have available to us.[24]

The critique of *Greening of America*—and perhaps an indictment of the Woodstock generation—thus returns in a criticism of its passivity, its trust in effortless inspiration and inevitable change. No doubt some forms of change are inevitable. No doubt also grace can come to us. But inspiration generally does not occur without prior effort and grace appears to require a certain receptivity. (David Crosby encourages clear interior radio reception on one of his songs on *Lighthouse*.) Contemplation can begin this awareness for the reception of insight. Indeed, a positive assessment of the interior way suggested by Reich's emphasis on consciousness was noted in 1971 by a Trappist monk, Anselm Adams. There is a long tradition of interiority and contemplation in Christianity, Adams observed; however, the trick is to balance this with the tradition of social action. Inner seeking must be balanced with action. To speak in neo-Marxist terms, there is a dialectic between reception and action and an urgency to praxis. It is figured in the movement from the contemplative act of Graham Nash's photography to the outward expressiveness of concert performance.

Crosby, Stills, Nash and Young speak to individuals. Adams noted that this was one of the strengths of Reich's narrative. He spoke to "you who brush your teeth, commute, and have one smoggy life to live." Adams writes that while Reich "does not situate his views within the history of ideas," neglects to recognize evil, and leaves out the problem of power, *Greening* is "in other respects commendable." Perhaps, his comments may suggest something about rock music: "Awareness, new consciousness, change of social goals toward humanistic values, community, meaningful work, innocence, wonder, and play are all to be highly prized." It is the spirit of play which ultimately gives *Greening* its authentically religious character, he says. "Play is irrelevant, non-achieving, impractical, useless. Like the sacred, and like contemplation, play is non-instrumental, disinterested, ultimate, an end in itself. It is adventure, delight, illusion, surprise, gift, amazement, grace." What is rock music, after all—apart from commercial ends—if it is not enthusiasm, spontaneity, and an expression of play?

One can critically discount the vision of *The Greening of America*, a text from the year that Crosby, Stills, Nash and Young emerged with *Déjà vu* at the forefront of American pop music. "To expect an actual greening of America would be to hope for too much," wrote Adams, but to dismiss the hope within it would be to throw away a healthy ideal. *The Greening of America* is about seeing the world new and contributing to making it new. Its admonishments to liberation echo a key theme that Crosby, Stills, Nash and Young have repeatedly returned to: freedom. Its encouragement of an adjustment of worldview can lead to attitudes which can be beneficial. The self's quest can be related—indeed is always related—to the meaning of one's life within the human community. The quest for the lost self, Adams tells us, is a search for the deep knowledge of who we are, what we have become, "of where we were and where we have been ... of what birth is and what rebirth."[25] This is the search and the dream of *The Greening of America*.

In 1974, Crosby, Stills, Nash and Young were again on tour. They played concerts at stadiums and arenas across North America. The dream of the sixties waned, as they continued to sing their hope and make large sums of money for their promoters and management and others along for the ride. For they had become an industry, a name brand, living the high life of material success. It was the age of narcissism, claimed the social critic Christopher Lasch. The Nixon presidency was consumed by Watergate. Bellbottoms gave way to distressed jeans. The sixties filtered away and Crosby, Stills, Nash, and Young again went off in their own directions.

5

On a Four Way Street
From 1975 to 1990

In 1975, Crosby and Nash joined forces again. Crosby had written "Carry Me" and Nash composed "Wind on the Water." And so, we return to that period following Crosby, Stills, Nash and Young's summer 1974 tour, when Crosby and Nash began to work together again. In *Long Time Gone*, Crosby recalls the 1974 stadium shows and that "relationships dissolved" at a pinnacle in their careers.[1] ABC Records promoted new albums by Crosby and Nash. *Wind on the Water* (1975) was recorded together. James Taylor was involved with *Wind on the Water* on several songs. Four songs on the album were recorded direct to tape, with no overdubs. *Whistling Down the Wire* came in 1976. Cameron Crowe followed their tour and wrote in *Rolling Stone* about their rock energy as well as their ballad harmonies. There was also *Crosby-Nash Live*. They turned to musician-friends as they worked on their project. Carole King played organ on "Bittersweet" and Jackson Browne provided background vocals on "Love Work Out." *Wind on the Water* would be the album's title and James Taylor sang on the title cut. They returned the favors. Crosby and Nash sang on James Taylor's "Mexico." Their vocals appeared on songs by many other artists: Art Garfunkel's "Breakaway," Kenny Loggins' "All the Pretty Little Ponies," Elton John's "Cage the Songbird," Dave Mason's "Every Woman," Gary Wright's "Love Awake Inside," Jimmy Webb's "These Old Walls." Jackson Browne introduced them to Tom Campbell of the Guacamole Fund, which was engaged with many social issues. They linked with Jackson Browne's benefit efforts, to raise consciousness in "anti-nuke" concerts, and issues that ranged from criticism of nuclear energy to concerns about the environment. They met Jacques Cousteau, with Linda Ronstadt as a guest.[2] They began to take issues of public education ever more seriously.

In 1976, Neil Young now re-entered the picture. He had completed *Tonight's the Night* and *Zuma* with his band Crazy Horse. He had four Stephen Stills songs with him. Before long, they were in Fort Lauderdale and Miami, at Criterion Studios. The Stills-Young songs provided a core for a record. Nash and Crosby looked for songs of their own besides those that would be on their record as a duo. When they went back to Los Angeles to compete that record, Neil Young went back to San Francisco and the proposed CSN&Y project remained incomplete. That was when Stephen Stills called for a Stills-Young record. Stills wanted to erase all of the Crosby and Nash background tracks and proceed with an album with Neil Young.[3] The album that resulted was *Long May You Run* (1976), a record by Neil Young and Stephen Stills that may be said to be a shared collaborative effort.

Crosby and Nash released *Whistling Down the Wire* in July 1976. While touring in support of the album they played at the Greek Theater in Los Angeles for three nights. On one of those occasions they brought out Stephen Stills onto the stage. They sang "Teach Your Children" together. Stephen Stills' marriage to Veronique Sanson had dissolved, and so had his band. His moment onstage with Crosby and Nash was fleeting but it sparked the possibility of another try for an album together.

In December 1976, Stills was at the Record Plant in Los Angeles. He recorded "See the Changes" and "Dark Star." Crosby and Nash were scheduled to add vocals. Nash brought his song "Cathedral," recalling Winchester Cathedral in London and the distant past. He also brought his songs "Carried Away," "Mutiny," "I Watched It All Come Down," and "Just a Song Before I Go," which would become a CSN hit. Crosby, although deteriorating, was still prolific and he brought "In My Dreams," "Jigsaw," "Anything at All," and "Shadow Captain," with his lyrics and music by Craig Doerge. Stills added "I Give You Blood" and "Run from Tears." Nash had recently been in England. He stood on the steps of the Midland Hotel where he an Allan Clarke had met the Everly Brothers on April 22, 1960.

CSN released their album in June 1977. They would tour that summer as a trio, true to their roots amid radio airplay that featured *Frampton Comes Alive* or Elton John as *Captain Fantastic and the Brown Dirt Cowboy*. Bruce

Springsteen had shattered preconceptions with *Born to Run* in 1975. Billy Joel had risen from airplay of "Piano Man" to his extraordinary break-through of his album *The Stranger*. Crosby, Stills, and Nash released their record as what could be heard on the radio was in transition. A disco phase, with the Bee Gees, Donna Summer, and K.C. and the Sunshine Band, was about to push aside the singer-songwriters of the early to mid-seventies. Stevie Wonder dazzled the charts with *Innervisions* and *Songs in the Key of Life*. The Eagles brought pop, country, and rock together with lush harmonies and began their string of hit singles. The rock of the late sixties and early seventies—Deep Purple, Led Zeppelin, Black Sabbath—had morphed into the corporate rock of Foreigner, REO Speedwagon, and Boston. In New York, Patti Smith was crafting her songs for *Horses* and punk/new wave bands—from Television and Richard Hell and Voidoids to the Ramones—growled in power chord protest at the insipid world of pop. The British punk bands soon would follow, growling and thrashing just as loudly, while acts like Madonna, Michael Jackson, and Prince were soon to dominate the charts in the newly visual MTV era of the 1980s.

Crosby, Stills, and Nash knew their sound and asserted it, not fol-lowing any of these industry trends. Stephen Stills continued to open shows with "Love the One You're With," a song about immediacy and con-nection with a title repeated emphatically, resolving in a bright, tuneful hook (dit-dit-dit) for which no words were needed. Neil Young, with his characteristic creativity, drew upon the primal energy of punk rock. Their personal lives were ever in change. Graham Nash married Susan Sennett in California. Group tensions continued. Crosby hoped for a Byrds reunion that was not to be. By 1978, he was often on the *Mayan*, adrift on drugs, as much as on the water. Stephen Stills had gone off to make music with others and the irrepressible Neil Young was busy creating his own music. Nash bought a home in Hawaii, had an exhibition of his photography at the University of California in Santa Clara, and gained his American cit-izenship on August 14, 1978.

The year 1979 brought participation in Jackson Browne's benefit con-certs. There were "No Nukes" concerts, including a show in Washington, D.C., with Bonnie Raitt, John Hall, John Sebastian, Dan Fogelberg, and Joni Mitchell. Radios across America were still playing "Running on Empty," which had hit #3 on the *Billboard* charts in 1978. David Crosby was scheduled to work on a solo album for Columbia Records, but he had declined under a cloud of drugs that took the edge off his singing voice and his focus. Nash was writing songs he would collect for another solo record, *Earth and Sky*: "Barrel of Pain," "In the Eighties," "Innocent Eyes," "Love Has Come," and his song about Hawaii, "Out on the Island."

Earth and Sky was the Graham Nash album with a cover design in which a rainbow led not to a pot of gold but to an infamous bar code. Nash had carefully brought together all of the musical and visual elements for the recording and its cover. The company had stamped on the album cover a Universal Product Code—those black lines in a white square that can be read by a computer. Nash rejected this and refused to let Columbia Records release the album. Capitol Records showed interest in the project and put out the recording.

The year 1979 also marks a time when David Crosby's drug habit began to deeply concern his friends. Crosby recalls that from 1979 on he was severely addicted.[4] At Britannia Studios he could not finish his recording project. He notes that Graham Nash was one of the few people around him who would confront him with "something real."[5] Bobby Columby, who supervised Crosby at Capitol Records, saw the problems Crosby was having and spoke with him about it. Graham Nash remained in regular contact with Crosby. Jackson Browne encouraged him to sit down at Warren Zevon's piano and then insisted that he was not to get up from the piano bench until he had finished the song "Delta," which he had started.[6] Browne continued bringing musicians together for work with MUSE: Musicians for Safe Energy, throughout 1979. Nash joined the organization's board and participated in the Hollywood Bowl concert of June 14, 1979. Promoters Ron Delsener and Tom Campbell backed a series of New York City shows, which included Bruce Springsteen and others. They urged Crosby, Stills, and Nash to participate.

A new decade, the 1980s, brought Susan and Graham Nash a son, born on January 12, 1980. It also brought *Earth and Sky*, which was personally relevant but less than commercially successful. Crosby, Stills, and Nash began jamming again. There was "no expression in David," Nash recalls; Crosby was at a low point and so were his vocals. Stills and Nash began to think it would be necessary to finish the album on their own, without Crosby. The record company would have none of that: they wanted a Crosby, Stills, and Nash record. Unable to give them a record immediately, they agreed to have Atlantic Records put out a compilation of their recordings. *Replay* drew upon their solo projects. The title was appropriate: the record offered nothing new.[7]

A new record, *Daylight Again*, featured "Southern Cross," which became a huge hit. The title song "Daylight Again" was a masterful song by Stephen Stills set in the American Civil War. However, the album was "a patch job," Graham Nash has said.[8] The album's pieces were painstakingly knit together. To fit David Crosby into the project was a difficult proposition because his singing voice was weak and his health was not good. Nash and Stills had several songs completed for a new album when they brought Crosby into the recording project. Crosby was unhappy that he was not involved in this project at first. Even though he was invited to join in the work, he was not on his game. Soon Stills and Nash realized that they would have to adjust to this deficit and improvise. They called in Timothy B. Schmidt, who had worked with the Eagles, Dan Fogelberg, and others, and added his clear tenor to Stills' song "Daylight Again." They incorporated Crosby tracks from his aborted Capitol Records album: "Delta" and the Craig Doerge-Judy Hensch song "Might as Well Have a Good Time." For "Delta" Nash and Stills placed their voices on Crosby's already multitracked vocals. However, it was obvious to them that it would be difficult to present the record in concert with Crosby in such a condition. If they had to perform anything live they would have Mike Finnegan sing Crosby's vocals from the shadows in the back of the stage. Nash, musing upon the condition of his friend, wrote "Into the Darkness," a song that Crosby recognized was directed toward him. Crosby has said that of all the Crosby, Stills, and Nash albums he is least happy with *Daylight Again*.[9] He knows that he was not in a good place—and that is an understatement.

During this period, Crosby functioned reasonably well at a show at Town Hall in New York and on several California gigs. However, arrests and drug charges soon followed in Costa Mesa and Santa Ana, California. For a Los Angeles area concert benefit for "No Nukes" outside an Orange County power plant, Crosby was late. He was arrested on drug charges, fined, and ordered by a judge to go into a rehabilitation clinic. He was becoming notorious: his reputation for drug use followed him. On April

12, Crosby was in Dallas for a solo show at Cardi's. He was busted when a policeman went backstage and drew open a curtain, revealing Crosby with his drug paraphernalia. Crosby's lawyers insisted that evidence was obtained by an invasion of his privacy and without a warrant.

On May 11, 1981, friends surrounded Crosby at his home in Mill Valley on Greenwood Way in a crisis intervention meeting in the living room.[10] Twenty people joined a psychiatric social worker and made their case to David Crosby. He and his girlfriend Jan Dance were in need of help, they asserted. They told him that they cared deeply about him and wanted him to go to seek help. Jackson Browne had arranged for a plane to fly David Crosby and Jan Dance to La Jolla, where they could enter the Scripps Clinic. They reluctantly agreed, succumbing to the concern and pressure of their friends, but once at the clinic in La Jolla they immediately decided to escape from it. They returned home. The downward spiral of drug addiction continued. People moved away from Crosby socially, increasing the alienation.

The Hollies reunited with Graham Nash in August 1981. The occasion of these concerts was prompted by the successful record release of *Hollieday* in England. The Hollies had achieved several hits following the departure of Graham Nash: "He Ain't Heavy, He's My Brother," "Long Cool Woman (In a Black Dress)," "The Air I Breathe." Nash found the reconnection with his childhood friend Allan Clarke and the other Hollies members a satisfying experience.

Crosby, Stills, and Nash went on a troubled tour in 1982, while Crosby was awaiting his court case in Texas. He was in deep into his habit at this time and had a supplier that he and Nash have named "Mort": a fine name for a death-shadow. The *Daylight Again* tour was often in a kind of darkness. At times, Crosby could barely function. Stills and Nash had to cover for Crosby with solos or by joining together in duos during concerts. Mike Finnegan sang from the shadows of the stage. They concluded their summer tour on September 6 in Irvine, California, where Crosby was again arrested on an older drug charge. They resumed concert performances in November on the strength of their hit "Southern Cross." Stills had taken a Curtis Brothers song, "Seven League Boots," and reworked it, adding a chorus and energy. Nash had written "Cold Rain," a song based in memory and personal history. His mother had recently told him about her own dream of being a singer and performer: a dream that he had fulfilled in his own life's work. In his song he looks at the brick and smoke of industrial Manchester where he once had lived. He reflects upon the lives of people, like his parents, who are stuck in their jobs but work earnestly for their families within the limits of their working-class circumstances.

On June 6, 1982, they played at the Rose Bowl in Pasadena and it was obvious that they now had many new fans. This was no sixties crowd. A whole new generation was listening to them as classic rock on the radio. Crosby was arrested again in Culver City California in September 1982, after a concert at Irvine Meadows. The warrant dated to 1980. When the "Wasted on the Way" video of CSN for MTV appeared in November, close-ups of Crosby were avoided. The May 1983 album *Allies* suggests the togetherness of a mutual effort. The image belied the true story. The work that Crosby, Stills, and Nash were doing remained lucrative and it took them across the United States, cities in Canada, and locations in Europe. However, the charges against David Crosby lingered. Crosby was a marked man; he was also a deeply addicted one. Crosby is an exceptionally talented musician, but he did not have the force of his vocal or songwriting skill when clouded by addiction. Crosby, Stills and Nash all remained vigilant, careful to avoid drug busts throughout their "Allies" tour. CSN made use of Houston show tracks for "Shadow Captain" as they developed an album. Some critics claimed that Crosby, Stills, and Nash concert tickets had become too pricey. At a concert in Philadelphia, Crosby disappeared backstage for about fifty minutes. Stills went backstage and poured a bucket of water on him to rouse him.[11]

Crosby's case in Dallas went to trial in 1983. The Texas court felony charges for Crosby came on June 3, 1983. Crosby was slapped with a five-year sentence on a drug charge to be served consecutively with three years for a weapons charge. It looked like Crosby, Stills, and Nash was over. They completed a European tour that included Paris, Rotterdam, Hamburg, Berlin, Rome, Milan and London. In October 1983 Crosby was arraigned on drug charges in Marin County, California.[12] An appeal in the Texas court hearing on December 9, 1984, rendered the decision that there had been an unreasonable search without a warrant. However, a variety of legal charges against Crosby held. Nash, concerned that Crosby would completely fall apart in jail, wrote urgent letters to attempt to get him into a clinic for rehabilitation. Crosby went into care at Fair Oaks in Summit, New Jersey.

In 1984, Stephen Stills recorded his solo album *Right by You.* Then he disappeared from public view. The first authorized biography of the group, by Don Zimmer, appeared that year. Early in 1985, CSN booked another tour. They appeared at the Live Aid Concert on July 13. As they continued on tour, Crosby made sure to stay out of Texas overnight. After any Dallas or Houston concert dates, he would stay at a hotel in Louisiana. However, the severity of the legal charges did not go away. He entered Huntsville Prison on March 6, 1986. Crosby's new home was C Block. He spent eight months in prison.

While Crosby was adjusting to the rigors of the penitentiary, Stills was following up his work on *Right by You* for Warner Bros. Records. Nash worked solo on *Innocent Eyes.* Neil Young, the most successful of the four in commercial terms, was promising a reunion if Crosby cleaned up his act. Nash sang at Hiroshima on August 6, on the anniversary of the nuclear bomb devastation there. A short time later, Crosby was released from jail.[13] He could finally join Jan Dance. She had been released from a facility in Kansas City and was receiving treatment at the Steinbeck Center in Salinas, California.

The occasion for the reunion of Crosby, Stills, Nash and Young was a benefit that Neil Young arranged for the Bridge School for children with cerebral palsy. Crosby joined Stills, Nash, and Young onstage for two concerts in October 1986. The new connection between them led to an album. They recorded at Neil Young's ranch south of San Francisco, an isolated place he that had settled into in 1971, and where he had recorded *Harvest.* Neil Young had an array of songs available for this album: "In the Name of Love," "This Old House," "Heartland," "Shadow Dance" and the title song "American Dream." To the sessions, Nash brought his song "Clear Blue Skies." Crosby had "Night for the Generals." He had faced death's door and had sought a still, sure spirit in his song "Compass." Stills brought the song "Got It Made."

American Dream is a recording in which Neil Young clearly is a full member of this group. The album is filled with the spirit of Neil Young, an artist who has always moved Crosby, Stills, and Nash "in a different direction," as Graham Nash has observed. With Young they moved toward a sound with "darker edges" and "tension and darkness," wrote Nash in his autobiography.[14] The record reached #16 on the *Billboard* charts.

The reunion that created the *American Dream* (1988) album and tour was one promised by Neil Young to encourage David Crosby's rehabilitation and revival. Crosby worked through his prison time in Huntsville in 1986. Young welcomed Stills, Nash, and Crosby to his ranch to work on the new recording. Neil Young was already involved in writing his critique of televangelists like Jimmy Swaggart and political campaigns derailed by extramarital affairs like that of Gary Hart. His song "American Dream" was recorded on March 3, 1988, and it led off the album. "American Dream" begins with high woodwinds, a bright clap-rhythm, and Young's vocal. Voices join as the singers point to things from above and join again on the title and then later in the song. "Name of Love" also brings us Young's vocal supported by the others singing the title, as a bright drum sound and guitar lines move through the song.

The *American Dream* recording was developed with the intention of exploring the goals and hopes embodied in the American dream. Stretching out across fourteen songs, the album did not fully make a solid, rousing statement. Critics, like Anthony DeCurtis writing a few years later, pointed out that while there were pleasant tunes and "the occasional interesting song," the album overall was more soporific than exciting.[15] The Stills-Young song "Got It Made" reached #69 on the Billboard chart but other releases did not make the top 100. In 1988, Crosby, Stills, Nash, and Young toured the United States, performing their hits and songs from *American Dream*. The concert tour made a lot of money, making promoters as well as fans happy. Often, they would move from an acoustic set into an electric rock set for the second part of their show. *American Dream* reached number 16 on the *Billboard* charts. Crosby, Stills, Nash and Young have not incorporated any of the 14 songs in their regular set lists since.

American Dream appeared between *Allies* and *Live It Up* (released June 11, 1990). *Allies* opened with two studio recordings, "War Games" and "Raise a Voice" by Stills and Nash, and then was assembled with live concert recordings. Crosby's performances of "Shadow Captain" and "For Free" were drawn from shows in Houston, Texas, in 1977. The other cuts emerged from the Crosby, Stills and Nash concert at the Universal Ampitheatre in Universal City California in 1982. Following "War Games" and

"Raise a Voice" on side one we hear "Turn Your Back on Love," "Barrel of Pain," and "Shadow Captain." Side two of the record begins with Stills' "Dark Star" and ends with his song "For What It's Worth." Paul McCartney's "Blackbird" and Joni Mitchell's "He Played Real Good for Free" also appear on side two. Graham Nash's "Wasted on the Way" entered VH1 and MTV video rotation, as did "War Games," with a video drawn from the movie that song was originally targeted for.

Live It Up did not sell well enough to reach gold record status, as previous CSN albums had done. "House of Broken Dreams" by Graham Nash and "Yours and Mine" by David Crosby and Craig Dorge would be performed in some subsequent concerts. None of the songs stuck strongly as regular repertoire in the CSN sets. Graham Nash takes the lead vocal on the first two songs, "Live It Up" by Joe Vitale and "If Anybody Had a Heart" by J.D. Souther and Danny Kortchmar. The album concludes with Nash's vocal on "After the Dolphin," a song written with Craig Doerge that points to war abroad. The album featured a playful cover with speared hot dogs. David Crosby wrote "Arrows" with guitarist Michael Hedges who, like Crosby, created songs with innovative alternate tunings. Even so, *Live It Up* did not leave a lasting mark. Rather than a scintillating and enduring record, it was more like an album of songs and performances passing through. Crosby, Stills, and Nash were again recording and performing together capably. The true revival and a new audience had by then only just begun to emerge.

6

American Dreams and Cultural Memory

The summer of 1989 brought a twentieth anniversary show at Woodstock. The concert was attended by about 30,000 people and it did not involve "name" bands. To repeat this a few years later, for a 25th anniversary, was empty and unnecessary: it was clearly a commercial ploy that fell flat. During this time, Crosby recorded *Oh, Yes I Can* and sang on "Another Day in Paradise" with Phil Collins. In November 1989, the Cold War was dissolving and changes were afoot in Europe. On November 18, Crosby, Stills, and Nash played music in the hall of the United Nations General Assembly. They flew from New York to Germany and on November 22 they were at the Berlin Wall, wearing jackets in the brisk air at Brandenburg Gate, singing "Long Time Gone" and a song Nash had just written called "Chippin' Away."

To return to Woodstock in 1989 after twenty years must have felt strange. Woodstock is symbolic. It has become myth or legend, a cultural reference point. For Crosby, Stills, Nash and Young it was their second show. It was a public beginning: one that was recorded. Yet, at this point Woodstock was a blip on the screen of a long career. In one respect, to celebrate again at Woodstock was an act of memorialization. It was a bit like Civil War veterans late in the nineteenth century returning to hallowed ground. On the other hand, cultural memory was an excuse for capital gain and commercialization. The event provided a marker at which one could question how the ideals crystallized at the 1969 Woodstock festival had fared across the years.

Picking up the Woodstock film soundtrack now, a listener can hear musical differences between then and now. The sound of Crosby, Stills,

Nash and Young, as a unit, has not substantially changed. In 1969, David Crosby commented, "The Rolling Stones are still a little bit 1965."[1] In what respect is Crosby, Stills, Nash and Young—even with all of their individual growth as artists—still a bit like 1969? They carry the weight and force of a memory. Yet, they have to appeal to an audience that includes thousands of listeners who were not yet born when they did that second gig at Woodstock. Sounds, tastes, styles have changed. Even so, when Crosby, Stills, Nash and Young returned to Woodstock they had acquired a lively, new audience that included younger generations of listeners. They were more than a museum piece, a recorded document, a statue on the town square. Their themes and songs, the ideals associated with them, had remained relevant and acquired a new urgency with the war in Iraq. That was the first of the encounters there and both would draw the ire and concern of Neil Young and bring together CSN&Y.

What is a band or an event when it becomes memory and symbol, a page in the records of history? If not for the lived impact of a life, the acts seem ephemeral. However, each life has an impact and the creative artist with a platform touches the consciousness of people. We are constantly interpreting that impact, that history, those sounds and stories. Rock performers and creators leave a cultural legacy.

Crosby, Stills, Nash and Young sounded a cultural moment. They were engaged in significant cultural work. Their artistry and awareness was deeply in tune with a transformation of culture and popular music within the period of the sixties. In memory, their music, image, lyrics, and ideas have created a cultural legacy that remains with us and continues to perform cultural work among us today. In continually evolving ways they each are a voice in popular culture fifty years after they first set foot on a wooden plank stage at Woodstock.

Because of their continuing relevance, it is necessary to explore how we view Crosby, Stills, Nash and Young and what they cause us to value and to remember. Memory studies provide us with a lens through which we can investigate their cultural impact upon the generation of listeners who first experienced them and those who encountered them later. CSN&Y signify a generation: the wonder, passion, and energy of people who met a world of change during the 1960s. Continually creative in the present, they are much more than this. Yet, one may also recreate a bit of the sixties in listening to CSN&Y. They act as a catalyst for remembering this time in specific ways. For many people, CSN&Y recall the vitality, dreams, and struggles of a not too distant past: a time of dramatic upheaval characterized by issues of war, civil rights, and shifting lifestyles. The significance of memory to CSN&Y themselves and to their listeners may be examined through theories of memory presented in Pierre Nora's *Realms of Memory* and Dominick La Capra's *Rethinking History*, both of which reflect on the interactions between text and historical context. The work of CSN&Y calls us to reexamine a few of the points that Nora and La Capra have made.

In his introduction to *Realms of Memory*, the French historian Nora tells us that "history is needed when people no longer live in memory but recall the past through the assistance of documents that help to recall it."[2] Crosby, Stills, Nash and Young are within living memory, but the band also exists in recorded documents that trigger personal memory. There are record albums, videos, interviews, autobiographies, and other material. The work that Graham Nash has been doing to compile retrospectives is a kind of archival activity: like that of an astute music librarian. Approaching Crosby, Stills, Nash and Young songs as documents or texts, we may consider them through La Capra's six ways of looking at the intersection between text and culture. La Capra's first two points issue a call for us to consider the relation between authorial intention and the text and the relation of the author's life to the text. He then points to the need to examine the relation of society to texts and the relation of culture to texts. Finally, we are encouraged to observe the relation of the text to the corpus of the writer, and the relation between modes of discourse and the text.

Memory is at the center of many of Crosby, Stills, Nash and Young songs. They set out maps of personal memory. An exploration of this personal memory may guide us in our assessment of the relation between authorial intention and the text. As songwriters memorialize their personal past and transform experience into song, they create a treasure of ideas and memories for their listeners. It is in conveying ideas and feeling that they might communicate with other consciousnesses to change the world. It is the life of the folksinger-tradition, in particular, that extends this with concern to the human family.

6. American Dreams and Cultural Memory

Audiences have used the music of Crosby, Stills, Nash and Young to remember things that they have lived through. For several decades they have been engaged with musical discourse and have created musical texts. In his reflections on cultural memory, La Capra points to the relation of society to texts and the relation of culture to texts. In becoming popular, each CSN&Y song has acted as a cultural marker for its audience, a thread amid the pattern of yesterday. As a widespread cultural phenomenon, Crosby, Stills, Nash and Young have participated in creating history and consciousness. Songs, as literary texts, continue to act as a framework for memory and have a role in the formation of cultural memory as they enter public discourse. The participation of their audience allows them to record that memory as people's lives intersect with CSN&Y songs. Thus, their music has entered what Pierre Bourdieu refers to as "the cultural field," a unique space of family frames, personal life-histories, and class and aesthetic differences.

Crosby, Stills, Nash and Young continue to be reinterpreted. Following La Capra's final two points, we may look at their body of work and the relation between modes of discourse and their texts. Listeners of these artists today continually re-read them, producing social knowledge and discourse. They circulate meaning through the interpretation of common texts and celebrate deeply felt emotions that emerge from memory. The original CSN&Y audience recalls the past with what Raymond Williams has called "a particular community of experience" and "the structure of feeling."[3] Subsequent audiences of CSN&Y interact with this recollection of a "common element." Yet, they experience them in new ways, some for the first time. They experience Crosby in the context with guitarist Jeff Pevar and songwriter James Raymond, or CPR. They attend concerts in which Stephen Stills sings with Judy Collins. Graham Nash is on *This Path Tonight* in venues throughout Europe and the United States. In a variety of new ways, they are expressive within the public sphere of communication. In this role, they retain a thread of the ambition to change the world for good that appeared fifty years ago in Graham Nash's song "Chicago." And so, benefits for the Bridge School, or for environmental causes, or for children in need—children who are the future, remain significant parts of their work that will be their legacy to mankind.

Change brings new perspective and new songs, or remixed treatments of old songs. Each time that Neil Young's songs are remixed, assembled, and distributed something else is going on besides repackaging. Rather, they take popular art and, as the poet Ezra Pound once declared, they "make it new." Editing creates a new product, a new cultural artifact. New placements of Crosby, Stills, Nash and Young songs prompt rereadings and revisions of cultural memory. This practice is consistent with revisions of history and recovery of areas of history that have brought increasing emphasis upon memory. Pierre Nora speaks of a sense of "belonging, collective consciousness ... memory and identity." He suggests for our period the term "the age of commemoration." As he puts it, "the most continuous or permanent feature of the modern world is no longer continuity or permanence but change."[4] For Crosby, Stills, Nash and Young themselves, rapid change or an "acceleration of history," to use Nora's term, appears to have prompted a desire for memory that appears in several of their songs and in collections of their work. This may also be true of their audience, for whom a reinvention of Crosby, Stills, Nash and Young in digital availability brings yesterday alive again in fresh and new ways. The relative permanence and familiarity of Crosby, Stills, Nash and Young enables their audience to cope with change. They remain a rock music fixture even as time plays its changes on the human body and dims areas of historical recollection. The remarkable thing is that their creativity persists in extraordinary fashion even as the golden age of eighty looms.

Oh, time has gone by—a long time gone. It goes by each day. Yet, the recordings of Crosby, Stills, Nash and Young continue today in a lively conversation with culture. Their work continues to be represented and documented in new media forms for today's listeners. They have crossed boundaries and cultures. They have had the means to reach out to the world and have entered "social frames" of memory. Consequently, it is important for us to consider how memory is embodied and enacted in the image, the lyrics, and the music of Crosby, Stills, Nash and Young. Additionally, by setting them within their historical and social context, we may further investigate through memory theories their lasting impact on their audience.

Crosby, Stills, Nash and Young emerged from a folk tradition that mixed with British pop, the blues, country, and the California sound. Their primary thrust was sheer creativity, an impulse to produce songs. They produced a vocal style of rich harmonies and participated in writing an integral portion of the soundtrack of the late 1960s and 1970s and beyond. Personal memory, transformed by imagination, acted as a through-line in many of their songs across their entire career as individual singer-songwriters and as a collective unit. Here we arrive at the cultural historian Dominick La Capra's first two points about text and context: the relations of texts with authorial intention and with the author's life. La Capra argues that life and text may challenge one another in a complex interaction. For Crosby, Stills, Nash and Young the increasing impact of the music industry at the peak of their success, the context of drugs, and the pressure of creative differences called for their separation that helped them re-situate themselves. Young was the deep, mysterious river, the stream pushing the edges of the land: unpredictable, moving the elements along. Crosby, the voice in the middle of the harmony, had to find his own way, for as much as he likes collaboration he is an intuitive stream of consciousness writer and musician. Stills' place was with the guitar gods in England and then with the formation of Manassas. Nash created *Songs for Beginners*, but soon found his way back to a successful duo with Crosby. They would sail away on the *Mayan* with the wind on the water.

Crosby, Stills, Nash and Young were one musical collective among several that had an impact on a generation of listeners. Following La Capra's fourth point, at the relation of culture to CSN&Y texts, it is important to consider the circulation of their songs across communities of discourse. These would include the interactions of Grateful Dead fans on the one hand and those who appreciated hard rock bands on the other. There was crossover between those who listened closely to folk and folk/rock and those who were pop music radio listeners with a more casual attitude toward CSN&Y. Then there are those people who did not care for Crosby, Stills, Nash and Young and those who did not like their politics. Within popular music, several songs of Crosby, Stills, Nash and Young may be regarded as being among the memorable texts of a specific cultural moment. In some ways, these songs reflect or correspond to the mentalities of a generation. (Certainly, this is the case with an album like *4 Way Street*. While somewhat hastily assembled the live album does reflect CSN&Y in a particular cultural moment.) This generation was engaged in an interpretive dialogue with Crosby, Stills, Nash and Young. Interpretation that takes on important texts is best done dialogically, in La Capra's view. As he puts it, "A text is a network of resistances, and a dialogue is a two-way affair; a good reader is also an attentive listener."[5] Texts address us in subtle ways, and we need to examine their relations with contexts.

Crosby, Stills, Nash and Young initiated a dialogue with their audience. This was exemplified with their a cappella call and answer pattern from the stage during their 2006 tour, which is described by Crosby in *Since Then*. Some people remember where they were when they first heard certain CSN&Y songs. The songs echo within their memories of their own experiences of love and relationship. Other songs trigger recollections of a time of social struggle. These personal memories intertwine with the collective experience of a generation. The pivotal year of 1968, for example, may be recalled as a time of student political activity, peace movements and feminism, the further escalation of America's role in Vietnam, the assassinations of Martin Luther King and Robert Kennedy, and the dawn of psychedelics. Crosby's *Long Time Gone* was prompted by the assassination of Robert Kennedy and dashed hopes and dreams. It is today one among many cultural markers that appear to grapple with memory and change, with issues of peace and war and the social turbulence that was part of the experience of this generation.

We may say that the trauma of Vietnam, the restlessness of 1968, and the turmoil of the decade were recollected through the soundtrack of the times. Crosby, Stills, Nash and Young addressed the upheaval of the time with a call to peace and to commitment. While The Beatles' stance of "All You Need Is Love" has at times been criticized as passive, a retreat from political engagement, that could not be said of Crosby, Stills, Nash and Young and pronouncements like "Military Madness" and "Ohio." Crosby, Stills, Nash and Young brought the changing world into their songs. They were attuned to the pulse and problems of the latter part of the 1960s. They engaged with their time and place. In doing so, they became part of an ongoing cultural dialogue and their words and music became a locus for interpretation. One may consider, in Crosby, Stills, Nash and Young, what Mikhail Bakhtin has called "carnivalization." This is particularly evoked in songs that engage a participatory audience.

---

6. *American Dreams and Cultural Memory*

The songs of Crosby, Stills, Nash and Young, entwined as they are with personal and collective memory, are a key to modern identity. For Nora, we commune with the past "through vestiges" that "hold the key to our identity, to who we are."[6] As cultural texts, CSN&Y songs have become part of personal memory for many of their listeners. As Nora explains, "The idea that collectivities have a memory implies a far-reaching transformation of the status of individuals within society and of their relationship to the community at large."[7] Crosby, Stills, Nash and Young are about this relationship with a "community" of listeners. From *Deja Vu* to *American Dream*, the albums of Crosby, Stills, Nash and Young have expressed the goal of connecting with their audience in a way that will encourage response to the needs of people in our world. Even as they withdraw into their own solo projects they have maintained a fan base. Even amid their times of personal division their songs encourage a community that could begin building toward peace and a more tolerant future. Crosby, Stills, Nash and Young, like many other bands, have become repositories of memory and a means for the community of listeners to situate their lives with respect to the present and the future.

The songs of Crosby, Stills, Nash and Young are, in a sense, articulated forms of personal or social history. Yet they are something more than only documentary records. The songs act as a trigger for memories, providing a kind of reassurance for some listeners and a challenge for others. Via these songs the older members of the audience may be working through events charged with meaning and value. They are engaging with the past. This assertion is not the same as a sense that survivors work through memories of traumatic times. However, it may be suggested that the songs provide a reference point for an audience making adjustments to modernity and postmodernity, an audience that may turn to memory and nostalgia for their youth when confronted by the pace of life and technological change. The sound of CSN&Y helps to situate these people. Perhaps they help some listeners to work through the stress of modern culture. This working through is an act of memory. It may be seen as a variation on what La Capra views as a "working through" of trauma. While the 1960s were perhaps times no more "traumatic" than those experienced by generations who experienced the American Civil War or the Second World War, they were uniquely jarring and unsettling for many. Thus, we can apply La Capra's thought to this fertile and difficult period and to the role of CSN&Y within it.

The songs need not be directly political or topical for us to situate them in their cultural moment, or to listen again and "re-read" them today. "Southern Cross," by Stephen Stills, for example, reverberates today on a radio station from Hyannis after rain has swept in for a few minutes across Cape Cod in Massachusetts. The song begins with Stills' voice across two verses. When he reaches the words "think about" a big chorus joins in and rides out with him to the word "forgotten." Then, almost jubilantly, the vocals jump and flow together in a declaration of circumnavigating the globe. They are not only recalling being all around the world, but they are all around us now, like the rain outside was moments ago. Chords punctuate this, two at a time, six of them, with stops and a final one extended. Stills returns to the lead vocal for another verse but is now joined by a higher vocal. Crosby and Nash are now in on the mention of a chain of silver and the word "chain" runs toward the off-rhyme of "name." It is music itself that is the narrator, speaking of its winding path around the world, into our minds and hearts. The vocals open and make an auditory circle on the word "around." We hear Stills' vocal return to solo, somewhat bare for a moment, and the punctuation of that chord pattern [// // // /]. The song leaves an imprint, a trace; played on the classic rock radio station across a beach, on an iPhone, or a system at home, it becomes familiar to us. When the radio DJ calls it up, we recognize it; we feel again with it. The song has the power of a remembered tune.

The reception history of Crosby, Stills, Nash and Young is available to us through reviews and commentary in newspapers, popular magazines, film, music trade papers, and on radio and television. It provides a marker for the group's impact on our times. Crosby has said that he appreciates when younger musicians cover his music. It is a reminder that CSN&Y has been leaving a legacy. Their music has become a resource for bands and songwriters who followed them and modeled themselves upon them. CSN&Y responded to a cultural and historical moment, to personal experience and imagination, creating songs that became sites of interaction and points of memory within the lives of their audience. The wide circulation of their songs and their celebrity made their presence culturally pervasive. In a setting where cutting edge creative rap/hip-hop and manufactured saccharine pop alternate on the airwaves, the authentic voice of committed aging rockers retains a place and a voice for our time. That voice is most resilient and most enduring, perhaps, in their benefits, in their commitment to children in need and to the future generations that will be left with the environmental issues, national debt, and politics that we are working through today. That is to say, that the memory that CSN&Y leave is filled with music, surrounded by song, but is ever something more. It is that spirit that says, even amid hard realities, we can change the world. Or, as Crosby once declared: "Oh, yes I can!"

For the audience, reconstruction of the past through memory is always occurring. But what does it mean to remember? To what purposes is CSN&Y and their music to be remembered? As La Capra notes, "The question of 'impact' is best seen in terms of a complex series of readings and uses which texts undergo over time, including the process by which certain texts are canonized."[8] Certain songs by CSN&Y have been "selected" in this sense. They have become part of the soundtrack of memory. These re-readings of CSN&Y are still occurring. Retrospective recordings and new song creations bring new assessments. Such reinterpretations continue because CSN&Y continue to have at least the echo of a platform. They have touched all strands of culture, from "high" to "low." Their music has reached across gender, race, class, and ethnic difference and intersected with lives internationally and continues to do so. The songs of CSN&Y, like documents, have what La Capra calls "worklike" aspects. Each song (and especially songs like "Ohio" or "Teach Your Children") is situated in history in a way that now gives it documentary dimensions. However, it also welcomes dialogue and our interaction with it. Following La Capra, one might say that one's own horizon is questioned and moved by it. One might say that these songs, like diaries or documentaries, are not free of their own historical consciousness. In turn, they linger in memory and continue to affect the consciousness of their listeners.

Memory sustains CSN&Y's continuing importance in the present. Their music has become a site of memory. This is true for people who lived through the 1960s and recall this music as well as for generations of listeners who have been born afterward. Parents and children have discovered in CSN&Y a common bond. In their time together, they transformed and recast themselves. Today, they are recast for new audiences in multiple ways. Their legacy is reconstructed and passed on to future generations.

Although La Capra reminds us that canonical texts can be seen as being in dialogue with "general popular culture," CSN&Y songs, which enable people to recall their lives and work through their personal histories, must be considered alongside their various interpretations in society, through discourse, and across time. This last point is particularly significant, as memory and reconstruction of CSN&Y's work has been enhanced by the digital information age. The remastering of early albums, and digital remixes preserve memory.

Yet, some traumatic memories linger for the sixties generation: the Vietnam war, the tumult at the 1968 Democratic convention, the assassinations of Dr. King and Robert Kennedy, Kent State, Watergate. The dreams, ideals, and personal histories of this generation of music listeners are tied together with cultural events that brought blues notes. Among the events that have been turned into symbols of the decline of fervor and hope is the concert at Altamont, a music festival in which Crosby, Stills and Nash participated in December 1969.

Woodstock and Altamont

Woodstock has been recalled, recorded and filmed, written about by participants, promoters, and musicians. The original Woodstock festival has been mythologized, turned into symbol and legend. It was a muddy affair, a tribal-like gathering, in the general vicinity of Woodstock, in Bethel. It was a huge gathering which came off fairly peacefully. Perhaps Woodstock got lucky. For set in contrast as its inversion was the fateful gathering at Altamont in California, December 6, 1969. That concert, at which Crosby, Stills, and Nash also played, has prompted dozens of interpretations, including the view that the idealism of the sixties was made ambiguous by violence at the event. Graham Nash, in his memoir, called Altamont "the weirdest date" that they have played. They appeared at the festival because Jerry Garcia of the Grateful Dead asked them to. While the titles of the songs in their set were a tad bit darker than those in their

Woodstock set, Crosby, Stills, and Nash had little to do with the debacle. Tensions became evident when Jefferson Airplane singer Marty Balin was punched in the head and the band decided that they would not play. Stephen Stills felt "the danger in the air," Nash writes. He appears to subscribe to the view that Altamont "more or less" acted as a sign of the end of "the Woodstock era."[9]

With the crack of a snare, the ring of a cymbal from Charlie Watts, and the distinctive riff of "Jumpin' Jack Flash" from Keith Richards' guitar and Bill Wyman's bass, the Stones began to play and the crowd became ecstatic. The Rolling Stones were finishing their first American tour since 1966 in a wave of publicity. Robert Cristgau called it "history's first mythic rock and roll tour."[10] Critic Dave Marsh would recall their tour as "part of rock and roll legend," one of the "benchmarks of an era."[11] The late sixties, like the Stones' tour, soon became mythical: a marker for an idealistic generation amid calamitous events. The years 1968 and 1969 had been troubled ones in America: the urban race riots and student protests of 1968 indicated tensions that were bubbling to the brim; the assassinations of Martin Luther King and Robert Kennedy lingered in the national consciousness; Nixon was a year in the White House and the war in Vietnam showed no signs of abating. Crosby, Stills, Nash and Young had joined the anti-war protest. Men had landed on the moon. Woodstock had been a triumphant musical celebration. The Stones were performing live, making music, in part, as a way to heal their loss of Brian Jones in the summer of 1968. Excitement had rippled through the rock music press and among Rolling Stones fans. The Stones were unfolding their newer songs: "Gimme Shelter" and "Sympathy for the Devil"; "Brown Sugar" had just been created in the days before Altamont. Now the Stones were back on stage: mythical, magical, doing what they did best, making music, and no one expected further tragedy, darkness, or shadows.

Yet, the darkness came. As the Rolling Stones played their set at Altamont, a tragic melee broke out in the crowd: one some critics would never let them forget. Across the past four decades a variety of attempts have been made to try to understand the tragic turn of events that accompanied the Rolling Stones' performance at Altamont Raceway in December 1969. For some critics, Altamont signaled the demise of the sixties; it was the day the music died, or idealism died. *Rolling Stone* blasted the band, their management, and the concert promoters, casting a litany of charges—more polemical than accurate. It was the day that an individual in the crowd died at the hand of Hell's Angels, at the front of the stage, and it became a symbolic moment in the annals of rock music.

For Crosby, Stills and Nash it was likely just another show. They had played at Woodstock. They had played at the festival at Esalen Institute, off Highway 1. The story of Altamont does not figure largely in their history. The shadows of Altamont have long faded. Yet, those of the tragedy at Kent State University linger. That was the troubled day that drew outrage from Crosby, Stills, and Nash. Neil Young's song "Ohio" still is associated with recollections of violence that occurred there in May 1970.

For years, the notion of a decline of sixties has been related to Altamont, Kent State, the deaths of Jimi Hendrix and Janis Joplin. Altamont has repeatedly been contrasted with Woodstock as the "twin evil sister" of the muddy gathering of peace and love. *Rolling Stone* magazine called Altamont "the product of diabolical egotism, hype, ineptitude, money manipulation and, at base, a fundamental lack of concern for humanity" (January 21, 1970). Eleven writers wrote across fourteen pages about the event, and most of the rhetoric was not pretty. The Rolling Stones were made guilty by association. *Rolling Stone* magazine and the rock press threw negative criticisms. Ralph Gleason claimed the Stones hated their audience because they were charging "high ticket prices" of $8, something that in 2019 seems like it should get a laugh from the Stones' logo when Stones concert tickets run to $850 or more. In response to Altamont, Keith Richards told the *London Evening Standard*, "A few tempers got frayed."[12] However, clearly something more complex was going on that frayed those tempers. Beyond this, the constructions of *Rolling Stone* magazine and by critics have made Altamont symbolic of something larger than a single rock concert. Robert Christgau wrote in *Newsday* in July 1972 that Altamont "provided such a complex metaphor for the way an era ended."[13]

Yet, Crosby, Stills, Nash and Young did carry on. They took separate directions, as their use of their name suggested that they would do. They gathered together again and were playing a concert the night that Richard Nixon resigned from the presidency. They announced that to the audience.

Neil Young played a song about it. They may have been disheartened by issues in America, by the war in Vietnam. They were liberal, vocal, and resilient. No doubt their message had an edge to it. Although they did not shirk from controversy, they were not threatening.

The Rolling Stones cut quite a different image. Altamont contributed to the Rolling Stones' myth. After all, these were the bad boys of rock, the ones with sympathy for the devil. Even if "Sympathy for the Devil" was not the song being sung when the stabbing incident at Altamont occurred, it was conflated with it. Stones manager Andrew Loog Oldham had promoted the band as rebellious and threatening. The rock press perpetuated that image. Licking lips and slipping zippers graced their album covers. Well before the release of *Hot Rocks*, their lauded collection of hits, the Rolling Stones were mythical. As Norma Coates has argued, the rock press itself was to blame for Altamont for making rock mythical and creating expectations among the rock music audience. She claims that violent economics played a role and that rock critics denied their own complicity in creating "mass mediated fantasies."[14] "That Altamont happened is not surprising," she writes; "Woodstock was the exception."[15] The rock star avatar is a creation of the press, Coates has argued, and these objects of attention sought money. In her view, the film by Albert and David Maysles that documented the Altamont concert, *Gimme Shelter,* showed "the sense of dread regnant at the festival."[16]

Such charges are part of the enduring speculation. Perhaps, all one can say for certain is that the Rolling Stones played their music at Altamont in December 1969 and a large crowd assembled to hear them and the other bands, like Crosby, Stills and Nash and their friends the Grateful Dead, that played there. Although the Grateful Dead, Crosby, Stills, and Nash, the Flying Burrito Brothers and others were all present, the incidents of Altamont are invariably associated with the Rolling Stones. Repeatedly, Altamont has been used by critics to suggest the dark side of the sixties generation, or an inherent violence that contrasts with the "peace and love movement" of that era.[17] However, what occurred at Altamont was not the "evil twin" of Woodstock. It had nothing to do with Vietnam, Mai Lai, or Manson. Altamont did not emerge from an underside of violence in the sixties generation. Nor were the Rolling Stones, or any of the other bands, responsible for those incidents. The Stones were no more responsible for a drugged audience member acting out, or Hell's Angels' acting out, than the Beatles were in any way responsible for a deranged psychotic's response to a song on *The White Album*. Altamont is an inadequate marker of an era. Crosby, Stills and Nash are better remembered for their appearance Woodstock, partly because of the film and soundtrack. Their story extends way beyond whatever these events are said to symbolize. Across the years, the music may have been corporatized and idealized, images co-opted and subsumed under business as usual, as in Woodstock 1994. However, the spirit of these bands and some of the ideals of the sixties remain with us.

Rolling Stone magazine blasted the promoters of Altamont as creating "a checklist for disaster": the promise of a free concert, a location change, the lack of sanitation sources, a poor sound system, and having Hell's Angels assigned as security guards. Lester Bangs and others called this "ineptitude." Ralph Gleason placed blame on Jagger and the Stones, saying Mick Jagger was either naïve or callous. Yet, Jagger was "angry" and "bewildered" according to other reports.[18] It appears that everyone in the press was reaching feebly for answers. Could this really be blamed on the Stones, or on a sound system and bad toilets? *Rolling Stone* clearly created its own narrative and its own interpretation. Indeed, we have "a masterpiece of rock mythmaking," as Norma Coates says.[19] As many as 300,000 people attended the concert. Hells Angels were hired for security and reportedly were paid with $500 of beer. Perhaps this was to be a limited role in protecting the generators, as some critics have said. Reportedly, Sam Cutler, the Rolling Stones' tour manager, had made a deal with Rick Scully of the Grateful Dead and Pete Knell of Hell's Angels San Francisco chapter. "There was no barricade," Scully pointed out in an interview in the *Canberry Times*, December 5, 2009.[20] Hell's Angels drank some of the beer as some members positioned themselves in front of the stage. Then came the scuffle in front of the stage.

Crosby, Stills and Nash were bystanders. Their own interaction with the crowd was without incident. Looking back, critics have wondered how this crowd became unpredictable. They have asked whether only a few people were antagonistic. A fight broke out in front of the stage. Some have claimed that it began during the third song, "Sympathy for the Devil." Mick Jagger was heard to say, "Just be cool down in front there. Don't push around."[21] While it may give a metaphysician shivers to think that pandemonium began with "Sympathy for the Devil," Meredith Hunter's death likely occurred as Jagger was singing "Under My Thumb." Hunter was wearing a bright lime green outfit and he had a .22 caliber revolver. Eric Saarinen took video footage of this. Cameraman Baird Bryant was on top of a bus filming the action. David Maysles later edited the film and you can see it for yourself in *Gimme Shelter*. Hell's Angel member Alan Passaro pulled a knife and charged Hunter. With his left hand pulling down on the pistol in Hunter's hand, he stabbed him twice. Hunter was high on metamphetemine. Passsaro was arrested and later acquitted. The Alameda County Sherriff re-opened the case in 2003, because it had been asserted that a second Hell's Angels member was involved. The review of the case was closed May 25, 2008.

The Sixties

Critics have sometimes held the concert at Altamont to represent the end of the sixties. It is a convenient date—December 6, 1969—with which to conclude the decade: perhaps too convenient. "American Pie" by Don McLean appears to refer obliquely to this as "the day the music died." Critic Ralph Gleason wrote, "If Woodstock is the flowering of youth culture, Altamont has come to mean the end of it" (August 1970). Perhaps Patti Smith has offered a clearer way of phrasing this as "the end of the idealism of the sixties." However, the features that historians identify with the sixties began before the decade and persisted several years after it. Others have set their marker for disillusion of sixties idealism at the death of four people and the injury of others at the Kent State University protests in May 1970. Yet, wasn't the vitality of CSN&Y's "Ohio" an expression of energetic protest and horror? Elements of the sixties had that kind of resilience, that kind of moral concern. Yet, the claims still linger: Altamont "brings the 1960s to a violent end." It was the day when "the counterculture attacked itself" (December 6, 2009, Huffington Post). Nonsense. This is, as Norma Coates has said, "a dubious claim."[22]

The sixties remain a source of debate for those who came to maturity during that period and now walk the corridors of political and economic power in the United States. This is true even as David Crosby's song "Capitol" questions the powers that be in Washington. What might "the sixties" mean? Does it refer to idealism, youth, commitment, a belief in the possibility of changing the world? Or was this a time of a disastrous war, civil rights strife, assassination, Kent State, and loss of faith in government: a national trauma? Was the sixties generation one of high ideals, democratic principles, quest for freedom and getting back to a prelapsarian, utopian garden? Or, was this a time of excess, moral relativism, slouching toward Gomorrah and anarchy? One's politics may hinge upon one's answer to this. Altamont is a convenient marker of the end of a decade when interpreted as a sign of disillusionment by some, or as a moment of turbulent excess and violence by others. The sixties went on beyond this point—at least to the mid-seventies, some critics say. The image of rock music as rebellious was easy to associate with the rebellions and aborted revolutions of the period. When rock music met with counterculture, it served as "a vehicle of protest."[23] Rock was a voice of difference for those who were young and looking for a place in the world that seemed not always compatible with their dreams and visions. Yet, it was also an aspiration to higher ideals.

The decade of the 1960s brought transformations in the areas of race and gender. A romantic millennial hope may have served to liberalize U.S. culture, but it also brought the immoderation that conservatives rejected and made political use of in subsequent decades. In the view of some conservatives, the sixties offered only a libertine carnival, attitudes of anything goes, and a politics of feminism, civil liberties, and gay rights that undermined family values.[24] Bands that were well-received by counterculture were associated by "silent majority" conservatives with this narrative of the demise of the true, the good, and the beautiful in the republic. Crosby, Stills and Nash became political. The Rolling Stones contested legal repression of their personal inclination toward drug use with "Mother's Little Helper," which pointed to the daily use of pharmaceutical sedatives by housewives in conventional culture. However, unlike CSN, they did not engage in the politics of the New Left. Meanwhile, as historians point out, the counterculture may have been unfocused, naïve, and at times indulgent, but most enjoyed rock music, and they aspired toward respect for individualism and Woodstock-like community.

---

6. *American Dreams and Cultural Memory*

By 1969, some rock bands, such as the Rolling Stones, had achieved both worldwide acclaim and notorious disdain. Their music was inescapable—crackling over transistor radios in the park, sounding from car radios, spinning on LPs in homes across the United States and Canada, as well as in Britain and Europe. Rock bands generated money—lots of it—and the music industry became increasingly commercial. By 1986, scholars like Allan Bloom, who didn't quite understand the rock music medium, were appalled. Bloom was dismayed that his young students were not reading Plato or listening to Mozart. They were being drawn into distraction by the siren call of rock music. This, he said, was the closing of the American mind.

Professor Bloom was reciting an ancient criticism of music. Plato, his own great intellectual icon, had not only kicked the poets out of his Republic, he had complained in the *Dialogues* about musical modes he adjudged disorderly; modes like the Dorian and Phrygian might assist warriors but others he believed generated ruinous dissonance in the body public (*Republic* III 396d-399 c). Bloom saw his students spending time on rock music and tried desperately to turn his students on to Mozart—who was, of course, as unconventional a genius as any era has produced. He lamented this state of affairs, as if high culture and popular culture were somehow mutually exclusive and one could not both read Plato and listen to rock music. In his view, the American mind was closing and all higher aspirations were being diminished. The central villain in his narrative was Mick Jagger. Prancing, singing about cavorting with gypsy barroom queens and divorcees in New York City, Jagger was notorious. Bloom did not spend hours listening to *Beggar's Banquet* and music alone did not trigger his response to Jagger, in 1986; Jagger's image did. Bloom's book, *The Closing of the American Mind* (1987), like those books on the Rolling Stones of 1984, underscores the effectiveness of Andrew Loog Oldham's publicity and the Rolling Stones' mythology.

Life in the United States changed profoundly between 1960 and 1970. With the British invasion of 1964 in pop music, the Rolling Stones, the Beatles, the Kinks, the Animals, the Who and others deeply entered the context and consciousness of the emerging youth culture. The Stones' "(I Can't Get No) Satisfaction" resonated with young people seeking satisfactions in this rapidly changing climate. Insofar as rock may be correlated with dreams of "the new frontier," as Kennedy had dubbed the hope of his administration in 1960, it was a music that reflected limitless expression and hope. So, it was associated at the end of the decade with the disillusion of dreams. Soon Hendrix was gone, Joplin was gone, and there had been Altamont. Rock co-existed with a mythology of disillusionment.

Given their visibility, the popularity of their music, and the power of their myth, the Rolling Stones were subjected to scapegoating, transference, and projection. Conservatives in the Bloom camp viewed them as a distraction, a disruption: a band of moral degenerates whose outlandish strutting, irrationality, drug problems, and sexual promiscuity would be imitated and lead to moral degradation. Their fans, however, saw them as a proud statement of independence, amplified energy, and in-your- face recalcitrance. Beneath these responses, a powerful mythology was at work.

Pushing the Boundaries

The Rolling Stones were born in rock and roll rebellion and have always reflected a subversive desire to transcend boundaries. Their dynamic performances continue to suggest the blossoming of possibilities and a revival of wonder and instinctual energy. However, conservative critics have charged that the breaking of boundaries is problematic for society. In his book *The Cultural Contradictions of Capitalism*, the conservative social scientist Daniel Bell criticized sixties radicalism as a form of hubris that included "the refusal to accept limits, the insistence on continually reaching out."[25] In this narrative, one that is rather like that of ancient Greek tragedy, the surpassing of moderation leads to nemesis. Icarus has flown too close to the sun and his wings melt and he falls. Orestes, seeking retribution, is pursued by the Furies. Narcissus, in love with himself and his reflection, falls into the pond and drowns. Excessive pride in Creon and Antigone lead to disaster. What goes around comes around.

At issue at the Altamont concert was the behavior of a few people in the area near the stage. There are a variety of explanations for what occurred but what prompted this crowd behavior is difficult to determine. Thousands of people present in those twilight moments had nothing whatsoever to do with the injuries that occurred and did not learn of them until afterward. They were at Altamont to see a show, to be part of an event. A rock audience like this may become a fellowship of spontaneity: *communitas*. In their pilgrimage to a concert, they will "distance themselves from mundane structures" and social roles and will reverse social hierarchies, as the anthropologist Victor Turner has pointed out. Following the views of Turner in *The Forest of Symbols* (1967), we may say that they enter a space in between, a threshold, a liminal space in the ambiguity of ritual. There is a tension in this zone. The trek to the muddy grounds of Woodstock or to Altamont may be compared with a pilgrimage to a sacred site. Victor Turner and Edith Turner examined pilgrimage as a liminoid experience as "a temporary liberation from profane social structures" that realizes renewal at the journey's culmination. When the Stones performed at Altamont, their audience was just beyond the apron of the stage, with minimal barriers and no seating. They were indeed lost in space, in the ambiguity of a liminal space, where audience and band were in a precarious balance and boundaries became indistinct.

The liminal has been described as a suspension, a deferral of resolution.[26] This is an atmosphere that can be felt by an audience. The Rolling Stones were scheduled to step onto the stage in the twilight: a time in between daylight and darkness. In Stanley Booth's account we read: "Night was upon us."[27] Booth writes that Jagger tried to walk around and see the show "but there was no way, it was too crowded, you could not move in the crush."[28] We are told of an announcement on the P.A. system before the Rolling Stones appeared: "The reason we can't start is that the stage is loaded with people…. The stage must be cleared or we can't start." The description continues with an image of the crowd: "Now they were one solid mass jammed against the stage." Booth adds: "One surge forward and people would be crushed."[29]

Similarly, Philip Norman writes that the stage was "like a bar at closing time."[30] He describes a very crowded space: "the slopes were solid with bivouacked bodies, each clinging to its precious inches of space with as much fervor as if the Earth were shortly to be turned upside down."[31] In inflated rhetorical style, he writes that stage side there were young people "naked in the dank cold, flinging themselves forward against the cracked leather cordon as puny white martyrs, almost begging to be surrounded, beaten, trampled, and kicked." It is doubtful that the crowd was that masochistic, or that the Stones, who "materialized in a demon red spotlight blaze," were any more aligned with satanic forces than they were with rock imagery and mythology.[32]

The incident may simply come down to a fact of human response: nobody likes to be pushed. In his account, Booth attempts to deflect off the Stones any charges of complicity. He blames the Hell's Angels. He claims that Michelle Phillips of the Mamas and the Papas observed the Hell's Angels "fighting with civilians, with women, and each other."[33] He notes that members of the Jefferson Airplane were disturbed by one of the Hell's Angels, "punching a blonde man in front of the stage" and that the band's singer Martin Balin was knocked out when he tried to intervene.[34] He repeats Jagger's exhortations to the crowd: "just be cool down in front now, don't push around."[35] As the Stones began "Sympathy for the Devil" a sound burst out, he says: "there was a low explosive thump." Booth writes: "People were pushing, falling, a great hole opening as they moved instantly away from the center of the trouble."[36] He suggests that this was the sound a motorcycle backfiring. Then he charges the Hell's Angels with "spinning like madmen, swinging at people."[37] Jagger, cast as a peacemaker, was calling out: "Who's fighting and what for? Why are we fighting?" Keith Richards asserted, either they cool it, or we don't play.[38] As the Stones broke into "Under My Thumb" the man was stabbed. Dr. Robert Hiatt, a medical resident at the Public Health Hospital in San Francisco, came to his aid and carried him off. A film crew recorded the incredible moments.[39]

Whether by force or design, crowds sometimes break barriers. At Woodstock in 1969, some people drifted freely, *au naturale*, into ponds, or sexually crossed emotional and physical boundaries into each other. At the attempted reprise of the festival in 1999, some audience members ripped plywood from walls and used a security fence for a bonfire. In 1979, at Riverfront Coliseum in Cincinnati, eleven fans of the Who died in a melee of pushing when they were pressed against the glass doors before even a single note had been played. In 2002, Marilyn Manson ended a gig when the crowd broke down a security fence in front of the stage in Kansas

City. At the Danish festival Roskilde in 2000, Pearl Jam's Orange Stage set was disrupted as people pressed against barricades. Questions arise whether the problems at such concerts are a few bad seeds, drugs, intolerance, or bad security—or some combination of these.

Aggression and uncivil behavior may have prompted some of these incidents. However, the media mythology that promotes rock music aspiration and instills excitement may have also played a part, as Coates has suggested. The audience's sense of space may have been another factor. The Rolling Stones' appearance, for some of the audience, was a highlight. The star status that the Stones had achieved played to an audience informed by film and television and the audience at Altamont was the first generation to grow up on both of these mediums. The movies give us epic space and intimacy. There is the grand panorama but also the close-up. The visual imagery of television had contributed to the election of a president in 1960. Star-making machinery in rock media had made the Rolling Stones bigger than life. People reached out to touch them, to vicariously live in and through them.

Yet, we may wonder what makes a crowd "act out." Is there some "collective consciousness" at work in a crowd, as the sociologist Emile Durkheim once theorized? The crowd at Altamont pressed toward the stage. Drug intake and beer loosened psychological barriers among some and, sadly, one who wished to touch ecstasy waved a pistol and touched death. There was a lack of physical space close to the stage. It was hardly the spacious society some of that generation dreamed of. The mythic hope of a continent of open spaces included, in the sixties generation, a rejection of the inheritance of a managerial, technological society. This, in part, was what the critics at *Rolling Stone* magazine were reacting to. They recognized that the vehicle for manufacture and distribution of rock music was the record company, an enterprise closely tied to corporate concerns. The critics of the Rolling Stones and of their promoters charged that they had sold out. They had become aware that the music industry had become a corporate enterprise emphasizing product and profits and the only garden the sixties generation would get back to was Madison Square Garden. The Rolling Stones, treated as rock royalty, were making a mint and Altamont was a rapidly constructed amusement park that turned into a disaster. The calliope had collapsed.

Some concertgoers likely went to Altamont to be part of the event, to be part of something, an audience, a temporary semblance of community. More than one sociologist has said that people like to be around other people and so people go to movies, or shopping malls. It is better than what Robert Putnam has called "bowling alone," the tendency to do things alone. Robert Bellah has sharply critiqued the fragmentation of modern society and the separateness of individuals in American society while also showing that competitive individualism is not the whole story: "The deep desire for autonomy and self-reliance" can be "combined with an equally deep conviction that life has no meaning unless it's shared with others in the context of community."[40] The counterculture represented what Dominick Cavallo has called "that strange paradoxical mélange of communal and 'do your own thing' individualism."[41] Simon Firth writes: "the violence of the Altamont Festival of 1969 was taken by rock fans ... as the final sign that a community could not be based on musical taste alone."[42]

Yet, music can inspire. Rock music may, on occasion, bring members of an audience to an experience of the sublime. Edmund Burke once indicated the effects of the singing and the "shouting of multitudes" in his *Enquiry Into the Origins of Our Ideas of the Sublime and Beautiful*. He wrote: "The sole strength of the sound, so amazes and confounds the imagination that in this staggering, and hurry of the mind, the best established tempers can scarcely forbear being borne down, and joining in the common cry, and common resolution of the crowd. "[43] This participation, he suggested, induces the feeling of the sublime. This is "a great and awful sensation" that stirs body and sense and mind and "fills it with terror."[44] Neil Hertz has likened this experiential transformation to religious conversion, leading to an altered perspective: "The awe of an external greatness is also an awe of what is within."[45] The energy of the Rolling Stones and an enthusiastic crowd responding to them may touch a kind of grandeur.

Icarus, in the Greek myth, must have felt that awe as he glided up toward the sun—just as a powerful concert experience may strike a sense of wonder in the listener. Such concert experiences are not based upon the kind of moderation Aristotle once advocated in the *Nicomachaen Ethics*, or that is encouraged by the Chorus in an Athenian play like Sophocles' *Antigone*. How does a rock crowd moderate its behavior when the idiom itself is beckoning to the soul to let go and exceed moderation? Perhaps, the issue is simple mutual respect: the ability to be loose and alive and free with others.

Neuroscience tells us that we have "mirror neurons" that fire when one imitates the actions of another.[46] In the dynamics of a concert, there is a rich social interaction. One may register emotion, empathic systems that respond to observing another's pain. The relationship between social phenomena and the experience of feelings is a concern of Antonio Damasio, who observes, "The study of social emotions is in its infancy." One might think of social emotions at a Rolling Stones concert and how those emotions are transmitted or shared. Damasio identifies emotions in three categories: background emotions (our emotional tone, regulatory and metabolic), primary emotions (our emotional experiences of surprise, happiness, fear, anger), and social emotions (sympathy, gratitude, shame, guilt, envy, embarrassment).[47] Damasio refers to social cooperation as something rooted biologically in us, which arises in social and cultural settings: "to some extent our brains are wired to cooperate with others in the process."[48] He calls this an inbuilt "human decree." However, there is a possible negative side our makeup, he observes: "The bad news is that many negative social emotions make the human decree difficult to implement and improve."[49] Were negative social emotions the cause of the incidents at Altamont?

Obviously, feelings may be altered by chemical substances and alcohol, narcotics, or psychotropic drugs may have been a factor at Altamont, as they may be at other rock concerts. Their use, notes Damasio, "accounts for the beginning of the chain of processes that lead to the alteration of feelings but not for the processes that eventually established the feelings."[50] Rather, there has been a changing of the "body sensing maps."[51] Concert security needs to be alert to those strained states, not a participant in them, as the Hell's Angels of San Francisco evidently were at Altamont.

A rock concert is a center of social interactions. Music affects human consciousness. People clearly have emotional responses to rock music, which is a communicative medium. As George Herbert Mead has pointed out, the social symbol is shared. Individual meaning is formulated, in part, through the perception of the gestures of others.[52] Psychologists and literary critics may offer a variety of other theories. Certainly, the sixties pushed social boundaries and intra-psychic ones.

There are subjective responses to the music of the Rolling Stones, to their mythical and iconic presence, and to the experience of a Rolling Stones concert. In his essay on Beethoven (1870), Richard Wagner wrote of "the oneness of our inner essence with that of the theatre world."[53] Interpreting Wagner's essay, Kiene Brillenburg-Wurth observes: "Listening to music is to open to the possibilities of losing one's borders or limitations as an individual and extending into an infinite life-force."[54] Rock music crowds may become ec-static (out of the body, or stasis); in this sense. Rolling Stones fans are moved to emotion. When Robert Pattison, in 1987, compared Jagger with Isadora Duncan, he wrote that when Jagger appeared after Tina Turner on that 1969 tour "again the audience was moved to frenzy."[55]

The death at Altamont may have principally been a response to one frenzied individual who was high and acting out. If unruly behavior in the crowd is cited, one might point to an array of things that may have prompted that. There may have been a loss of control, boundaries, or borders. There may have been toxic social emotions of aggression that swept through the crowd. If we begin to extrapolate from the incident and consider it symbolic of the loss of idealism of the sixties, and the spirit of the times, it is interesting to ask if the peace and love of Woodstock bore the undercurrents of war and hate. Critics may suggest this, while others lament the waning of ideals of peace and community. Yet, Jagger seems to have expressed it pithily: War is often just a shot away, but love is a kiss away. It matters what individuals, crowds, and nations will choose.

Meanwhile, it is true that by 1969 rock music had become about hagiography as much as about music, as Norma Coates has observed.[56] Pressure was placed on rock artists to conform to a vision created by the critics and perhaps this "spirit of the times," as she calls it, contributed to Altamont. However, this seems a vague phrase, recalling those early nineteenth century writers about the zeitgeist. This also does not answer our questions. After all, what was this ill-defined "spirit of the times"? It is fine to say that rock critics, or label public relations managers, were mythmakers. What did the mythology surrounding the festival at Altamont have to do with audience behavior? Yes, money and reputation created the concert; it helped to move the location and set the stage. Rock criticism helped to construct the mythology. But this was no utopian space apart from the world. Nor were Woodstock and Altamont some bipolar experience of a generation. Such a view is misleading. A critical game of pass the blame does not get at what happened. Nor does it help anyone to get beyond it. Perspective and healing are gained across time.

The decade of the 1960s was no dream, no mere drugged haze over Lethe, the river of forgetfulness. The music was alive. The commitment to causes, the yearning for freedom, the challenges to authority were real. So too, for some, was an almost bi-polar ecstasy and disillusion linked with Altamont, Kent State, and Watergate (of the long 1960s). Yet, to suggest any causal continuum between the Rolling Stones' appearance at Altamont and one stoned individual's death and to extrapolate this as a sign for an era is a position fraught with illogic. To search for causal relationships leads one into a quandary. There will always be those who engage in a blame game. Yet, it seems appropriate to ask: ought the Stones to have never played the gig? (Of course, they should have!) Should the promoters never have changed venues? Was it a mistake to hire the Hell's Angels of San Francisco and San Jose to watch over the generators and act as security, or to have paid them with beer? Critics have blamed everything from the band to the sound system to the toilets. They have cast Altamont as the inversion of idealism, contrasted the concert with Woodstock, making them binaries, even as others have argued that Woodstock was not all that different. Altamont immediately became myth and moral lesson. California was a mythological west of promise, a haven for the American dream that had erupted like an earthquake. Altamont was where a frontier and those primitive roots of a nation's identity suddenly disintegrated. But, paradoxically, this moment in the Rolling Stones history was merely the end of a chapter, and the beginning of a new phase for one of the most enduring and extraordinary bands in the world.

For Crosby, Stills, Nash and Young, the attempt to redefine an American dream persisted. Their musical creations took further new turns as they entered the 1990s. In 1990, David Crosby re-emerged on the CSN album *Live It Up*, an album produced by Joe Vitale and J. Stanley Johnson with the band. This began as a Nash-Crosby project. Nash has said that the goal was to have fun, as the cover appears to indicate: we see hotdogs speared above a blue earth. Along with "Live It Up," listeners heard "If Anybody Had a Heart" and "Yours and Mine" and Crosby's restored high tenor on "Third World Wars." More seriously, "Arrows" was soul-searching: a song about turning misfortune around. Jazz saxophonist Branford Marsalis added solos. "After the Dolphin" emerged as an intriguing song about a World War II broadcast that announced a bombing hit on a pub. The song ends with a recording of Harry S. Truman announcing the bombing of Hiroshima. The song raises the question: will anyone survive the twentieth century?

Closer to home for David Crosby was the potential for natural disaster: a California earthquake. Crosby and his wife Jan were living in Santa Ynez, about thirty miles north of Santa Barbara when they experienced an earthquake that shook the house and disrupted the area. He recalls the empathetic response of people to them and people in the Encino area who were affected.[57] In 1991, he had a motorcycle accident. His recovery intersected with CSN tour dates in Europe. In 1992, the CSN&Y album *4 Way Street* was reissued and expanded with bonus tracks. Crosby, Stills, and Nash played a series of summer concerts. Crosby worked on a recording. Neil Young recalled his 1972 album *Harvest* with an album in a different mood, *Harvest Moon*.

In 1994, David Crosby experienced serious health issues. Hepatitis C affected his liver and he had to have a liver transplant. He was ill for the Woodstock event that was scheduled for July. Not only had his health collapsed but much of his money had vanished also. Crosby belonged to the guild for music performers and had AFTRA/SAC health insurance. To the UCLA Medical Center came friends to visit him. Illness and recovery brought time for reflection. There was an up side to this. He had a child and he met his adult child from an affair he had had long ago. James Raymond, a talented musician in his own right, sought out his father, David Crosby, through the assistance of Michael Finnegan.[58] That reunion not only brought a new lease on life to David Crosby; it produced some extraordinary music from CPR (Crosby, James Raymond, guitarist Jeff Pevar, Steve Di Stanislao on drums, Andrew "Drew" Ford on bass).

There was now also an extended Crosby family: his wife Jan, his son Django, his daughter Donovan, and his daughter Erika. Bailey and Beckett were born to Melissa Etheridge and Julie Cypher, to whom he was a sperm donor.[59] Now there was also his adult son, James Raymond, his wife Stacia, and their daughter Grace. James Raymond was a fine musician in his own right and the band CPR would add a new collaborative dimension to Crosby's music.

After the Storm, produced by Glynn Johns, was released in August 1994. This was the last Crosby, Stills and Nash album released on Atlantic Records. Soon afterward, country artists Suzy Boguss, Kathy Mattea, and Allison Kraus recorded "Teach Your Children" for an AIDS benefit album. On May 6, 1997, Crosby, Stills, and Nash were inducted into the Rock and Roll Hall of Fame. James Taylor provided the induction speech. Buffalo Springfield was also inducted the same evening, making Stephen Stills the first individual to enter the Rock and Roll Hall of Fame twice on the same day. Joni Mitchell, the Bee Gees, the Jacksons, the Rascals, Parliament Funkadelic, and bluegrass legend Bill Monroe were all inducted that day. Crosby would subsequently be inducted, for the second time, with the Byrds, and Nash with the Hollies.

The most visible and commercially successful member of the CSN&Y lineup in 1997 was Neil Young. Young's support led to the album *Looking Forward* (1999) on his label, Reprise, and a tour in 2000. A CSN&Y tour of America in 2002 was very financially successful. In 2006, the Freedom of Speech tour followed the Neil Young protest album *Living with War.* They continued to make solo recordings. Crosby's *Voyage* provided his chronicle of his solo work and work with bands. He had begun working on music with CPR. Nash offered his *Reflections* as he approached his 67th birthday. He started writing his autobiography. Stills recorded *Man Alive!* In 2005. On July 30, 2008, they sang "Teach Your Children" on television on the *Colbert Report* with Steve Colbert appearing in the guise of Neil Young. In 2009, a collection of CSN song demos was set to appear but did not. They thought about developing a recording, "Songs We Wish We'd Written," but Crosby could not see eye to eye with Rich Rubin, the producer assigned to the project. They participated in a Bridge School benefit October 27, 2013. However, there has since been some falling out between Neil Young and David Crosby and more recently between Nash and Crosby. In 2014, Crosby recorded and issued *Croz,* arguably one of the best solo albums of his life. The richly textured recording demonstrated that he was in fine voice and had embraced a new sound, accompanied by his son James and band. The CSNY 1974 anthology box set compiled by Joel Bernstein for Rhino Records was released on July 8, 2014, but it would not be followed up by any concerts or tour. DJs on XM Radio announced that Young and Crosby were not talking to each other. It was yet another turn in a long story of music making and conflict.

7

Speaking Out
Political Activism

The work of Crosby, Stills, Nash and Young has been indissolubly linked with political activism. This goes back to their beginnings as a group. In 1967, Nash was growing restless with the pop songs of The Hollies and Crosby was on the outs with the Byrds and composing works that did not fit with their musical direction. In January 1967, Buffalo Springfield's "For What It's Worth" was released. The song, created by Stephen Stills, is connected with the Vietnam War in many videos. Stills responded to Sunset Strip riots in Los Angeles, more as a matter of concern with civil liberties than Vietnam.[1] By 1970, Graham Nash was writing songs like "Chicago" and "Military Madness." David Crosby was speaking out, letting his views be known. Neil Young wrote "Ohio." Crosby, Stills, Nash and Young were singing "Find the Cost of Freedom."

The contribution of Crosby, Stills, Nash, and Young has been through music. Their political pronouncements have been intertwined with their public voice. However, songs are not essays. Neil Young's "Ohio" or Stephen Stills' "For What It's Worth" may stand high among rock's protest songs but they operate more through emotion than through an explication of rational inquiry and argument. The music is fundamentally related to each statement. The voice, the atmosphere, and the force of a song touches the listener. A song like Graham Nash's "Chicago" speaks of freedom and justice. The bright forward movement of the song's rhythm and the assertion of capacity to change things evokes optimism and determination. The song lyric offers a sentiment and allows the listener to interpret it.

Chicago was the site of the 1968 Democratic National Convention. This was a time when the Tet Offensive signaled an escalation of the war in Vietnam. President Lyndon Johnson had declined to run again for office and hopes were raised about the Eugene McCarthy campaign against Hubert Humphrey for the Democratic nomination. There were disturbances at the convention. The Chicago Eight were charged on April 9, 1969, with conspiracy to riot at the convention and they pled not guilty. They were vocal at trial about war, racism, and Nixon and were charged numerous times with contempt of court. The conspiracy charges did not stick. A 1972 court of appeals overturned the convictions.[2] To write about this resistance in song was an act of courage and a declaration of sympathy with the anti-war movement.

Crosby, Stills, Nash and Young are part of a long line of folk music engagement with issues of social justice and politics. In the twentieth century, these ranged across the traditions exemplified by Woody Guthrie, Joe Hill, Josh White, Pete Seeger, Phil Ochs, Bob Dylan, Joan Baez, Harry Belafonte, Peter Yarrow and others. The troubadour is the town crier: a cultural loudspeaker, a voice of the people making announcements and pronouncements in the public square. R. Serge Denisoff reflected upon the social engagement of folk and folk/rock music in his book *Sing a Song of Social Significance*. Denisoff examined the folk music of the left and the sociology of dissent.[3] That tradition continued to find its voice in the work of socio-politically aware artists like Neil Young, Bruce Springsteen, Billy Bragg, Tracy Chapman, Jackson Browne, Bruce Cockburn, Holly Near, Ani DiFranco, and Steve Earle.

Crosby, Stills, Nash, and Young, collectively and individually, became voices to raise consciousness and promote awareness about political issues and social causes. Bob Dylan was at the center of the folk protest song in 1963–64, when the Hollies had begun recording tuneful and innocuous cover songs. There was Joan Baez. There was the essential Phil Ochs sounding the note of protest. Pete Seeger, with his guitar and banjo, spoke for the common man and woman. He maintained concern with civil rights, ecological stewardship, working men and women, and he extended the work of his friend and fellow musician Woody Guthrie. Barry McGuire sang P.F. Sloan's song "The Eve of Destruction." The Byrds recorded Dylan's "Mr. Tambourine Man," with harmonies and Roger McGuinn's electrified 12-string guitar. "Eight Miles High," with their stirring vocals, was a hit in 1966. There was war in Vietnam. The Great Society had not brought great equality.

---

7. *Speaking Out*

In *Chronicles* (*Volume One*) Bob Dylan writes that whatever the counterculture was he'd "seen enough of it." He was tired of hearing his lyrics misinterpreted, wrenched into attempted meanings, or turned "into polemics."[4] Besides, what about the tunes, the melodies, the folk music song structures and atmospheres, the musical innovation that makes a song a song? Yes, most people are not musicians, as Dylan recognizes. But timbre and tonality, the vocal attack and rhythm, the simple twist of fate expressed on a guitar are inextricable from any of the lyrics. Like Graham Nash, who addresses in his memoir the art of "seeing," Dylan points out that creativity has to do with experience, imagination, and observation of life. The artist needs alone time, apart from the rush and haste. Why else would Neil Young live on an isolated ranch? Dylan lived at Woodstock for a time, seeking that space, and was eventually unable to find privacy there. He missed the Woodstock Festival ("just wasn't there") and Altamont ("missed that one too").[5] Yet, Dylan was (and is) himself an iconic figure of the counterculture of the sixties. When he writes that his family was his "light" that could be David Crosby talking too, expressing his gratitude in songs on *Sky Trails*. Both Dylan and Crosby, in their own ways, had to find renewal. Back in 1987, both Dylan and Crosby had admitted, they felt a bit off track.

In 1987, David Crosby was released from prison. However, he had to deal with the diagnosis of type 2 diabetes. He became more conscious of nutrition and diet. In 1987, Crosby, Stills, Nash and Young resumed contact to work on the album which would become *American Dream*. Neil Young was central to the project. While they were crafting that recording in California, Bob Dylan was on tour with Tom Petty and the Heartbreakers. One of the organizers of that tour was Elliot Roberts, who had been manager for Crosby, Stills and Nash. He set up a series of concerts that joined Bob Dylan with the Grateful Dead. This came at a time when, as Dylan tells it in *Chronicles*, he was feeling out of sorts, a "troubadour, a folk-rock relic" moving through "the bottomless pit of cultural oblivion."[6] He was not connecting emotionally, spiritually, with his own songs. The Grateful Dead wanted him to play songs of his that they liked, some of which he could barely remember. How could he find the heart to sing truly and with grace?[7] He writes about wandering into a place to hear a jazz band and how the singer's performance reminded him of how to find his

---

power.[8] Crosby, Stills, and Nash were regaining that inner strength with Neil Young. The Greenpeace concert in Santa Barbara was in 1987 and Neil Young joined them for that. When they followed *American Dream* with a tour the next year, David Crosby, amid his struggles, had to rest a bit during some concerts, but he was making a recognizable contribution. Watching such a concert one might wonder: where did he go? The others sang solos, giving Crosby a chance to rest. On the rock songs, Stills and Young were trading guitar leads like two ego-driven fiends.

"Talk about déjà vu," Nash writes in his memoirs about returning to Woodstock. The flashback to Woodstock in 1989 will inevitably generate reflections. Nash suggests that Woodstock was "the end of something and the beginning of something else."[9] So, yes, it was a pivotal point. Yet, he does not indicate what that something else might be. Did Woodstock serve as a marker of the culmination of an era? What might it have begun among those who listened to the music? What changed afterward? There was some recognition that the youth movement had gathered into a force. Meanwhile, as Nash points out, this also meant that corporations identified a large new wave of customers. Like others, Nash seems to have regarded Woodstock 1989 as a bit odd. How could anyone recapture an event that had been so associated with the spirit of the times in 1969? Nash called it an echo. (An echo is an interesting auditory metaphor to describe music and memory, a moment that reverberates again in the present.) Fewer people attended the 1989 show: about 30,000. Of course, that is a substantial amount of people. They were greeted by rain. Some sunlight broke through before Crosby, Stills and Nash were to perform their set.[10] An era of rock music had brought more attention to the sound of outdoor concerts. Crosby, Stills, and Nash could hear themselves across the monitors and the audience could hear them clearly across the P.A. system.

While there had been advances in technology, there had also been developments in commercialism. Writing with David Crosby in *Since Then*, Carl Gottlieb noted the "obvious commercialism" of the 1994 attempt at a 25th anniversary Woodstock concert.[11] Crosby called the 1994 show "as strange a gig as any we've ever done."[12] Nash sharply criticized the 1994 event as "completely overrun by corporate interests."[13] Of course, he is entirely right on this count and not alone in that view. How could any concert promoter be so crass as to require people to leave their water behind on a scorching hot August day and then sell bottled water for $12? This pathetic attempt to increase revenues at the expense of humanity reflects callousness, selfishness, and the mercenary indecency that Crosby, Stills and Nash themselves argue against in their work. One might pay for access to entertainment, for items at a concession stand, or a meal. But a couple of liquid ounces of basic necessity ought not to cost $12. It was "an utter rip-off," says Nash. More than this, it was immoral.

Moral engagement intersects with folk or folk/rock music, which expresses itself as a voice of the people. Songs stand-in for the ideals of every day working people and their sense of right and wrong. In 1969, this ethos linked with a quest for community, a search for naturalness, and a dream of freedom. Joni Mitchell's thoughts were imaginatively linked to Woodstock although she was not there. She remained in a Manhattan hotel room, for a taping of the *Dick Cavettt Show*. Her song "Woodstock" was arranged by Stephen Stills into the rock song we continue to hear today. It is shot through with vocal harmonies, given force, and creased along the top by Neil Young's ragged guitar line. The song became a clarion call to freedom and dignity, the celebration of the dream that resided in the great gathering. The child of God who walked along a road was each member of a generation and those not yet born: the human community reaching toward an ideal. This was not retreat into a prelapsarian dream but hope of forward progress, a cosmic view penned in a Manhattan hotel room that now became an anthem to the human spirit.

That was the core of the folk music tradition: that concern for the people. And it took on new colors and sounds with folk/rock, with the electrified chords of Dylan and the Byrds and Buffalo Springfield. Many other musicians would follow with commitment, facing the challenges of modern society and individuals in need with song, spoken words, and benefit performances.

Stand and Be Counted, the book and documentary, is a gathering of interviews with musicians who have turned their attention at one time or another to peace activism, social justice concerns, or environmental issues. They play across a variety of musical styles, but all have been moved by a sense of purpose to use their platform in popular music for worthwhile causes. The folk music tradition of Pete Seeger, Woody Guthrie, Josh

---

White and others lies behind this. An orientation toward "the people" and an artistic sensibility make a contribution also. The sixties protest voices of Joan Baez, Bob Dylan, Peter, Paul, and Mary, and Phil Ochs are wrapped up in this principled support of people in need. For someone like Pete Seeger this amounted to an embrace of all, a celebration of voices and ethnicities and ecological sensitivity that could be seen at his annual Clearwater Festival along the Hudson.[14] Folk music also connected with the civil rights movement and song became inspiration, from gospel in churches to affirmations like "We Shall Overcome." In someone like Harry Belafonte, calypso intersected with civil rights commitment. Crosby has recognized what he has called "a chain of influence" from Thoreau to Gandhi to Martin Luther King. Clearly, there is also a chain of influence from one generation of musicians to the next, as *Stand and Be Counted* effectively shows.

Déjà Vu emerged amid changes. They had moved from Los Angeles. Crosby went to a country house in Novato and he found freedom in sailing on *The Mayan*. Young moved in to his ranch. Nash found his place in a Victorian 1890s house in San Francisco near Buena Vista Park West. San Francisco was a haven for the counterculture. Haight-Ashbury hippies kicked back with a joint held between the fingers on damp windswept days. Nash could walk past building where music "poured out" over "hippies, head shops, record stores, fortune tellers."[15] There was a new vibe here. There was a musical community, including the Grateful Dead and Jefferson Airplane. There was Wally Heider's studio where the sounds of CSN&Y were recorded. Crosby, Stills, Nash and Young traveled to Chicago for their first public concert in August. Then they boarded a plane that took them to the East Coast. From Teterboro, a small airport off Route 46 near Hackensack, New Jersey, they took two helicopters up to the tribal gathering at Woodstock.

Not long after, back in California, a chance accident brought tragedy, sorrow, and cosmic absurdity. The loss of Christine Hinton punctured David Crosby's spirit. Yet, somehow, he sang, and music and the support of friends sustained him as the drugs anesthetized him. Stephen Stills had broken up with Judy Collins. Young apparently had a tense relationship at home, according to Nash's account in his memoir. He addresses the tensions between them as they continued to make the record.

Nash tells us that he was looking for a song that could kick-start the album. "Suite: Judy Blue Eyes" by Stephen Stills was a remarkable four-part song that had provided a powerful introduction to their first recording. Nash turned to Stills again, seeking something bright, forceful, or striking. Stills delivered.[16] "Carry On" bursts out on the record with vibrant energy and remains one of the group's most memorable tunes.

In October 1969, Nash accompanied Crosby to New York and to London and then back to San Francisco. The trip was intended to distract, to change scenery, to shift gears: anything that might serve to heal a broken spirit. Then they returned to the recording project. Toward the end of the year, Nash recalls, Joni Mitchell's song "Big Yellow Taxi" was probably written. With its twist of satire, it was one of the first of popular environmental songs. In her song, Mitchell wrote wittily that even the trees had become museum pieces. While America was paving paradise for more malls and parking lots, what Mitchell and Nash had once was soon gone. The branch gone, the songbirds had somewhere new to fly to. Relationships change. Chords move and the melody shifts. A records spins and the song is done.

On January 1, 1970, President Richard Nixon signed the National Environmental Policy Act. While Crosby, Stills, Nash and Young apparently detested the political Nixon and the war in Vietnam, the dark side of Nixon was mixed with intelligence, a knowledge of foreign affairs, and some sense of public service and his historical role alongside political calculation. He would violate the public trust with Watergate, but also contribute to the public good by initiating or signing legislative reforms and with his post-presidential writings. When Nixon signed the National Environmental Policy Act and followed it up with the formation of the Environmental Protection Agency at least some of paradise was spared from parking lots.

Nixon represented the authorities, the intransigence of institutions and bureaucracy, the so-called "silent majority," and the persistence of a painful war that went on interminably. There was tax reform for lower middle-income families, an increase in Social Security payments, aid for education, and the development of the Occupational Safety and Health Act (OSHA). Nixon supported the right of Native Americans to self-determination. Yet, Nixon was a complex man. On the one hand, he was square, manipulative, suspicious, musical at his piano at home, a family-oriented man committed to his wife and two daughters. On the other hand, he could be a pragmatic political operative and he hated the media digging out dirt, revealing classified information he believed should stay hidden, and casting aspersions on him. There was Earth Day, the EPA, the Clean Water Act: genuine achievements to preserve the environment for future generations. Yet, there were the horrors too: Nixon was coming with tin soldiers to Ohio, declared Neil Young's song "Ohio." With that image of Tricky Dick came repression. Nixon had nothing directly to do with a mayor's call to the Ohio governor to send the National Guard to Kent State. He had nothing to do with their use of live ammunition and firing into a crowd of protestors and innocent bystanders. Yet, it occurred on his watch. He had initiated the incursion of the American military forces into Cambodia. It appeared to many people that he was escalating the war. That was never the plan. The goal was to ferret out the North Vietnamese forces that had taken positions near the border. It was a contained and limited military operation. However, news of the military move appeared on page one of the *New York Times* and spread across the country. It was like a crack of thunder, a flash of lightning. College campuses across America lit up in protest.

It was in March of 1970 that the military in Cambodia launched a coup, denying Prince Sihanack his throne. This caused the Vietcong to respond and the Khmer Rouge to march on Phenom Penh. To a U.S. administration with a policy of containment this was a recipe for disaster. Communism must be contained, or the nations of Asia would fall like dominoes, one after the other. The pressures of the war had tormented Lyndon Johnson and now with Nixon in his second year in office they played upon him too. The flag-draped caskets still came home.

"Find the Cost of Freedom," Crosby, Stills, Nash and Young sang. Why this pitiful loss of life? They sang as voices linked with the peace movement opposing the war. An appalling event was about to transpire in northeast Ohio. It would reflect the fear and the violence in Asia. To contain the resistance assembled forces would march up a hill and use deadly force.

In Washington, D.C., back behind that fence that surrounds the grounds of the White House, Nixon was surely in conversation with Henry Kissinger. They had no foresight of the future collapse of Cambodia, no crystal ball in which to see the genocide that would follow. They responded to the Cambodian problem with a strategy: one that worked for a time and secured the border through 1970 and 1971. It was intended to be limited in scope. The counterculture roared that Nixon was escalating the war like Johnson had done. This was unacceptable. It was outrageous. In the first days of May demonstrations vented sound and fury. In Ohio, in the town near Kent State University, windows were broken. The ROTC building on campus was set ablaze by firebombs. The mayor appealed to the governor, who called out the National Guard.

It was Nixon's Gethsemane, writes biographer John Farrell.[17] One evening at the Lincoln Memorial, the president met with a few protestors who had gathered to rest and reconnoiter before the march they had planned for the next day. He attempted a dialogue with them, recalling his own youth to sound a note of sympathy. Nixon did not like the protest movement, or the press accounts. However, he was not without concern for humanity. He was, of course, no angel. Enmeshed in politics, bedeviled by worldly cynicism, how could he draw upon his mother's values or his family's Quakerism? The world of realpolitik demanded strength. Beyond the president's gloomy meditations, dedicated young men and women, some of whom believed in the cause and some who wavered, went to risk their lives in an increasingly unpopular war. Amid the domestic unrest and vehement protest, "tin soldiers" came to Kent State to quell the rebellion. They came not merely with tear gas and a human wall of strength but with live ammunition and jittery, fearful hands. Shouts and stones were answered with bullets. Lives were shattered. Four died, one was paralyzed for life, and others were seriously injured. Two of the people who died were simply walking by to go to another day of classes. Could not those on opposing sides see the humanity in each other's faces? As David Crosby has recently sung, fear is indeed the antithesis of peace.

It seems that the moral core of Crosby, Stills, and Nash matured across the years. Flattered by acclaim, suffused with pleasure, they were, like all of us, flawed creatures: free and far-seeing, but at times blinded and bound with their Promethean energy to the rock that was the rock music business. The business is like a Beethoven symphony: one with outrageous dynamics, bipolar swings of riding high and falling low back into the hotel room. Pride or overconfidence may blind one toward weaknesses.

Drugs lift but over time may diminish faculties. The road is long with many a winding turn. Brothers need to lift each other up. Brothers get on each other's nerves. And so, Crosby, Stills, and Nash are endowed with moral imagination. But they are only human, curmudgeonly independent souls, each with a gift, open to life, but struggling heroically with divorce and medical issues, art and character. The tasks assigned to them are great. The recognition by an audience, a business that seeks profits, and a world that needs their message pushes them outward. The devotion to their craft is wrapped up in their songwriting. Family and friends, or new loves and inspirations, move them along this path tonight. They've known the external journey up the mountain of success and they've been through the valleys. As a group they have had to try to achieve coherence. As individuals they may seek the grace and gratitude that comes in wholeness. Men with scope are anchored to meaningful attachments. They are open to the flow of music and life that moves through them. That is the compass that David Crosby wrote and sang of: that grounding in what matters most. It is the gratitude and self-realization of finding oneself at last that we hear Graham Nash sing of in his second song on *This Path Tonight*. It is a homecoming of the heart. And from this comes the authentic music.

Even with the money that has flowed through Crosby, Stills, Nash and Young concerts and recordings, the social commitment to something bigger than themselves has persisted. Crosby, Stills, Nash and Young have always been attuned to the humane gesture of utilizing popular music to support benefits for meaningful causes. As both Nash and Crosby have written in their memoirs: if it involves children, the future of our world, and a real need, they will be there. They will sing to raise money for a clear purpose. They will be selective and will never sing merely for the administrative costs of a non-profit organization. But if it is evident that there is genuine access to providing support for children's education, for the preservation and renewal of the environment, or for the cause of peace and justice, they will make a contribution. This is true of Stills and Young also. Young has been deeply committed to the Bridge School project and Stills has sung for them. Young is regularly involved with Farm Aid. He has demonstrated that he will not hesitate to sound a clarion call against war for profit, or for opposition to ecological disruption in the name of profit.

---

7. *Speaking Out*

When Graham Nash, in *Wild Tales*, segues from his critical brief about the Woodstock memorial concert in August 1989 to thoughts on benefit concerts and a visit to the Berlin Wall in November 1989, this is not only a matter of chronology holding a narrative together. Nash is also connecting the dots thematically. To sing at the United Nations General Assembly and with a crowd chipping away at the Berlin Wall stands in marked contrast to greed. It is also a movement from the grounds of upstate New York out to a wider world of change and transformation.

In 1989, changes were afoot in Eastern Europe. The Soviet Union was disintegrating, transforming with perestroika and glasnost to meet the modern age. An older world order that brought us the Cold War was shifting. The *New York Times* Russia correspondent Hedrick Smith wrote that the year 1989 was "of enduring significance" for Eastern Europe and that those nations "in what seemed like barely an instant ... threw off Soviet rule."[18] The process had begun with the social and economic transformation initiated by Mikhail Gorbachev in 1985. Even so, there were longstanding systemic issues that Gorbachev and the Soviet Union needed to confront.

Crosby, Stills, and Nash did not only witness the changes from afar. As the events in East Germany gained momentum, at the suggestion of Stephen Stills, they bought plane tickets and sought to see things firsthand. On the heels of their U.N. General Assembly performance for the "Children of the Americas" benefit, they headed for Germany without their entourage. On November 22, 1989, wearing jackets to buffer themselves against the cool wind, they stood with thousands of people outside the Brandenburg Gate. There was no P.A. system. There were no roadies or crew. Just three men and an audience tuned in to radios to hear "Chippin' Away," a song by Tom Fedora, that was sung by them. Crosby took a piece of the wall as a souvenir. The world had changed. Crosby, Stills and Nash were there, participating in the end of an era. A fundamental need for economic and political adjustment had generated widening momentum. The determination of people from Poland's Solidarity movement to East Germany and to the Baltics had spread the communication of ideas of freedom and democracy. As Nash recalled the transformation in his memoir he wrote: "No walls can stop ideas for very long."[19]

Situations may become humanized when people communicate. Nash italicizes the word in his memoir.[20] Music is communication, of course.

Dialogue is communication. Reconciliation and change may come through communication. Of course, this may be difficult. The communication has to be real. The walls between people are an interpersonal reality. If I built a wall, writes the poet Robert Frost, I'd ask to know what I was keeping out or keeping in. The Berlin Wall was built to keep in, not only to keep out. It was a repressive barrier of control. The walled city has otherwise, since ancient times, been conceived of as a means of protection.

Woodstock was an open field. However, that very openness may have been a security issue at Altamont. Walls and bleachers would not necessarily have contributed stability to a hastily organized festival, however. Crosby, Stills and Nash were not at the center of the disruption. They prepared a four-song set. In the first months of 1970, Crosby, Stills, Nash and Young were already a loose connection, drifting their separate ways. In May, Neil Young was with David Crosby when they heard the news of the shootings at Kent State and were presented with that dreadful photograph of a girl screaming over the fallen body of a slain student. Neil Young went out and wrote "Ohio," that memorable classic of outrage and protest that was quickly recorded and forever associated with Crosby, Stills, Nash and Young's spirit of protest.

All is not protest, however. Much of their concern is directed into an embrace. During the 1990s, Crosby, Stills and Nash were involved with numerous benefits. Neil Young was in and out of some of those occasions with them. Nash lists benefits for homeless people, victims of earthquake, drug education, Greenpeace, Farm Aid, the Bridge School, UNICEF, and the California Environmental Initiative.[21] There have been recognitions and awards: Nash's being recognized with order of the British Empire; Stills being honored by institutions of higher education like the University of Florida. There have been interviews, appearances of popular late-night national television shows, and awards. However many awards, appreciations, or recognitions one receives, the work goes on. Crosby, Stills, Nash, and Young continue to perform individually. Neil Young eats music for breakfast and grandpa rocks in Crosby, young in spirit, and surrounded by family and talented younger musicians. Nash is ever at his artwork. Stills keeps playing a mean guitar, gathering up past and notes of nostalgia with Judy Collins on tour.

Graham Nash has been accomplishing a great deal of retrospective work during the past decade or so. The double CD set of 2018 follows *This Path Tonight*, his autobiography *Wild Tales*, and CSN archival projects, begun in 2003 with Joel Bernstein. Songwriting with Shane Fontayne has brought a variety of new material with which Nash continues to touch and spark awareness and feeling in listeners. Of course, that begins with the courage to create, the desire, even the necessity, in an artist like Nash to listen to life and "see" the world. We need to listen and to see, he says in his writings and interviews: to train our eyes and ears to awaken to the wonder around us. An artist is engaged in observation, in ways of seeing, and then translating experience, releasing feeling like butterflies from a net. It is to grasp life's wonder imaginatively. "Learning to see that way has been a lifelong education," writes Nash.[22]

Songs arise from experience, from imagination, from emotion. They sometimes come in unexplainable ways. A song may begin with a phrase, a cool riff, a rhythm, playing around with a melody, or just making sounds. Yet, often enough songs are drawn from life, from love, from wonder. Stills writes from life and his musicianship and workmanship place his imprint upon whatever he composes. Crosby's "Guinevere" recalls his early love Christine Hinton. Recent songs have Jan, his wife, in them, Nash's "Cathedral" emerged from experience. His father is referred to in "Military Madness." And as a bird is born to fly, so Neil Young, the musician, makes music.

Sometimes Young's music is simple, and it is words and emotional fury that carries a listener along. We keep rocking in the free world. In 2006, the Freedom of Speech tour of CSN&Y was essentially launched by Neil Young's vigorous response to war in Iraq with his music for "Living with War." Young's songs were directed against the military-industrial complex, military solutions to conflict, and war for profit. He pushed toward an outcry of "Let's Impeach the President." (However, it is really difficult for most listeners of a liberal persuasion to understand why anyone would impeach George W. Bush if that would result in Dick Cheney in the Oval Office.) Charges were directed against companies they viewed as profiteers: Halliburton and Boeing among them. As Crosby, Stills and Nash embraced these positions there was some disagreement among some of their audience (about 10 percent, Nash estimates).[23] Of course, if you're going to a Crosby, Stills, Nash and Young concert, what do you expect?

In 2006, Crosby, Stills, Nash and Young circled Neil Young's newer songs with poignant, familiar songs that carried a message, like "Long Time Gone," "For What It's Worth," and "Teach Your Children." Crosby wrote that there is, for CSN&Y, an "obvious continuity from before and into the future." That continuity included their progressive political commitment.[24]

In 1994 Crosby faced hepatitis C and significant liver problems that required a liver transplant. The Northridge earthquake of January 17, 1994, shook the house where he and his wife Jan, lived. They were conscious of the damage a natural disaster like that could wreak upon their neighbors. Crosby, Stills and Nash recorded *After the Storm*. The 25th anniversary of Woodstock came that August. On September 24, Jan and David Crosby learned that that Jan was pregnant; they were going to have a child. Django was born in May of 1995. Meanwhile, he met his son James Raymond. That was also a discovery of a fine musician, one attracted to jazz like David Crosby and that able to sing that middle harmony part also. CPR, the band with James Raymond and guitarist Jeff Pevar, opened up a new world of collaboration for David Crosby. He played new songs with them and their drummer Steve Di Stanislao and bassist Andrew "Drew" Ford.

There is a clear line across folk music into folk/rock music of the song of conscience. Crosby, Stills, Nash and Young have never forgotten that. They maintain a commitment today to making music work on behalf of people through benefit concerts. They also stay current with the political news and can be heard expressing their opinions in interviews. In "Ohio," CSN&Y decried the drumbeat of pain, the march of unformed tin men and Nixon coming. In concert one night they applauded the resignation of the beleaguered president. However, in Graham Nash's view, there is a perceptible contrast between the paranoid, crafty politician Richard Nixon and today's Tweeter of 1600 Pennsylvania Avenue. Nash contrasts Nixon with Trump, saying: "At least Nixon had a brain. As divisive as he was, at least Nixon had a heart." Nixon started the EPA, he observes. Trump would strip it away.[25]

In 2000, David Crosby and David Bender published an important book and documentary, *Stand Up and Be Counted*. The authors considered the commitment to activism and engagement with social and political concerns by a wide range of music performers. They considered the work of these musicians on behalf of benefit causes, their involvement in civil rights and the anti-war movement, and in more recent concerns. In an interview with Ken Paulsen of the First Amendment Center on "Speaking Freely," available on YouTube, you can see them and hear them cogently discussing their project. They mention the work and commitment of Pete Seeger, Peter Yarrow, Harry Belafonte, and Joan Baez, among others. Crosby refers to Graham Nash's courage to speak out for justice, including in his song "Chicago." Bender tells the story of his connection with the Robert Kennedy campaign when he was only twelve years old and how much Crosby's song "Long Time Gone" meant to him. Crosby recalls wondering as a child at the song "Strange Fruit," sung by Josh White, and the racism and murderous hostility toward blacks that it conveyed. When asked if the sixties generation has retained the spirit of their time and their ideals, Crosby recognized that "it is hard to generalize." However, he affirms that peoples' lives were touched by this spirit. So, the answer he gives is "largely yes."[26]

In 2006, while performing with Neil Young, Stephen Stills, and David Crosby on their Freedom Tour, Graham Nash unequivocally stated their dislike of the Bush Administration. Neil Young's "Living with War" was performed on this tour. Nash added a new twist to his song "Military Madness." Crosby sang "What Are Their Names." When asked if a music performer ought to be politically informed and to voice an opinion, Nash responded that he believes that it is the responsibility of songwriters "to write about what happens to them as human beings." He added that this includes expressing their "disappointment" about how things in the country are going.[27]

In 2012, Crosby, Stills and Nash sang "Almost Gone (The Ballad of Bradley Manning)." The song begins with Nash's vocal emphasizing the working man, blowing the whistle, doing his duty. We later hear Crosby calling for human treatment. Stills' guitar leaps, drives, and burns throughout the song.

In 1970, Graham Nash recognized the need to pull his hit song "Teach Your Children" from radio rotation to make room for the message of "Ohio." Nash's high-ideals and concerns today come with an opposition to the administration of the Trump presidency. What has been occurring, Nash has said, could "undermine" the efforts of the past thirty years. It is so outrageous, he told one interviewer, that if a writer had submitted a proposal for a Hollywood screenplay a few years ago, before this, he or she would be laughed out of the studio or business office. Even so, Nash concludes, people must stay "positive and alive."[28]

In recent years, some concerns have been voiced about whether democracy has been sold out to pragmatism and economic ends dictated by persons in power. Critical voices ask: Is America losing its center, the moral soul of America? Crosby, Stills, Nash, and Young are engaged in this discourse. David Crosby asserted in an interview with Sean Kaye that intelligent discourse in the public forum is "a lost art." He told Kaye that he speaks out because "that's who I am." Nash told him, "Every song needs a reason to exist." In that interview, Crosby groused that American's votes do not matter. "This is not a democracy," Crosby said of America. Rather, he said, it is "a politics of fear."[29]

The era of Donald Trump gets under the skin of individuals like Graham Nash and David Crosby. They have been clear about their support for the progressive politics of Bernie Sanders and Elizabeth Warren and their disdain for Trump. The slogan "Make America Great Again" assumes that there is a better "then" that we can go back to. The unsettling changes of postmodernity and globalization, economic changes from industrialism to the information age, and the diminishment or loss of old securities prompt anxiety, the desire for change, and the quest for a mythical time. There is what J.D. Vance has called a "hillbilly elegy" sounding from the South and the Appalachians up through the Rust Belt states of Ohio and Michigan. People are struggling to make ends meet. From the evangelical right there is a call for the anchor of traditional values and faith. From the left come concerns about veracity and falsity, Watergate-like obstruction, callous disregard of ecological balance, racial insensitivity, insulting chauvinism toward women, or crushing blows to human rights and civil liberties. The slogan "America first" ensures dedicated patriotism and holds the hope that auto workers, coal miners, and Walmart shoppers will not be stranded and hopeless. To others it sounds like jingoism and authoritarianism. For them, to turn away refugees at the border and separate children from their parents is inhumane and un–American. It is to selectively quote a passage from St. Paul while placing of the letter of the law before the spirit of the law. Football players are prohibited from exercising their

First Amendment rights of protest against the injustice of racial profiling. There is a lockstep left-right march off the edge of a cliff.

This clash between progressives and traditionalists was spelled out in 1991 by James Davison Hunter, a University of Virginia professor, who coined the phrase the "culture wars." That phrase was repeated by Pat Buchanan the following year. These were the culture wars to define America and we continue to experience the movement of the pendulum. Hunter undertook a sociological analysis of public discourse. He argued that this is not only a conservative-liberal dichotomy. However, a spirit of individualism, "rationalism and subjectivism" and one of "traditionalists" is in collision. There is a quest that is moved by a concern with sources of moral authority.[30] There is a struggle over the meaning of America.

Recognizing the polarized camps in our political discourse, David Crosby has written songs like "Capitol," in which he says that, despite the vote, the will of the people is ignored. Hunter observed the conflict of perspectives at work in the attempt at definition of America. Another observer, Alan Wolfe, in *One Nation After All* (1998) claimed that the argument across America was about values and personal freedoms and most Americans were not taking sides.[31] Twenty years later, the lines of opposition are drawn. Hunter's awareness of the culture wars came in the 1980s. He argued that realignment creates conflict about our "core institutions." Even moderates are divided by different political leanings. Americans are aware of limitations to the recognition of their voices in a democracy like those David Crosby points to. Crosby observes that elites promote their own self-interest and many politicians who are in the pocket of corporate interests are ineffectual as representatives of the people.

Crosby is outspoken about American politics at his concerts, voicing his dislikes and his "low opinion of politicians." He uses his Twitter account actively to voice his opinions. In an interview with *Variety*, he called Donald Trump "a horror show" and "a badly behaved child." He recognized that people wanted a change but added that "they tossed the wrong grenade." Crosby praised the students at Marjory Stoneman High School in Florida who have spoken out about gun issues. For Crosby, one bad apple in the Big Apple or in the White House doesn't spoil the whole bunch. Crosby has called Trump "the orange disaster" and says that "the daily barrage of outrage is exhausting."[32]

In *The Nation*, Eric Alterman interviewed Graham Nash when *Wild Tales* went into paperback. They began, of course, with politics. Nash said that the goal of any song is "to move hearts and minds."[33] He asks the interviewer if a song like "Ohio" can be called politics, or if it is about humanity. There was hope as well as concern for future generations in this conversation. Even the Koch brothers must have children and grandchildren, Nash said. So, what is greed doing to our planet? Nash then focused upon climate change in this interview. With scientific studies indicating the human role in the shifting of the earth's climate, he sees sheer self-interest in the deniers. He observed that the Rockefeller family has divested from fossil fuel and is supporting the exploration of alternative energy. It is a wise business move, as well as ecologically sound: profit can be gained from developing alternative energy sources.

In recent interviews Graham Nash often shares his political thoughts and anger at the Trump Administration. Nash has dual citizenship. He addresses personal freedom in the United States and "the right to speak our minds." He recognizes that people who run large media conglomerates do not want a lot of protest in the media. During the "Living with War" tour of 2006, Crosby, Stills, Nash and Young realized that some members of the audience would disagree with their political stance regarding the Bush administration.[34] However, they chose to speak their minds.

Graham Nash spoke about the presidential election to *Billboard* (January 22, 2016). He said that he liked what Bernie Sanders stood for. In the article he is called "one of music's most astute and outspoken chroniclers of the political scene." Of Donald Trump he said, "We're just feeding his show." Nash holds that artists must be true to their politics as well as to their art. Artists have "a responsibility to reflect the times in which we live," he said.[35] Stephen Stills added his own "Message for Trump" on November 4, 2016, and it appears on his website at www.stephenstills.com. Stills indicates that he is not overly fond of the political protest song genre but will speak out if the need arises.

A house divided against itself cannot stand, Abraham Lincoln once said. That may be true of a broken family, a pissed off and burdened band, or a divided nation. At a time when it seems to some people in America that anger has replaced values, can Crosby, Stills, Nash and Young look to a higher principle and practice enough conflict resolution to speak out together again from their substantial platform? Can they set aside their differences to again sing their truth and encourage us to believe "we can change the world"? As of this writing, it appears that each of them is quite busy with their own tours and their present musical collaborators.

David Crosby, while on tour with his group, appeared onstage at the Newport Folk Festival during Jason Isbell's set on July 30, 2018. He resumed touring with James Raymond, Jeff Pevar, Steve Di Stanislao and the others in his entourage. They took off for a show in Reykavic, Iceland, on August 23 and began a European tour with dates in Scandinavia. On July 30, Graham Nash was travelling from a show at Salford in the U.K. to his concert date in Dublin, Ireland on July 31. He headed back to the United States and picked up his tour again in Austin, Texas. After several shows in Texas, he journeyed on to Colorado to play another series of concerts. Meanwhile, Stephen Stills continued his concert tour with Judy Collins through November 2018. A remastered Buffalo Springfield compilation first appeared in May 2018 and on CD and vinyl on June 29, 2018. Those recordings recall the past. What will appear in Stephen Stills future? With his work with the Rides throughout 2017, it is likely that Stills will soon be returning to that blues-based group to work again with guitarist Kenny Wayne Shepherd, keyboard player Barry Goldberg, bass guitarist Kevin McCormick, and drummer Chris Layton. Neil Young played some summer solo concerts in 2018, beginning in St. Louis and continuing through Detroit on July 3 and two shows in Boston, July 11 and 12. He also contributed his talents again to Farm Aid in September 2018 and played some additional band concerts. Young has focused on his Neil Young Archives website where you can find his well-documented work from across the years. The site is available by subscription and Young has said that he will present his new material first on that website prior to its wider release. Crosby is booked for concerts through 2019 and Nash is also booked for shows through March 2019. With all of that activity, it appears less than likely that all four musicians will reconcile or enter a temporary truce long enough to speak their minds collectively about politics and society in 2019. Yet, who knows?

8

Crosby, Stills, Nash and Young Now

Individually, Crosby, Stills, Nash and Young continue to create. Their recent efforts again affirm that they are artists, songwriters, voices for today, not only a legacy or merely a trademark or a brand. Creatively, going their separate ways in recent years has been a blessing. If Crosby, Stills and Nash tried to salvage their group amid arguments between 2016 and 2018, there might be no Stills-Collins tour. *This Path Tonight* and the songs written by Graham Nash and Shane Fontayne might have taken longer to emerge. The creative burst that began with *Croz* and the recordings *Lighthouse* or *Sky Trails* by David Crosby might not have been quite so extraordinary. These are artists who need breathing room.

Neil Young continues to be on the cutting edge of popular music. His creativity has been expressed in his work with Promise of the Real and in his film *Paradox*, directed by Daryl Hannah. In spring 2018 he reunited with Crazy Horse for a few shows for the first time since 2014. He played a series of solo shows beginning in St. Louis on June 28, continuing in Chicago, and then extending to other cities. He headlined at Farm Aid with Dave Matthews in September 2018. He continues to be an exceptional songwriter. In an interview several years ago with Paul Zollo on songwriting, Neil Young observed that he has written several songs in minor keys (E minor, A minor) and "D with no thirds." Zollo recognizes the "striking imagery" of some of Neil Young's songs. There is a suggestion that, along with creating images, Neil Young likes to leave space in his songs.[1] He also leaves a little space between his tours but continues to be an active songwriter, filmmaker, and performer.

Miles away Stephen Stills is on tour with the angel voiced Judy Collins.

8. *Crosby, Stills, Nash and Young Now*

Stills released a box set, *Carry On*, in February 2013 and began to think about writing his autobiography. In 2018 he completed his recording with Judy Collins, *Everybody Knows*. Leonard Cohen had his unique way with that song of his. His low, conversational delivery told us something about what was happening. Stills and Collins grace it with a new treatment. Their album brings new life to some older songs. They cover Bob Dylan's "Girl from the North Country," with Stills' vocal leading the way, as if in a recollection of their folk roots. They also cover "Handle with Care," which was originally recorded by the Traveling Wilburys (Bob Dylan, George Harrison, Jeff Lynne, Roy Orbison, and Tom Petty). Judy Collins's voice remains as clear as crystal. Stills' vocals are less compelling but they have an edge that works in a complementary way with Collins' vocals. Stills, who is a fine (perhaps underrated) guitarist, contributes his solid instrumental support. One might wish for fresh, new material from Stills. However, one may also be grateful for this reunion and the dusting off of lesser known gems from the past.

David Crosby has often said in recent years that he is happy now with family and music. His productivity seems to bear that out. He told *The Hollywood Reporter* that he wants to make the best music he can in the time he is given in life.[2] There is a rare gift in this man. He is an intuitive stream of consciousness writer and musician. When Crosby speaks one hears intelligence. He speaks his mind—maybe too much, when a blurt or rash comment seems to hit emotional buttons. The down-going to hell and back, like Dante through the Inferno, has brought a deepening to his music.[3]

When Crosby appears the house breaks into applause. *Sky Trails* has already told us that the music will be charming, arresting, and by turns vigorous or introspective. There are smooth bass lines from Mai Agan and clever musical blessings from the guitar of Jeff Pevar and voice of Michelle Willis. There is the pulse of Steve Di Stanislao's drums. And what can you say about James Raymond, who writes wonderful songs? He is that surprise who returned into David Crosby's life and became a musical gift to ours. Is there something genetic that led him to jazz and melody? There's Crosby, that golden voice again, the songwriter who has come back to life. Graham Nash has said he might consider performing with Crosby again if Crosby would write some songs that would knock him on his ass. Yet, some of these songs are like beautiful flowers you might buy on a spring day and put in a vase. The gray hair flies. The notes stream out. Will the weight of the words match the heft of the waist? The politics may rankle some, declaimed as they are as if from a Ciceronian soapbox. One might imagine Crosby as some monumental bronze figure exposed in rays of light. Call him the enduring man, radiant with beams of melody.

Surely there is someone in the audience thinking: Can they reconcile? Should they? What was it that Bernie Taupin wrote with Elton John about the word sorry? Jangled nerves. Crosby still gnashing. Nash still cross. But there is a higher purpose, a greater cause ... if they can just sing together without choking each other. An outsider cannot possibly know the sensitivities, tensions, and hurt that may arise within a family or fracture the alliances of friends. Conflict and pain is part of the human condition. Yet, Crosby, Stills, Nash and Young fans hold out hope as *Rolling Stone*, *Billboard*, and other periodicals publish news of the latest strains in the ongoing soap opera. They know that when these voices come together and the Stills and Young guitars go to work there is magic.

Crosby told Bill Robinson that he likes playing with a band and being able to stretch out and "head toward Steely Dan" (Huffington Post, October 26, 2015). For example, listen to "She's Got to Be Somewhere" on *Sky Trails* and you'll hear musicianship and production that sounds a bit like Steely Dan. Crosby is about exploration—like a sci-fi imagination. He's read Heinlein, Clarke, Bradbury, von Vogt, Asimov and others. He likes reading stories by Iain M. Banks. He has watched *Star Trek* with his son. He enjoyed a conversation with Neil de Grasse Tyson on the cosmos.

In an interview with David Crosby *American Songwriter Magazine* editor Paul Zollo immediately points out Crosby's talent with words and music. Crosby tells Zollo that he has always preferred collaboration. Musically, he and Nash have sometimes entered what he calls "a telepathic exchange." Zollo observes that their vocal parts intertwine so much that when they sing alone a listener hears the melody line a little differently. The interview gravitates toward Crosby criticism of George W. Bush in an exaggerated Texan accent.

The "Lyrically Speaking" interview is entertaining and informative. One can appreciate the ease with which Zollo proceeds to encourage an investigation of songwriting. Crosby explores the spontaneity of his song

"Shadow Captain." He reflects on the hypnogogic state, in which one drifts before sleep. A songwriting goal, Crosby says, is to help the audience to "feel something." He sings a cappella and encourages the audience to sing with him. Then Crosby demonstrates the alternate open tuning and picking pattern for "Déjà Vu." His left hand slides in the direction of the 12th fret for the slow section of the song that includes the word "feel." (How could Crosby have ever done "Déjà Vu" with the Byrds?) Zollo comments on the raw emotion and straight out rock of "Almost Cut My Hair," which was recorded live to tape. Crosby tells Zollo and the audience that Stephen Stills built the tracks for "Long Time Gone." When Stills and Young "get it right" in their guitar exchange they are extraordinary. (Of course, the audience for CSN&Y does know that already.) Crosby is coaxed into playing a bit of "Long Time Gone." It looks like this is coming off the fifth fret down to G to F in barre chords.[4]

The melodies, colors, and moods of Crosby's recent albums display a kind of musical reawakening. Yes, Crosby has told interviewers that he is happy. Of course, his former bandmates—Nash, Young, and Stills—are not happy with him. In 2014 they were still working together, as Crosby created his first solo album in two decades.

Croz

Little did anyone know in 2014, when *Croz* appeared, that Crosby's new album would signal the beginning of an incredible burst of creativity and musical revival. Three albums emerged in quick succession between 2014 and 2017. Throughout these albums we see Crosby's inclination to engage in collaboration. This creates newfound ground and extends his art. James Raymond is central to *Croz* and to *Sky Trails* and his musicianship and aesthetic touch to these albums is everywhere present. Michael League brings a light jazz touch and reverbed chorus vocals to *Lighthouse*. Crosby sounds younger than his years on these recordings, which come to us as a late-career renaissance.

Along with David Crosby's vocals, which sound youthful and vital, the production and arrangements on *Croz* by James Raymond, Daniel Garcia, and Crosby make this album a treat. "What's Broken" immediately places the band behind Crosby's vocal. "Time I Have" starts with congas, acoustic guitar, and Crosby's vocal. To reduce cognitive dissonance appears to be a personal goal. The crowded city of concrete is a zone where fear is the opposite of peace. We are presented with images of social and racial violence, like a Native American being shot, or obstructions to life, that are contrasted with the search for inner peace. A word of forgiveness and the phrase of Jesus, "They know not what they do," echoes with the rhetorical question: does that sound familiar? Of course, it does, and the facts of urban anxiety and the experiences of cognitive dissonance must be met with positive thinking and hope. Call this a therapy song, an affirmation of hope despite the city's dissonance. We can get on in the modern world. Despite the brokenness in the world, healing and wholeness can be found in the time we have. Okay, so that's an interpretation. It may not be exactly what Crosby means but this song can encourage us to take a look inward and take a look around. While introspective, the song projects itself outward.

Crosby then brings this down with a reflective vocal accompanied by a simple guitar strum on "Holding on to Nothing." A sunny day can trick us, bringing rain, birds in the sky, sketches of pencil and traces of cloud. A muted trumpet provides a lovely solo and the vocal chorus surrounds the reference to a sunny day. "The Clearing" brings a strong picked guitar pattern with a riff above it. The drums kick in and the song opens up. Crosby's vocal enters at about 38 seconds into the song. He points to a love that is independent and free, shadows like giants looming from the trees, and a fierce storm setting in. Lay down the past, let it go, he declares. There is a 12-string guitar sound, an acoustic guitar interlude, and with drum hits the band returns and plays out.

Following a brief pause there is "Radio" and a message, a call. The music is more briskly uptempo, vital and steady. We are asked to look down and to rescue someone from the sea. For there is an S.O.S. on the air and humanity needs to reach out, to pull out the forsaken. There is a lovely drift of piano and guitar at the end of this song.

In "Slice of Time" the song title comes to us in the first words that are sung. Piano and slow, steady drums and bass lead the way. A listener might picture a voyage on *The Mayan*, or some steady vessel on the water. The word "images" is repeated, almost with an urgency as the melody climbs. The teacher or guru has advised that time itself is elastic. We move into a slow 6/8 and there are tasteful guitar touches. The singer concludes, saying he has returned from the edges of the night. And surely Crosby himself has. He has set at least some of the baggage down.

The next song encourages anyone listening to "Set That Baggage Down." It begins with those distinctive guitar chord sounds that have Crosby written all over them. Then it unfolds into a declaration, an anthem, an assertion: put your baggage aside. There is almost a Native American war-chant about it. Tambourine and bass join in and the bass answers the hollow body guitar. There is a call to rise up. A crescendo declares, "no more".

The next song, "If She Called," tells a story. An acoustic guitar on a pickup begins this sympathetic portrait of a lonely woman. It seems that she deeply feels the absence of someone who had been her lover and she is imagining their lovemaking while all alone. She feels tired and steps out into a gray day in the rain. A man is splashed when a bus goes past through a puddle and he curses aloud at the world. She laughs at the sight and then cries. At home she sits sadly on the floor with the television on and it broadcasts in a foreign language. She recalls the past of hopeful love lost in the busy city morning. There is a dreamy quality to the arpeggio guitar picking and poignant vocal.

"Dangerous Night" begins with light chords, and a pulse as Crosby sings. Amid people, oceans, weather, how to make life's pieces fit? Peace is elusive. The intention to adopt the spirit of Buddah lapses and falls into guns. What can be given to future generations if truth gets lost? To seek peace in your heart does sound right. Can a troubled soul find peace on such a dangerous night? The singer asks who has the integrity to walk with him across the fields and orchards and grain of life's journey? Is there someone who has been through it and will not give up in the times of rain? There is a beautiful chorus vocal part meeting in that frozen rain.

On "Morning Falling" from the distance come tones, then an up-tempo guitar. His vocal floats on this song in a melodic, dreamy way. Music that is bright, tending toward bossa nova, not quite Spanish flamenco, moves along rhythmically. Pull out the shakers. Crosby's voice sounds youthful. With "Find a Heart" the band turns into a jazz ensemble and the music takes on a jazz quality. This moves into a kind of group chorus scat singing as a saxophone is playing out to the song's conclusion.

Lighthouse

Lighthouse was released October 21, 2016. *Lighthouse* is clear and spare, an album that features Crosby's voice and his guitar playing. It was produced by Michael League of the large jazz fusion group Snarky Puppy. On a CD cover the lighthouse stands at the edge of the ocean with white clouds floating nearby. On the opening song , "Things We Do for Love," finely played acoustic guitar patterns are joined by Crosby's voice. The song's chorus lifts into a male group harmony, drenched in echo, that suggests things we do for love are valuable. This create a pleasant, reflective space. This is a keynote for an album in which guitar meets voice in enchanting melody. We are listening to a performance that is fashioned and textured with gentle touches in vocals and arrangement.

"The Us Below" begins a guitar pattern with Crosby's voice in a bit higher melody. The setting brings attention to the words. Chorus vocals return in a bit of echo and a guitar chord line climbs. "Drive Out to the Desert" encourages meditation, finding a quiet center, a space from which to finally see. The music may take you to this quiet place. Next, a subtle texture is created behind a rhythmic jazz guitar pattern. "Drive Out to the Desert" comments on meditative receptivity: tuning in like a radio dial. He seems able to be spontaneous that way, like a musician who listens for the muse and allows himself to go with it. Life unfolds like a jazz phrase. There might be something like a fishing line dipping into the depths and ideas emerge and maybe something happens. He surely knows how to be aware of that intuition, or suggestion of a song. From Crosby have come songs of the heart, songs of the spirit, haunting songs that sing, sail on waves, filled with feeling.

"Look in Their Eyes" brings a jazzlike melody and a chorus vocalizing on the title, blending, and moving into a counter in which some sing the title and others a line of response. These melodic phrases end in a voice in a higher bell-like tone. The vocals seem to surround and caress the melody. The chorus sings the words of the title and Crosby responds with a line each time. "Somebody Other Than You" has a lyric that is harsher and "The City" follows. The movement into these songs begins with light guitar picking on a riff, again jazzy. This is just vocal and guitar with a lightly tapped rhythm. Then a vocal hum is met with the sound of an organ and joined by a chorus singing together. There are some guitar riffs with Crosby's solo voice and we go back to the hummed vocals and organ and on into joining a vocal chorus above the strummed guitar. There is gentle snapping-like rhythm with gentle guitar tones. A slightly distorted guitar line adds an accent to this for a moment and the vocal chorus and acoustic guitar continue. One should leave a light on—like the lighthouse, perhaps—as the chorus hums. The song concludes on a clean harmonic.

"Paint You a Picture" immediately follows with a reference to winter and creates an atmosphere. This is a song that ought to be a Crosby classic: one with melodic intention and a peaceful, centering vocal. Led by a soft guitar and piano touches, this song is rich with imagery: a winter skyline dashed by drifting chimney smoke, a hawk in the gray sky. This moves in the direction of a Joni Mitchell verbal painting.

The tempo picks up on the next song, ever so gently behind the vocal. A Dobro fills in and an organ plays behind vocals that are subtle, arising in chords. The tone here is a bit darker. The recording moves on into the final song, "By the Light of Common Day." The opening melody is like a scale that rises with Crosby's vocal out front. You could pick out the notes. This melody line is later given to us in guitar chords and in chorus vocals. Crosby's voice is joined by others, male and female. There is almost a children's song quality, a clear simplicity. "Ooo" vocals are reverbed over guitar lines on lower strings and Crosby's evocative singing moves the song forward, then joined by the female voice and other vocals. The guitar patterns are nicely played. A softly echoed electric guitar chord ends this album.

Sky Trails

Sky Trails, like the other recent albums, reminds us that David Crosby is, perhaps foremost, a singer. He seems to have deepened in spirit along with this expressive voice. There is collaborative quality to *Sky Trails*. The album begins with "She's Got to Be Somewhere." A keyboard riff on electric piano sounds along with light touches of high-hat and cymbals on drums. A sustained whole note provides a rest for a moment and a drum fill follows and we are brought back to the keyboard riff-pattern. Crosby's vocal enters, referring to a fallen frozen angel. With the jazz-like phrasing of the vocal, the emergence of a Fender Rhodes electric piano sound, horns, and harmonies, we are into something that sounds a bit like Steely Dan.[5] Background vocals join on the chorus which announces the title, "She Got to Be Somewhere." We hear of clear blue skies over Santa Ana, California, and we're taking a ride in the open air with a light jazz breeze. Later a saxophone comes in and an electric guitar responds, and she is on a mission, going somewhere. Got to be.

An acoustic guitar brings us into the title song, "Sky Trails," which is like another breath of air lifting, drifting, pretty. The immediate surprise is the appearance of a female vocal. Becca Stevens joins Crosby on this song. There is a pleasant scale-like melody, like going up and down a ladder, and the music caresses the listener as the duet-ballad proceeds. The light, drifty vocals ask please, can someone tell me where I am, and seem to beckon toward the sky itself in a search of wonder.

"Sell Me a Diamond" pulses up next and the jeweler claims the jewel is conflict free. Or maybe this is Crosby in a therapeutic moment acknowledging that to be a little more conflict free would be a good thing. His vocal is clear and strong and if there was a single to emerge from this album it might be this one. A piano introduces the next song, "Before Tomorrow Falls on Love." The song has a beautiful melodic quality and Crosby delivers a gentle jazz vocal. The piano guides this tune along but the vocal rides along above it with a beautiful quality. The song is reflective of an older style, perhaps the 1940s and 1950s jazz Crosby listened to as a child. He has brought it into his heart and made personal these jazzy, evocative tones. And this song reminds us: the man can sing.

A string bass-guitar sound, as from a guitar-synthesizer, meets with drums and saxophone on the next cut, "Here It's Almost Sunset." The song has a beautiful melodic quality. The vocal asks: Why is there more brightness in the sky at sunset? Does that make sense? The song creates an atmosphere, with a good deal of instrumental space and the saxophone lines drift over the bass and strings sound toward the end.

"Capitol" is more feisty and brazen, or critical and biting. This is a song of protest at the inefficacy of the U.S. Congress. The lyric charges Congress with playing politics while the will of the people is ignored. Position, power, and money appear more valued than their responsibility to legislate.[6] The lyric presents us with images of people visiting the Capitol and National

---

8. *Crosby, Stills, Nash and Young Now*

Parks and seeing shining marble floors and guards at the door. Deals are made behind closed doors without reference to democracy or public needs.

Paste reviewer Morgan Troper indicated his disappointment with the track. He critiques "Capitol" as having a "stock jazz groove." Rather than acting like a "vital and provocative protest song" to this critic it sounds like "something you might hear over the speakers at Nordstrom."[7] Maybe the song does not have that raw, cutting edge of "Ohio." However, Troper seems to miss that there is enough in Crosby's well-sung performance to raise questions even among the shoppers in the department store, if they care to listen. Crosby's words are not platitudes. The song works in images and in the brightness of a band's mobile expression, trading musical statements from keyboard, guitar, and saxophone as bass and drums hold a steady rhythm. "Capitol" extends the comment of Crosby's "What Are Their Names," as NPR's Jim Allen noted in a review of the album.[8]

Crosby's vocal treatment of Joni Mitchell's song "Amelia," which follows, is a highlight of this recording. There is a flawless beauty to this faithful rendering, with crystal vocals and sensitive piano phrasing. This song from Joni Mitchell's album *Hejira* is melodic, painterly, and artful. Crosby's resurrection of it is a joy. The comparison of six white trails of vapor from aircraft in a blue sky to a hexagram and to the strings of a guitar is arrestingly clever and opens the inner eye to the rich palette of this song. Crosby seems to glide across the melody like Icarus on silken wings rather than waxen ones. The lyric and melody land on the repeated mention of what has happened being only a false alarm.[9]

"Somebody Home" begins slowly with guitar picking and vocal melody line, a singing that is present, almost spoken, and intimate. This seems to be a love song to Jan and the vocal tones flow like a woodwind or horn line. The voice is joined by distant keyboard-organ sounds and some piano. It is drifting and atmospheric, as if through clouds and sun, with jazz-like touches. When the next tune comes up the guitar seeks a Spanish feel, like that of a bossa-nova and is joined by some bass and percussion. "Curved Air" features guitar work well-played. The lines are moving and rise to three bluesy notes that chorus vocals join on the word "found." The music plays out breezily, in a joyful dance.

"Curved Air" and "Here It's Sunset" are called songs of "vaporous beauty" by *Rolling Stone* reviewer Richard Gehr (October 27, 2017).[10] Morgan

---

Troper in *Paste* does not much care for the Auto-Tune added to Crosby's vocal on "Home Free" and believes this causes one to not take the song seriously. I disagree. The song is a fine reflective, sentimental note of gratitude about home with which to conclude this album. Guitar and keys come up from under a tone that sets a quiet atmosphere, one of reflection and appreciation and a calming spirit. "Home Free" sets out images of rain, lighting a candle, taking a bath, lapsing into reverie, looking out the window and wondering at the big world full of people going about their business. He stirs his coffee with gratitude, like a tree finally rooted, as people travel across America. A restless life has found its grounding. There is security in home, in a simple a row of flowers, and one can see the magic of things together with a lifelong friend. This is a celebration of that love and trust, that dear companion, a sense of gratitude for togetherness and for home.

In November 2017, David Crosby spoke with Jeff Slate of the *Quartzy Newsletter*, who had met him at a Brooklyn recording studio the previous year. "Crosby has opened his creative energy in gloriously unexpected ways," Slate writes. True enough.[11] As Crosby realizes, Michael League, James Raymond, and Becca Stevens create a greater palette for him. The musicians carry forward the vision well.

David Crosby is a survivor. He is also a reader. The *Tampa Bay Times* asked David Crosby about his reading in November 2017.[12] Crosby commented on re-reading Carl Hiassen's *Skinny Dip* because he like the humor in it. He was also reding *Espedair Street* by Iain Banks, who was a science fiction and mystery writer. When asked if he had read David Yaffe's biography of Joni Mitchell he said that he had not done so yet. Crosby said that it was hard to write about Joni Mitchell.

This Path Tonight

Nash's contributions to CSN&Y were often fairly straightforward, melodic songs that were closer to folk songs than the Crosby creations like "Déjà Vu" with its changing time signatures, vocal overlays, and alternate tuning. Nash's songs are well-structured. While a song like "Marrakesh Express" is undeniably catchy and bounces along like a train ride through Morocco, a song like "Our House" is pleasant and simple. "Teach Your Children" is a meaningful folk-based song that can be played with a few chords, whereas some Stephen Stills or David Crosby compositions require dexterity and some accomplished guitar playing. Even so, Nash's songs came a long way from Hollies pop song fare. He had learned the art of the song hook. However, he sought to experiment musically, but it was clear that The Hollies simply weren't going to do any more songs like "King Midas in Reverse." Graham Nash was stretching out and had to move on. Songs like "Military Madness" and "Cathedral" were not ever going to be Hollies songs. What they lost with Nash was a great harmony singer and a true artist open to exploring creative impulses.

Nash went on to signal hope with the fierceness and determination of "Chicago" and the beauty of "Wind on the Water." There were the quickly conceived and enduring gems like the melodic "Just a Song Before I Go." Nash told interviewer Paul Zollo that he penned the lyric at an airport, after recently traveling on the Concord at twice the speed of sound.[13]

On June 16, 2018, Graham Nash talked with Brad Tolinski and a live audience at the Cutting Room on East 32nd Street in Manhattan. David Crosby was on his way from Connecticut to the Berkshires for a show at Tanglewood. The next day, he arrived in Morristown, New Jersey, for a show on June 17, Father's Day. Meanwhile, Stills pulled into Tanglewood for a show. Neil Young was in Santa Barbara with Promise of the Real for shows on June 19 and June 20. Nash prepared for a European tour, beginning in Italy on June 30. He had just released *Over the Years*, a career retrospective, on June 29.

Nash's retrospective set seems to have been issued for posterity, a recollection of history. Atlantic Records owns the early albums. Warner and Rhino own masters. However, a case could be made for private recordings that were never released. These days, Nash can tour and also enjoy New York City galleries and a new relationship. For whatever nostalgia there is in creating a new collection of his songs, Nash appears to have his eyes set on the future. On July 8, 2014, the Associated Press reported that Nash had told an interviewer that he had much optimism that young people will change America for the better. Likely, he still holds that view. Nash. Nash told an interviewer for *The Journal of Roots Music* that people need to speak out.[14]

For Graham Nash, as he has said, what could be really meaningful after London air raids, the Second World War, and facing the prospects of sudden death? With the Hollies life became quite different from the daily working class labor that a young man from his time and place in the world might have been expected. Yet, there was something to be sought, something meaningful to be found beyond the pop song and sixties pop acclaim. The masterful harmonizer was pulled away, drawn to discovery. Life was beckoning elsewhere. When it came time for Woodstock with Crosby, Nash, and Young, he already knew the experience of crowds, media attention, fan adulation, and the collective energy of audiences. The Hollies had more of that than the Byrds or the Buffalo Springfield. Nash was apparently still like an open-ended tune, one now still connected with Joni Mitchell, with Crosby and Stills and Young. There was America. There was Laurel Canyon. There was this concert they'd flown in to do and the tribe of bobbing heads and muddy feet and hearts and minds taking it all in.

Even so, now's the thing, a new phase, a new day: New York and the East Village and a slant of sun across the buildings and onto the sidewalk on the way to another gallery. Catch him in the photo frame: jeans and denim, sure stride, white hair flying back in a breeze. Girlfriend Amy Grantham is taking photos that speak of life. They practice that visual art.

This Path Tonight seeks to simplify and focus as *Songs for Beginners* did. There is more recorded material that has yet to be released. Shane Fontayne recorded some twenty songs with Graham Nash. Graham Nash's *This Path Tonight* begins on a chord and a pulse begins to tick underneath. There is another chord and the pulse persists. The vocal begins with a question, asked twice. Chords chime twice and drums begin their march. The verse is conversational, underscoring a song that addresses a quest, a self-reflection, the heart and mind of someone on a journey. It signals what one reviewer called "a more intense type of trip" than "Marrakesh Express"[15] (Jim Allen, NPR, April 7, 2016). The lyric is filled with questions and the path is fiery. We push forward, return to the chorus, which asks where we're going, and then the music heads out again in its drum and bass march. The trek is Dantesque, one of seeking the light of meaning. The unmistakably passionate artist, Graham Nash, is here walking the talk, taking the path less traveled. His marriage of 38 years has concluded

---

in divorce. He is soon to sever ties with longtime musical partner David Crosby over conflict that has arisen between them. Yet, this is also a continuation, it seems, of the journey and quest motif that appeared in Nash's first album *Songs for Beginners*. Only now, there seems to be more depth, maturity, and the vital intensity of a song like "Chicago" has condensed, focused, and faced more of the darkness. A *Rolling Stone* review (March 23, 2016) is subtitled: "A veteran sings as he ponders his road's end." Will Hermes characterizes Graham Nash as "one of the 60s great can-do optimists" and calls this record "haunted."[16] Yet, it is possible to disagree with the reviewer's implication that that the dark songs suggest anything like resignation. Rather, there is yet optimism here, even in the face of a universe's apparent Darwinian indifference. The recording may indeed sound "haunted," as this reviewer says, but it never gives up. There is a decidedly forward thrust and movement in the music. It is not merely nostalgic for "Golden Days." It embodies a sense of transition and a claim to freedom and direction. Even as the pensive masterpiece "Back Home" is a tribute to Levon Helm, a threnody for mortality, it is an affirmation of life as the band plays on. There is realization, completion, and dedication as the song rests on its final word: home.

From the opening song, "This Path Tonight," we proceed to a gentle folk-song of intimate spirit, "Myself at Last." We hear a phrase from an acoustic guitar and a reflection upon the past. Again, traveling on the road, there is recollection, wondering at what is gone. People have been "a kind of test" along life's journey. This sounds like a confessional song. He directs an emotion at the universe, seeking answers. A lonesome harmonica provides an instrumental bridge. Someone has come to his rescue, like Dante's Beatrice to the drifting traveler amid the pace of passing life. She is a lifeline, the rescue of a soul. At last, he has found himself.

"Cracks in the City" begins as a ballad with a 3/4 time feel. The word "cracks" repeats with suggestions of the city and "voices." There is a pretty ascending line that follows the word "above." This returns in the chord pattern at the end of the song. There is something transcendent rising above the cracks of the city and the textured chorus descending in "oh." Drums—the soft pulse of tom-toms—take us into "Beneath the Waves" and move into a double-time pattern. A roll of drums and guitar introduces Nash's reference to fifty years before the mast. The nautical metaphor probably has little to do with Richard Henry Dana's novel. Instead, it seems to focus on the waves and vicissitudes of life and hope before things may sink beneath the movement of the sea. The vocals meet on "ah" descending with a drum pattern and a bit of guitar underneath them. "Fire Down Below" begins in an electric blues. It unfolds in step-like motion with a few power chords thrown in as accents before the lyric says the dogs have come announcing that something is coming. The soft pops and pulse of the drums move into a march and Nash's voice rises above. Could there be a prayer here to the unknown God, some eternal force to whom is addressed a request for a personal love? Or, to be a bit less metaphysical, is this addressed to someone who can offer love and rescue him from the fire down below?

When Graham Nash created his first solo recording a listener would flip it over at this point to listen to side two. The MP3 download, CD, or streaming video is continuous. The next song is addressed to someone who is slipping into darkness. The song asks, who is there for you? Can love be worth a try? No more broken hearts are needed. Despite the whispery dark and the cry and tearing apart in the verses, the chorus music lifts to something that sounds almost optimistic. A lot of emotion and concern seems to be packed into the small space of this song.

"Target" brings a clever lyric that seems to be addressed to a new love and expresses a clear direction. This is a romantic troubadour song with strings that sound like a uke or an autoharp at times. This blends into a harmony vocal that might resemble one of the gentler Eagles songs. A harmonica and organ mixed back joins the vocals and strings. Nash moves on to a meditative place recalling songs with soul and provides a moody recollection on golden days with the Hollies or CSN&Y. And where are we now, he asks. "Back Home" follows with a well-structured, haunting and moody composition that pays tribute to the Band's Levon Helm while drawing the larger universal meditation on mortality and cherishing life. No one knows the future, so breathe. There is the connection of life and eternity, of memory and the circle of passing and renewal, a soul's transmigration, and the band plays steadily on.

Following this meditation is another reflection. Who is the popular singer when he steps off the stage? When the encore ends, what is really meaningful? Questions linger. The song again seems self-reflective. Yet, this could be for any performer, or metaphorically, it could represent most anyone if all the world's a stage. And when the last song is sung and heard, the last chapter written and read, what do we find meaningful? What has one given to life, in the encore?

The rhetoric of the sixties found a way into song lyrics and the commitment of performers like Crosby, Stills, Nash, and Young. The sixties could reference the truths that we hold to be self-evident: equality, freedom, peace and justice which are expressed in the Declaration of Independence and the U.S. Constitution. Will there be an encore?

In the early 1970s "[t]he sixties receded into haze and myth," wrote Todd Gitlin. The dream evaporated and "the upheaval was over—as mysteriously as it had appeared."[17] He wrote his book, he said, to reclaim "the actual sixties." That "actual sixties" may be reclaimed in CSN&Y also, in a new setting. If Crosby, Stills, Nash and Young continue to hold that political thinking matters to the fate of American democracy and that there may be yet hope for care and decency, can they be useful? Can they make a new start with a critical spirit? Or, are they better off approaching this separately rather than together? What is the best way for them to remain fiercely independent and true to themselves? Could they consent to joining in a collective effort to address and highlight the issues of humanity that are the order of the day? Rock empowers the affective life. It connects musician and listener in human community. When we look at Crosby, Stills, Nash, and Young we can see that each prickly individualist, each gifted musician, singer, and writer, has given us musical treasure and has had the courage to stand for a truth that he sees and believes. May the music and a passion for justice reconnect this powerful collective voice and enable them to sing! For life is short and the future beckons and the children of the world who are its future surely need to hear their voices. Crosby, Stills, Nash and Young: maybe tonight they will come again. Certainly, they will not fall silent. Not yet. Tonight, their voices will ring out—four together or four alone. They will signal a hope of community and possibility. And listening, we too will be one for each other.

Video and Print Resources

Our access to the work of Crosby, Stills, Nash and Young has been greatly enhanced by the availability of videos and recordings on YouTube. Obviously, to buy their recordings and to attend their concerts is the best path to appreciating and enjoying their music. To read their autobiographies, interviews with them, and commentary about them is also valuable and can provide us with a path to understanding their art. However, videos of interviews provide us a sense of immediacy, or virtual presence, and a glimpse into their thoughts. Performance videos allow us to see and to hear them. This is a sampling:

In summer 2018, YouTube provided Crosby and Nash's "Carry Me" from *Wind on the Water*, "Lay Me Down," "The Last Whale," "Where Will I Be," "Cowboy of Dreams," "Out of the Darkness," a performance at Berkeley in 1975. You could listen to the entire *Wind on the Water* album, if you could put up with the pop-up commercials. Crosby's recent "She's Got to Be Somewhere" was also to be found on YouTube. Crosby was on his way to Lenox, Massachusetts. "Carry Me" had 218,873 views on YouTube. There is the solo voice and the harmony breaks out with high harmony joining on the line that brings us the title. "Lay Me Down" begins with a guitar picked intro and an up-tempo folk music. The song is reflective, pretty, with gentle harmony. "Foolish Man" from *Whistling* is slow and easy, dips into some jazz in a mellow movement. Nash's high harmony comes in along with guitar leads fills. Crosby's vocal becomes bluesy and breaks out. "Southbound Train," a Nash song from the first Nash and Crosby album (1972) is also on YouTube. It begins with a harmonica and moves in 3/4 time as an image of the album cover slowly spins. It is clearly a Nash folk ballad that moves into some nice harmonizing.

You can hear "This Path Tonight" and "Marrakesh Express" performed by Graham Nash at City Winery on September 24, 2013. For Stills, you can find a performance of "Black Queen" (June 16, 2011), "You Can't Catch Me" (1983), "Southern Cross" (1980), "4 and 20" (from 1971) and "Helplessly Hoping" (2014). Stills and Judy Collins appear in clips to promote *Everybody Knows* (Associated Press upload 1:35, CBS.com trailer 2.06). See www.stephenstillsjudycollins.com. A David Crosby recording of "Sell Me a Diamond" appears at https://www.npr.org/2017/08/01/540538554/songs-we-love-david-crosby-sell-me-a-diamond.

David Crosby

Interviews with Crosby abound. You can go back to a radio interview from August 30, 1967. There is an interview with Bob Costas from 1979. There are also interviews online that Crosby did to promote *Stand and Be Counted*, his book and documentary with David Bender. Among the best on Crosby's songwriting is Paul Zollo's interview with Crosby for "Lyrically Speaking" from the Aspen Writers Foundation on April 14, 2015.

One can appreciate the ease with which Zollo proceeds to encourage an investigation of songwriting. Crosby explores the spontaneity of his song "Shadow Captain." He reflects on the hypnogogic state, in which one drifts before sleep. A songwriting goal, Crosby says, is the help the audience to "feel something." He sings a cappella and encourages the audience to sing with him. Then Crosby demonstrates the alternate open tuning and picking pattern for "Déjà Vu." His left hand slides in the direction of the 12th fret for the slow section of the song that includes the word "feel." Zollo comments on the raw emotion and straight out rock of "Almost Cut My Hair," which was recorded live to tape. Crosby tells Zollo and the audience that Stephen Stills built the tracks for Long Time Gone. When Stills and Young "get it right" in their guitar-exchange they are extraordinary. Crosby is coaxed into playing a bit of "Long Time Gone." It looks like this is coming off the fifth fret down to G to F in barre chords. See Stories and Songs from David Crosby, Aspen Times.com (https://archives.org/details/story_and_songs-from-david-crosby).

The Film Archives-Book TV on C-Span with Brian Lamb is a serious interview with David Crosby that promotes *Stand and Be Counted*. Crosby affirms that he has "always been sort of an activist." Crosby's book with Bender took a look at how music artists have responded to issues. A subtitle tells us that this will be "A Revealing History of Our Times Through the Eyes of Artists Who Helped Change Our World." There is no studio audience for this interview, which seems to contribute to the serious tone. Crosby admits to disciplinary problems in school. He addresses psychedelics as "a way" toward insight. However, as of 2000, he recognizes that it does not serve him to take drugs. He does not agree with how drugs are policed in America or the incarceration of drug users for minor drug offenses. The interview appears to force introspection, or recollection, and the difficult days seem to be a bit closer in recent memory. There is some throat clearing—of course that could be a cold. Crosby acknowledges the contribution of Bender to the book. This politically astute friend drew upon transcriptions of conversations. He appeared with Crosby on an interview with Charlie Rose (March 10, 2000) (http://www.charlierose .com/videos). Before the interview with them begins there is a film excerpt that begins with Neil Young singing. Then follows brief interview comments with a who's who of rock luminaries: Melissa Etheridge, Peter Gabriel, Bruce Springsteen, John Mellencamp, Jackson Browne, Bonnie Raitt, Phil Collins, Sting, and Carlos Santana all have something to say. The folk music-activism tradition is represented by Pete Seeger, Harry Belafonte, Arlo Guthrie, and Tracy Chapman. Fragments of performances by Jackson Browne, Tracy Chapman, and U2 are interspersed. In the interview, Crosby speaks of his appreciation for people of courage who stand for their beliefs. He says that the engagement of artists like Eddie Vedder and Michael Stipe suggests that a younger generation of rock performers can pick up the causes of social concern because this "occurs naturally." When asked if this "does any good" Crosby reflects on societal inertia and how it takes time to break through that.

- Crosby's political disagreements with conservative Ted Nugent are featured on YouTube, October 28, 2016.
- "Stories and Songs from David Crosby": NPR Artist Page http:www.npr.org/artists/153968471.
- Several interviews with David Crosby appear online. There is an interview with Crosby at Kent State transcribed by Taylor Pierce: https://BlackSquirrel Radio.com/interview-david-crosby.

- PBS provides the text from an interview on *Frontline*: "The Way the Music Died," www.pbs.org/gbh/pages/frontline/shows/music/interviews/crosby.html.
- "You Hope to Wake People Up": https://www.oregonlive.com/music/index.ssf/2017/04/david_crosby_interview_lighthouse.html.
- Bill Robinson's interview with David Crosby from the *Huffington Post*: "David Crosby: A Certified Anti-War, Folk/Rock Icon" (October 26, 2015). There are some photos of Town Hall and Robinson comments that he experienced an easy conversation and that Crosby was affable and not a curmudgeon at all.
- Spin magazine: www.spin.com/featured/david-crosby-interview-sky-trails, September 28, 2017.
- Crosby's 1970 interview as a member of Crosby, Stills and Nash appears in an article by Ben Fong-Torres in *Rolling Stone*, July 23, 1970. This is available at www.rollingstone.com.
- Crosby's most recent recording is *Here If You Listen*, created in collaboration with Michael League, Michelle Willis, and Becca Stevens.

Other interviews are noted in the text and bibliography.

Stephen Stills

Stephen Stills can be heard speaking from a stage to an audience in an auditorium at the University of Florida in Gainesville. This clip is audio only. Someone introduces him with some biography, reminding the audience that CSN sold 2 million copies of their first record in the first year of its release. Stills has played at many benefits, he says, and he has recently made a contribution to the University of Florida band facility, which is now named for him. This talk by Stills is fairly improvised. He plays his songs and he talks a bit about them and about Florida. Search for Stephen Stills, University of Florida "Lecture."

There is an Australian television interview with Stills and Manassas from 1972. The pace of the interview is slow, with Stills doing the talking. He seems reflective and there an almost pot haze quality to this one. He says that playing at an Australian music festival is a way of opening a new market. When asked if he plans to go back to Crosby and Nash and Young he hesitates. This band he has now has all the tools, including the voices, to make a good sound. Then he concedes that "when the time is right" may CSN&Y will "put it back together."

There is a 1980 interview with Jim Ladd, when Ladd was a deejay in Los Angeles. In the Ladd interview, Part 4, a bearded Stills wearing a football jersey holds a guitar and sings "Southern Cross" with three background vocalists.

Stills is in Paris in 1983 in another video, with Veronique Sansone. One might learn a little bit of French from the subtitles. In one segment, Stills, in jacket and tie, sings a song about Paris.

Stills is with Jeff Baxter to discuss guitars in 1991. There are five parts to this video. Stills holds a D-45 Martin that he says is about sixty years old.

Graham Nash

We can find Nash interviews on YouTube: With KUTX, Austin, "Myself at Last," June 24, 2016. He appears on Sirius XM, March 31, 2018. On YouTube you can find a Graham Nash "On Stage" interview with Nick Forster, interviews from 2016 and 2017, and comments on the Crosby issue from June 21, 2016. There is a clip of Nash singing "This Path Tonight" (1:52) and one of "Myself at Last."

Neil Young

Neil Young interviews on YouTube are also plentiful. Young is the deep, mysterious river, the stream pushing the edges of the land: unpredictable, moving the elements along. That makes Young an intriguing character for interviewers. There is the so-called "Big Interview" with Dan Rather in which Neil Young expresses the intuitive moment of creation as a "cool breeze." It is that point at which the musician becomes the music, or the music simply fills the musician. It is a point where there are no strings for one reaches a "mindless" state of being there. When Rather asks why Young, who is so accomplished, continues to do the music, Young turns the question back on him. They agree that there is a passion they have for doing what they do. It is who each of them is. Rather asks Young about his childhood struggle with polio and tells him of his own experience of rheumatic fever, which he believes might have become something that contributed to his drive.

In a Neil Young interview on *Late Night with David Letterman* (July 2008) the subject is cars and a collaborative project to develop capable, economical vehicle. The utterly serious topic of ecological destruction arises in Young's interviews with the Canadian Broadcasting Company about oil sands development and the dilemma of the Chipewyan First Nation. In one clip on Q-TV Young forcefully objects to the claim that musicians should stay out of politics. He asks: Does that take away from the right to free speech? Haven't I always written about what concerned me? A six-minute video includes comments by Alberta's Energy Minister and a bureaucrat named David Collyer who says that Young has "a lack of understanding." There is voice-over from a CTV reporter. Young asserts that Canada is placing money before integrity. John Bennett, Sierra Club Canada's executive director, supports Neil Young's view and affirms that celebrity can be used toward "good ends." The assertion is made that the development of oil lands is not about supplying Canada but about supplying the Asian market. Young's calling this destruction of the land to Hiroshima is more a metaphor than a comparison, Bennett says. It is, Bennett says, a "slow motion devastation."

Rolling Stone refers to Neil Young's interview with Howard Stern at https://www.rollingstone.com, "12 Things We Learned from Howard Stern Interview with Neil Young."

DVDs

CSNY: *Déjà Vu: A Film by Neil Young* (Bernard Shakey).
CSN: *Daylight Again*, 1983; *The Acoustic Concert*, October 1991; *Box Set*, October 1991; *The DVDs*, October 2004; *Long Time Comin'*, 2005; *Demos*, 2009; *CSN 2012*.
Crosby: *David Crosby from the Front Row Live!*, Philadelphia, April 1989.

Crosby and Nash: *Crosby and Nash in Concert,* October 11, 2011, Palace Theater, Stamford.

Stephen Stills: *Stills Live at Shepherd's Bush, London;* Stills and Manassas Live, December 13, 2005; *Stephen Stills and Manassas Live at Musik-Laden.*

Graham Nash: *Graham Nash,* concert from St. Louis, 2015, includes two UK performances and two interviews, September 2018

Neil Young: His catalog is extensive. Volume I of the Neil Young Archive is available on Blu-ray (10 DVDs, 8 CD set). Projected but yet to be completed are: Volume II, 1972–1982; Volume III, 1980s; Volume IV, 1990s; Volume V, 2000s. There are many DVDs of performances, including *Weld,* with Crazy Horse, 1991; *Live at Massey Hall; Neil Young and Crazy Horse; Neil Young: Heart of Gold* by director Jonathan Demme; Neil Young *Journeys; Journey Through the Past; Hurricane* with Crazy Horse; *Human Highway,* 2016; *Rust Never Sleeps,* 2016; *A Tribute to Neil Young,* MusiCares.

Chronology

1968: Crosby, Stills and Nash meet in Los Angeles area. They sing "You Don't Have to Cry" at Joni Mitchell's house.

1969: *Crosby, Stills and Nash* album. Neil Young joins. Their first concerts are performed at Chicago Auditorium and at Woodstock in August. Young releases *Everybody Knows This Is Nowhere.*

1970: *Déjà Vu.* All four work on solo albums. Young's *After the Gold Rush* appears in September. Stills' first solo album appears in November.

1971: Crosby's *If I Could Only Remember My Name* is released in February. Nash's *Songs for Beginners* appears in May. *Stephen Stills 2* features the songs "Change Partners" and "Marianne." Young begins work on *Harvest*. Crosby and Nash go on an acoustic tour together. The live performance album *4 Way Street* is released.

1972: Young's *Harvest* is released. Two hits, "Heart of Gold" and "Old Man, emerge from the album. Stills joins with Chris Hillman to form Manassas and their album, *Manassas*, charts at #4. The *Graham Nash-David Crosby* album is released. Young and Nash release Young's "War Song."

1973: Young records *Time Fades Away*. His recordings for *Tonight's the Night* are held back. Crosby is involved with a Byrds reunion album. Stills and Manassas release a second album in April.

1974: Nash's *Wild Tales*, his second album, appears in January. A summer tour is arranged by Bill Graham, including stadium performances by Crosby, Stills, Nash and Young. Their attempt at creating an album to be called *Human Highway* brings them to Young's ranch and to Hawaii. However, the album plans fall apart. CSN&Y's *So Far* is a bestselling compilation of their work to date. Young releases *On the Beach*.

1975: Crosby and Nash, signed to ABC Records, create *Wind on the Water*, which goes to #6 on the *Billboard* chart. *Stills Live* and *Stills* are released. Young's *Tonight's the Night* and *Zuma*, with Crazy Horse, are released.

1976: Crosby and Nash record *Whistling Down the Wire*. Stills and Young join forces in the Stills-Young Band and record *Long May You Run*. Stills removes Crosby and Nash vocal tracks. Stills does not want Young's band Crazy Horse on the tour. *Illegal Stills* also appears.

1977: *Crosby-Nash Live*, a concert album, is released. Crosby and Nash have been

Chronology

contributing vocals to recordings by Jackson Browne and James Taylor. *CSN* marks the return of Crosby, Stills and Nash and becomes their bestselling album. Nash's "Just a Song Before I Go" is a soft-rock hit with captivating harmonies. They tour. Young and Crazy Horse record *America Stars 'n Bars.*

1978: Crosby, Stills and Nash again go on tour. They receive Hollywood stars on June 21. Young releases *Comes a Time.*

1979: Young records *Rust Never Sleeps* and releases *Live Rust.*

1980: Nash attempts a recording with Crosby, *Earth and Sky*, but Crosby is in no shape to complete the project. *Earth and Sky* is essentially a Nash record. Young creates the album *Hawks and Doves.* The CSN recording *Replay* appears.

1981: Crosby, Stills and Nash make plans for their *Daylight Again* album. Young creates *Re-ac-tor* with Crazy Horse.

1982: The recording and mixing of tracks for *Daylight Again* is led by Stills and Nash. They insert some Crosby when asked to make a CSN record by the record company. They sweeten the Crosby vocals on his song "Delta" and on "Might as Well Have a Good Time" by Judy Henske and Craig Doerge. The album includes two hits, "Wasted on the Way" by Nash and "Southern Cross" by Stills. "Too Much Love to Hide" by Stills also reaches the charts. CSN attempts to tour. Crosby is arrested on drugs and weapons charges in May 1982. Young records *Trans.*

1983: *Allies* was another effort by Stills and Nash to bring together an album with Crosby. It begins with two studio recordings: "War Games" and Stills and Nash's "Raise a Voice." The rest of the album includes live performances. The Crosby performances of "Shadow Captain" and "For Free" go back to a Houston concert in 1977, when he was strong of voice. Other songs come from a Universal City concert in 1982. Neil Young produces *Everybody's Rockin'.*

1984–1987: These are the missing years for Crosby, Stills, and Nash. There is an appearance at Live Aid in 1985. Stills records *Right by You* (1984). Nash records *Innocent Eyes* (1986). Young records *Old Ways* (1985), *Landing on Water* (1986), and *Life* (1987).

1988: *American Dream* is recorded by Crosby, Stills and Nash with Young. The album reaches #16 on the *Billboard* chart. There is a video of the title song by Young. There is no album tour. Young records *This Note's for You.*

1989: Young records *Freedom.* Crosby records *Oh, Yes I Can.*

1990: *Live It Up* is recorded and released. Young records *Ragged Glory.*

1991: A box set of four CDs featuring Crosby, Stills, Nash and Young is issued. *Stills Alone* is released. Young releases *Weld.*

1992: Young's *Harvest Moon* is released, twenty years after his *Harvest* album

1993: Crosby records *Thousand Roads.*

1994: Crosby, Stills and Nash's *After the Storm* is recorded and released. Young records *Sleeps with Angels.* Woodstock II is a commercialized event. Crosby records *It's All Coming Back to Me Now*, and it is released in December.

1995: Young records *Mirror Ball.*

1996: Young records *Broken Arrow.*

1997: Crosby, Stills, Nash and Young are inducted into the Rock and Roll Hall of Fame.

1998: CPR records their performance at Cuesta College and puts out an album.

1999: Young, who has had considerable solo career success, orchestrates the means to bring together Crosby, Stills and Nash to create *Looking Forward*. The album is released in October on Reprise Records.

2000: Crosby, Stills, Nash and Young go on a well-received concert tour. Young records *Silver and Gold*.

2001: CPR records *Just Like Gravity*.

2002: CSN&Y resume touring and the tour is again financially successful. Nash records *Songs for Survivors*. Young records *Are You Passionate?*

2003: Young records *Greendale*.

2004: *Crosby and Nash*, a double album, is released.

2005: Stills records *Man Alive!* Young records *Prairie Wind*.

2006: The Freedom of Speech tour connects with Young's *Living with War* album, his response to the war in Iraq. There is new material from Crosby and Nash.

2007: Crosby's *Voyage* appears as a career retrospective, including some Byrds performances, solo album cuts, and Crosby, Stills and Nash material. Young records *Chrome Dreams II*.

2008: Crosby, Stills and Nash sing "Teach Your Children" on the *Colbert Report*, with Steve Colbert joining as "Neil" on the Neil Young harmony part.

2009: Nash produces *Reflections*, with recordings from across his career. He works through the Crosby, Stills and Nash tracks not assigned to Atlantic Records or Rhino Records and the result is *Demos*. Crosby, Stills and Nash perform at the Glastonbury Festival in June. Stills produces a live album and *Manassas Pieces*.

2010: The "Songs We Wish We'd Written" album projects falls apart amid tensions between Crosby and producer Rick Rubin. Young records *Le Noise*.

2011: Crosby, Stills and Nash tour. A CD remastering of their first album appears in December.

2012: Young records *Americana*.

2013: The *CSNY 1974* anthology, released on July 8, captures recordings from a summer tour. Crosby, Stills, Nash and Young perform at the Bridge School Benefit on October 27. Also appearing is Nash's *Love*.

2014: Crosby releases *Croz*, his first studio album in twenty years. Crosby comments anger Young.

2015: Crosby, Stills and Nash tour the United States, Canada, Europe, and Japan. They sing at the holiday tree lighting ceremony in Washington, D.C., on December 3. Young records *The Monsanto Years*.

2016: Nash is in conflict with Crosby. Nash divorces from his wife of many years. He completes *This Path Tonight* (April 15 release) and moves to New York City. Crosby's album *Lighthouse*, produced with Michael League, is bright and spare and his voice sounds younger than his years. Young records *Peace Trail*. *Earth* is a live album with Promise of the Real.

2017: Nash remains in conflict with Crosby. There are media reports that CSN&Y dislike the new president, Donald Trump, so much that they would set their differences aside for the higher purpose of protest. Crosby's *Sky Trails* appears on September 29. Stills joins with Judy Collins to record *Everybody Knows*, with its title song by Leonard Cohen. Young releases *Hitchhiker* and records *The Visitor* with Promise of the Real.

2018: Stills tours with Judy Collins. Nash continues on tour in the United States. Upon the release of a career retrospective he begins a tour of Europe. Crosby continues his *Sky Trails* tour. Young releases the film and soundtrack *Paradox*.

2019: The fiftieth anniversary of Woodstock.

Chapter Notes

Introduction

1. Alexander Bloom, *Long Time Gone: Sixties America Then and Now*. Oxford: Oxford University Press, 2001. p. 9.
2. Bloom, p. 7.

Chapter 1

1. Todd Gitlin, *The Sixties: Days of Hope, Days of Rage*. New York: Henry Holt, 2013. xiv.
2. Philip Jenkins, *Decade of Nightmares*. Oxford: Oxford University Press, 2008; Stephen Paul Miller, *The Seventies Now: Culture as Surveillance*. Durham: Duke University Press, 1999. p. 13 ("transition"), p. 16 ("incorporating mores"), pp. 16–18 (we still debate the sixties), p. 19 ("unfinished business"); Alexander Bloom, *Long Time Gone*. p. 4, 7.
3. Brenda Laurel, *Utopian Entrepreneur*. Boston: MIT Press, 2001. p.10; Mark Massa on "Chicago" in *The American Catholic Revolution: How the Sixties Changed the Church Forever*. New York and Oxford: Oxford University Press, 2010. pp. 120–126; Diane Snyder Cowan, *Music Therapy Perspectives* 9, no. 1 (January 1991): 42–45.
4. Lloyd Jansen Review of Don Zimmer, *Four Way Street*. *Library Journal* (February 15, 2004): 128.
5. Graham Nash, *Wild Tales: A Rock and Roll Life*. New York: Crown, 2013. p. 116.
6. Nash, p. 126.
7. Nash, p. 132.
8. Nash, pp. 134–35.
9. Nash, pp. 146–150.
10. David Crosby and Carl Gottlieb, *Long Time Gone: The Autobiography of David Crosby*. Garden City, NY: Doubleday, 1988. pp. 152–53.
11. Crosby and Gottlieb, p.140.
12. Crosby and Gottlieb, p.155
13. Nash, p.113.
14. Michael Lang with Holly George-Warren, *The Road to Woodstock*. New York: HarperCollins, 2009. p. 234.
15. *Ibid.*
16. Lang with George-Warren, p. 235.
17. Pete Fornatale, *Back to the Garden*. New York: Touchstone, 2009. p. 239.
18. Fornatale, p. 240.
19. Fornatale, p. 244.
20. Fornatale, p. 46.
21. Fornatale, p. 245.
22. Thomas Kitts, *John Fogerty: An American Son*. New York and London: Routledge, 2016. pp. 113–14.
23. Nash, p. 173.
24. Nash, p. 203.
25. The lyrics of Robert Hunter were an integral part of the Grateful Dead. See Bob Sarlin, *Turn It Up! (I Can't Hear the Words)*. New York: Simon and Schuster, 1975. Also see "Eyes of the World," on *The Annotated Grateful Dead Lyrics*, A Web Site, Santa Clara, University of California. http://arts.ucsc.edu /GDead/AGDL.

Chapter 2

1. David Crosby and Robert Gottlieb, *Long Time Gone.* p. 164.

2. Andy Greene, "Track by Track: Crosby, Stills, and Nash on Their Self-Titled Debut, *Rolling Stone*, August 18, 2008.

3. *Ibid.*

4. C. Michael Bailey, "Crosby, Stills, Nash, and Young: Four Way Street," *All About Jazz*, September 10, 2004.

5. Neil Young's *Harvest* was reviewed in *Rolling Stone* by John Mendelssohn on March 30, 1972.

6. Paul Zollo, pp. 358–59. See Paul Zollo, *Songwriters on Songwriting*, Da Capo Press, 2003: Neil Young 351–359, Graham Nash 361–370, David Crosby 371–383. We learn from the Young interview that "Comes a Time" was "fun to make."

7. *Mirror Ball* was Neil Young's twenty-first album and was released June 27, 1995 on Reprise Records.

8. Peter Glenn, *The Calgary Herald*, January 18, 2014.

9. Tom Kershaw, "Religion and the Political Views of Neil Young," *The Hollowverse*, www.hollowverse.com, September 2, 2012.

10. Sharks lurked in the waters to rob The Turtles blind. By 1970, the first phase of the Turtles' musical life was over. Mark Volman and Howard Kaylan moved on to another creative phase of work with Frank Zappa into 1971. The Turtles were "Happy Together" in 1967 but not so happy when sound recording rights failed to be honored and they lost deserved royalties. Contract clauses and management issues prohibited their use of their given names. They became Flo and Eddie. They sang with their friend Marc Bolan (T. Rex), most notably on "Get It On (Bang a Gong)" (1971).

11. During the commercial boom of the singer-songwriter from about 1970 to 1975, there were still folk music purists. Folksingers played at coffeehouses. Folk music has appeared on small labels like Rounder, Philo, and Red House.

Chapter 3

1. Anthony Lane, "High Crimes," *The New Yorker*, June 18, 2018. P. 64. This is an essay about the Bill Clinton-James Patterson collaboration *The President Is Missing.*

2. "The 40 Greatest Stoner Albums," *Rolling Stone*, June 7, 2013. Contributions from Jon Dolan, Patrick Doyle, Joe Gross, Will Hermes, Christian Hoard, Michelangelo Matos, Jonathan Ringlen.

3. The vocalists on "Chicago": Rita Coolidge, Yanetta Fields, Shirley Matthews, Clydie King, and Dorothy Morrison.

4. In 1985 Chris Hillman, Herb Pederson, and others joined Dan Fogelberg on his "High Country Snows" tour. This led to the formation of the Desert Rose Band. In 1985 CSN&Y toured and appeared at Live Aid, July 13, 1985. There they performed "Southern Cross," "Suite: Judy Blue Eyes," "Teach Your Children," "Only Love Can Break Your Heart," "Find the Cost of Freedom," and "Daylight Again."

5. Dave Thompson, *Heart of Darkness: James Taylor, Jackson Browne, Cat Stevens and the Unlikely Rise of the Singer-Songwriter*. Montclair, NJ: Backbeat, 2012. P. 253. Jackson Browne's "Rock Me on the Water" was recorded by Johnny Rivers and by Linda Ronstadt, "Jamaica Say You Will" by the Nitty Gritty Dirt Band. Linda Ronstadt was joined for a recording by the musicians who would become the Eagles: Glenn Frey, Bernie Leadon, Randy Meisner, and Don Henley.

6. Anthony DeCurtis, Review of *For Everyman. Rolling Stone*, August 5, 1999.

7. Dan Fogelberg's *Souvenirs*, produced by Joe Walsh, brought the hits "Part of the Plan" and "The Long Way" and catapulted his career. J.D. Souther had recently had a hit single with Souther, Hillman, and Furay. The Eagles released *On the Border*, including "Already Gone" and "Best of My Love." Henley had a relationship that year that may have contributed something to his lyric for "Hotel California."

8. Graham Nash, *Wild Tales*. Pp. 200.
9. Nash, p. 183.
10. Nash, p. 223–24.

Chapter 4

1. Jeremy Varon, M.S. Foley, J. McMillan, "Time Is an Ocean: The Past and Future of the Sixties," *The Sixties* 1. They refer to historian Robert Darnton's phrase that the French Revolution was an argument for "possibility against the givenness of things."
2. David Farber, "Building the Counterculture," *The Sixties* 6 (2013). Elsewhere, USC Professor Alice Echols reflects on neglected constituencies. *Daring to Be Bad: Radical Feminism in America, 1967–1975*; *Scars of Sweet Paradise: The Life and Times of Janis Joplin*.
3. Ninian Smart, *Dimensions of the Sacred: An Anatomy of the World's Beliefs*. Berkeley: University of California Press, 1996.
4. Alan Wolfe, *New Republic*, June 2018. *Le Monde* reported that there were 1,205 demonstrations in France and 63 in West Germany.
5. Peter Braunstein and Michael William Doyle, *Imagine Nation: The American Counterculture of the 1960s and '70s*. New York and London: Routledge, 2002. They divide up the 1960s: The Beatles in 1964 to Nixon's election in 1968 is phase one; 1968 to about 1974 is phase two. At this time cultural liberation movements splintered. They point out their own dilemma in writing about this period. Academics tend to rely upon a reason and logic in argument that the counterculture tended to reject.
6. George Will, *Newsweek*, August 21, 1995.
7. The *Rolling Stone* Interview with Bill Clinton. *Rolling Stone*, September 17, 1992.
8. David Brooks, *The Road to Character*, p. 103. For an overview of the historiography of "the sixties," see Simon Hall, "Framing the American 1960s: A Historiographical Review," *European Journal of American Culture*, February 1, 2012; Irwin Unger with the assistance of Debi Unger, *The Movement: A History of the American New Left, 1959–1972*, 1974; Allen Matusow, *The Unraveling of America: A History of Liberalism in the 1960s*; Todd Gitlin, *The Sixties: Years of Hope, Days of Rage* (1987); James Miller, *Democracy in the Streets: From Port Huron to the Siege of Chicago* (1987). For the conservative movement, see Mary Brennan, *Turning Right in the Sixties: The Conservative Capture of the GOP* (1995), Rick Perlstein, *Before the Storm: Barry Goldwater and the Unmaking of the American Consensus* (2001); Lisa McGirr, *Suburban Warrior: The Origins of the New American Right* (2001).
9. Hannah Arendt, *The Origins of Totalitarianism*. New York: Schocken, 1951. p. 430.
10. Theodore Roszak, *The Cult of Information*. Berkeley: University of California Press, 1986.
11. R. Serge Denisoff. *Youth and Society* 2, no. 1 (September 1, 1970).
12. R. Serge Denisoff. "Protest Songs: Those in the Top Forty and Those of the Streets," *American Quarterly* 22, no. 4 (Winter 1970): 807–823.
13. Thomas Franks has often written on political conservativism in America. Robert C. Cottrell, *Sex, Drugs and Rock 'n' Roll: The Rise of 1960s Counterculture*. Lanham, MD: Rowman and Littlefield, 2015.
14. Crosby, Stills, and Nash were joined by John Sebastian for their performance on Saturday, August 13. Original Woodstock performers included Joe Cocker, Country Joe McDonald, Jorma Kaukonen and Jack Casady, members of Sweetwater, The Band, and Bob Weir of The Grateful Dead. The lineup of bands included Metallica, Nine Inch Nails, Green Day, Red Hot Chili Peppers, Melissa Etheridge, Peter Gabriel, Santana and Bob Dylan.
15. M. Scott Peck, *The Different Drum: Community Making and Peace*. New York: Simon and Schuster, 1987. p. 17.

16. These writers are associated with the Frankfurt School.

17. John Kenneth Galbraith, "Who's Minding the Store?" *New York Times*, op. ed., reprinted in *The Con III Controversy*. Ed. Philip Nobile, New York: Pocket, 1971.

18. Emil Capouya, "The Myth of Ecstatic Commentary," *The Nation* 1971. One might explore how much of rock audience enthusiasm can be related to *en-theos*, that is, to something "spiritual." See Deena Weinstein's references to Mircea Eliade's notion of hierophanies in *Heavy Metal: The Music and Its Culture*. New York: Da Capo, 2000. See also *Finding God in the Devil's Music: Critical Essays on Rock and Religion*, ed. Alex DiBlasi and Robert McParland, Jefferson, NC: McFarland, 2019.

19. Robert Pattison, *The Triumph of Vulgarity: Rock Music in the Mirror of Romanticism*. New York and Oxford: Oxford University Press, 1987. Also see James Rovira, ed. *Rock and Romanticism: Blake, Wordsworth and Rock from Dylan to U2*. Lanham, MD: Lexington, 2016.

20. Charles Fried, *The Con III Controversy*. p. 91.

21. Andrew Greeley, "The Redeeming of America According to Charles Reich." *America* 124 (January 9, 1971): 14–17.

22. Charles Reich, *The Greening of America*. New York: Random House, 1970. A reprint was issued in 2012. Jesse Kornbluth reflected on its current relevance in *The Huffington Post*, March 26, 2012, www.huffingtonpost.com.

23. Reich, *The Greening of America*. p.75.

24. Michael Novak, "No New Spring in America," in *The Con III Controversy*. p. 119.

25. Anselm Adams, *The Con III Controversy*.

Chapter 5

1. Crosby and Gottlieb, p. 265.
2. Crosby and Gottlieb, p. 232.
3. Nash, p. 236.
4. Crosby and Gottlieb, p. 310.

5. Crosby and Gottlieb, p. 313.
6. Crosby and Gottlieb, p. 266.
7. The album includes Stills' songs "First Things First," "Love the One You're With," and "Change Partners," on which Jerry Garcia plays pedal steel and Fred Neil and Henry Diltz sing background vocals; "So Far," "To the Last Whale" on which James Taylor plays guitar; "Critical Mass" by Crosby; "Wind on the Water" by Nash. Stills edited "Carry On," getting rid of the "Questions" tag and putting in a new lead guitar part. Cass Elliott sings background vocals on "Pre-Road Downs."
8. Crosby and Gottlieb, p. 374.
9. Crosby and Gottlieb, p. 354.
10. Crosby and Gottlieb, p. 431.
11. Crosby and Gottlieb, p. 338.
12. Crosby and Gottlieb, p. 385.
13. Nash, p. 302.
14. Nash, p. 308.
15. Anthony DeCurtis, Review of *American Dream*. *Rolling Stone*, January 12, 1989.

Chapter 6

1. David Dalton, "Altamont: An Eyewitness Account," p. 279.
2. Pierre Nora, *Realms of Memory*, i–iv.
3. Raymond Williams, *Preface to Film*. London: Drama Film, 1954. See also reprint in *Drama in Performance*. Open University, 1991.
4. Nora, *Realms of Memory*, v–vi, 1–3.
5. Dominick La Capra, *Rethinking*, p. 80.
6. Nora, *Realms of Memory*, p. 5.
7. Nora, *Realms of Memory*, p. 7.
8. La Capra, *Rethinking*, p. 65.
9. Nash, p. 177.
10. Robert Christgau, "The Rolling Stones Can't Get No Satisfaction," *Newsday*, July 23, 1972. p. 12.
11. Dave Marsh, p.15.
12. Burks, *Rolling Stone*, February 7, 1970.
13. Christgau.
14. Those "mass mediated fantasies"

promoted sales of recordings. Re-issued albums and compilations supplement the Rolling Stones' ongoing creativity and studio recordings. In 2009, *Time* magazine reported: "In May, Universal will begin reissuing the Rolling Stones' 14 most recent albums... Most reissues are by acts with rabid fan bases... that have both cash and nostalgia in abundance." Josh Tyrangiel, "Old Masters, New Income," *Time* 173, no. 16 (April 27, 2009): 53.

15. Norma Coates, pp. 59–60. Some estimates place Altamont attendance at about 260,000, others at 300,000.

16. Coates, p. 64. The term "twin evil sister" was used by Norma Coates in her essay "If Anything, Blame Woodstock: The Rolling Stones, Altamont, December 6, 1969." In *Performance and Popular Music.* Ed. Ian Inglis, Aldershot: Ashgate, 2006. Norma Coates repeats the "twin evil sister" phrase to argue that Woodstock was not more ideal than Altamont and that the vision of a rock culture in *Rolling Stone* magazine was "blind to the practical realities" (59). Anthony Scaduto claims that the only time the crowd quieted was during the country set of the Flying Burrito Brothers. *Mick Jagger, Everybody's Lucifer.* New York: Berkeley, 1975.

17. Brown, p. 85.

18. Booth, p. 373.

19. Coates, pp. 59–60.

20. Rick Scully, *Canberry Times*, December 5, 2009. p. 2.

21. Quoted in Scaduto and Norman, p. 332, Booth pp. 358–59.

22. Coates, p. 59.

23. Cavallo, p. 4.

24. Cavallo, p. 252.

25. Daniel Bell, *The Cultural Contradictions of Capitalism.* pp. 87–88.

26. Brillenburg Wurth, p. 26.

27. Booth, p. 356.

28. Booth, p.354.

29. Booth, 356–358.

30. Philip Norman, p. 333.

31. Norman, p. 327.

32. Norman, p. 332.

33. Norman, p. 354.

34. Norman, p. 333.

35. Norman, p. 358.

36. Norman, p. 355.

37. Norman, p. 359.

38. Norman, p. 359–360.

39. Norman, pp. 324–339.

40. Robert Bellah, p. 150.

41. Dominick Cavallo, p. 2.

42. Simon Frith, p. 222.

43. Edmund Burke, *Enquiry into the Origins of Our Ideas of the Sublime and Beautiful,* pp. 75–76.

44. *Ibid.*

45. Quoted in Brillenburg Wurth, pp. 80–81.

46. Mark Rose, p. 166.

47. Antonio Damasio, p. 43. Damasio expresses the hope that in the exploration of social emotions "the cognitive and neurobiological investigation of emotions and feelings can join forces with, for example, anthropology and evolutionary psychology." p. 169.

48. Damasio, p. 173.

49. Damasio, p. 174. Damasio uses the term "conatus," from the philosopher Baruch Spinoza, to describe our striving for self-preservation and to enhance human vitality. He asserts that it is important for us to know how emotions and feelings work and how this "makes a difference to the governance of social life" (p. 268). We have feelings of empathy, "our emotive sympathy with the other" (p. 270). Consciousness allows for anguish and memory. Disruption of the homeostatic state because of suffering brings this down and we may seek to correct the balance, or "to find compensatory strategies" (pp. 269–70).

50. Damasio, p. 120.

51. Damasio, p. 124, pp.131–32.

52. George Herbert Mead, pp. 180, 253–54.

53. Richard Wagner, *The Art-Work of the Future and Other Works.* Lincoln: University of Nebraska Press, p. 71.

54. Brillenburg Wurth, p. 80.

55. Robert Pattison, p. 65.

56. Norma Coates, p. 69.

57. David Crosby and Carl Gottlieb, *Since Then: How I Survived Everything and Lived to Tell About It.* New York: Berkeley/Penguin, 2006. p. 16.

58. Crosby and Gottlieb, *Since Then,* p. 144.

59. Crosby and Gottlieb, *Since Then,* pp. 94–95.

Chapter 7

1. John Einarson and Richie Furay, *For What It's Worth.* Lanham, MD: Taylor Trade, 2004. p. 126.

2. The Chicago Eight were Abbie Hoffman, Jerry Rubin, Rennie Davis, Tom Hayden, Dave Dellinger, Bobby Seale, John Froines, and Lee Weiner. Froines and Weiner were penalized for intent to riot.

3. R. Serge Denisoff explored the record industry in *Solid Gold* and in *Tarnished Gold,* in which he recognized some decline in its business "since 1979." He recites the story that a disc jockey in Boston played America, thinking it was Crosby, Stills, and Nash and "Horse with No Name" was then on its way to becoming a hit. See *Tarnished Gold,* Transaction, 1986. p. 39. America in the 1970s was Gerry Beckley, Dewey Bunnell, and Dan Peek. Willie Leacox played drums. Michael Woods was brought in on guitar in 1977. Peek left the band and turned toward contemporary Christian music.

4. Dylan, *Chronicles,* p. 120.

5. Dylan, *Chronicles,* p. 122.

6. Dylan, *Chronicles,* p. 147.

7. Dylan, *Chronicles,* p. 149.

8. Dylan, *Chronicles,* pp. 150–51.

9. Nash, p. 321.

10. *Ibid.*

11. Crosby and Gottlieb, *Since Then,* p. 54.

12. Crosby and Gottlieb, *Since Then,* p. 53.

13. Nash, p. 321.

14. Pete Seeger was man who walked the talk and did so in many ways. As we walked across a field following one festival day in June, I saw a man picking up litter from the lawn and said hello to him. It was Pete Seeger.

15. Nash, p. 171.

16. Nash, p. 176.

17. John Farrell, *Richard Nixon: A Life,* p. 404.

18. Hedrick Smith, *The New Russians,* p. 652.

19. Nash, p. 653.

20. Nash, p. 324.

21. Nash, pp. 325–26.

22. Nash, p. 328. The word "artist" is tossed around glibly in pop music. Everybody is an artist. That may be true, but not everyone is Michelangelo. It takes a lifetime to be an artist.

23. Nash, p. 335.

24. Some of the less politically inclined listeners, like one of my own friends who enjoys their music, said of Crosby, "I wish he would just shut up and sing."

25. Wayne Bledsoe, "Graham Nash on Life, Nixon, Trump and the Everly Brothers," Interview with Graham Nash, *Knoxville News Sentinel/USA Today,* September 12, 2017.

26. David Crosby and David Bender, *Stand Up and Be Counted* interview on "Speaking Freely," 2000.

27. Melissa Newman, "Crosby, Stills, Nash and Young Exercise Their Freedom," The Beat, *Billboard* 118, no. 22 (June 3, 2006): 57.

28. Steve Baltin, "Crosby, Stills, Nash and Young Could Reunite Because They Hate Trump More Than They Hate Each Other," *Variety,* April 20, 2017, https://www.variety.com/music/crosby-stills-nash-young-reunion-trump/12023913.

29. Sean Kaye, "Rockin' in the Free World." See Crosby's comments: p. 222 ("a lost art"), p. 116 ("it's who I am"), p. 16 (Graham Nash's comment: "songs need a reason to exist"), Crosby's comments p. 51 ("not a democracy"), p. 222 ("politics of fear"). Crosby and Nash are quoted extensively in Sean Kaye's *Rockin' in the Free World* (2017). He interviewed Crosby in June 2014. See

their definition of peace and concern for people affected by war, p. 113.

30. James Davison Hunter, *Culture Wars: The Struggle to Define America*. New York: Basic, 1991. p. 54.

31. Alan Wolfe, *One Nation After All*. New York: Viking, 1998.

32. Jeff Slate, interview with David Crosby. "Riffin' with the Croz," *Rock Cellar*, January 12, 2017.

33. Eric Alterman, interview with Graham Nash, *The Nation*, November 14, 2014.

34. Chris Varias, "Donald Trump Could Inspire Crosby, Stills, Nash and Young Reunion," *Cincinnati Enquirer*, March 9, 2018.

35. Steve Baltin, "Graham Nash on One of the Strangest Presidential Elections Yet, Supporting Sanders and Donald Trump Playing Upon Fears," January 22, 2016. Also see, "Crosby, Stills, Nash and Young Could Reunite." *Variety*, April 20, 2017.

Chapter 8

1. Paul Zollo, *Songwriters on Songwriting*. New York: Da Capo Press, 2003. pp. 358–59. *Songwriters on Songwriting* includes interviews with Neil Young (pp. 351–359), Graham Nash (pp. 361–370), David Crosby (pp. 371–383).

2. Paul Bond, "David Crosby on Donald Trump, New Songs, and Possible CSN&Y Reunion," *Hollywood Reporter*, February 2, 2018. In this interview David Crosby comments on the song he and James Raymond wrote for the independent film *Little Pink House*. In *Long Time Gone*, Carl Gottlieb refers to David Crosby as an "instinctive musician," p. 269. An example of this is "Almost Cut My Hair," which was recorded live.

3. Drugs may have contributed to the shifting of perspective for CSN&Y but it is debatable whether the drugs ever truly enhanced their creativity. The ability to make music and a capacity for openness must be there prior to any pharmacological input.

4. "Lyrically Speaking" interview. For the "Lyrically Speaking" interview, see You Tube.

5. The similarity to Steely Dan is evident in the instrumentation and jazz movement of this song.

6. Crosby did not have the advantage of seeing the July 2, 2018, cover of *The New Yorker* before he wrote this song. But he's obviously seen enough to spark some annoyance and disgust. On the eve of the Fourth of July, readers could see a cover illustration in which immigrant children, refugees facing deportation, separated from parents and held in camps, are hiding, tucked away in the skirts of the Statue of Liberty.

7. Morgan Troper, "Sky Trails Review," *Paste*, September 29, 2017.

8. Jim Allen, "*Sky Trails* Review," NPR, September 21, 2017.

9. *Ibid.* This song and this album recalls Joni Mitchell's jazz phase to the NPR reviewer, but credit is due not only to Mitchell's *Blue* and beyond but to Crosby himself for absorbing and exploring jazz sweetness a great deal himself.

10. Richard Gehr, "David Crosby, A Late Career Marvel Embraces His Steely Dan Side," *Rolling Stone*, October 27, 2017.

11. Jeff Slate, "David Crosby Thinks America Can't Be Wiped Out by One Bad President." *Quartzy*, November 22, 2017.

12. After a Boston Winery show the Crosby *Sky Trails* tour would next go to Florida. Some of Crosby's family lives in Florida, a daughter and two grandchildren. That provided the occasion for this interview with David Crosby by Piper Castillo, *Tampa Bay Times*, November 2017.

13. Zollo, *Songwriters on Songwriting*, p. 369.

14. "Graham Nash on Trump, Clinton, the Beatles and More," Graham Nash interview, *The Journal of Roots Music: No Depression*.

15. Jim Allen, "*This Path Tonight* Review," NPR, April 7, 2016.

16. Will Hermes, "*This Path Tonight* Review," *Rolling Stone*, March 23, 2016.

17. Gitlin, p. 3.

Bibliography

ABC Radio. "Graham Nash Says He's Not Talking with David Crosby." March 20, 2018.

Allen, Jim. Review of *Sky Trails*. NPR. September 21, 2017.

_____. Review of *This Path Tonight*. NPR. April 7, 2016.

Alterman, Eric. "More Wild Tales: An Interview with Graham Nash." *The Nation*, November 14, 2014.

Altschuler, Glenn C. *All Shook Up: How Rock' n' Roll Changed America*. Oxford and New York: Oxford University Press, 2004.

Anderson, Terry. *The Movement and the Sixties: From Greensboro to Wounded Knee*. New York and Oxford: Oxford University Press, 1995.

Aristotle. *Nicomachean Ethics*. Trans. W.D. Ross. New York: Macmillan, 1972.

Bailey, C. Michael. "Crosby, Stills, Nash and Young: Four Way Street." *All About Jazz*, September 10, 2004.

Baltin, Steve. "Crosby, Stills, and Nash Could Reunite Because They Hate Trump More Than Each Other." *Variety*, April 20, 2017.

_____. "Graham Nash on the Strangest Presidential Election Yet: Supporting Sanders and Donald Trump Playing Upon Fears." *Billboard*, January 22, 2016.

_____. "Stephen Stills Has a Message to Deliver to Donald Trump." *Forbes*, November 3, 2016.

Bangs, Lester, Rony Brown, John Burks, Sammy Egan, Michael Goodwin, Geoffrey Link, Greil Marcus, John Morthland, Eugene Schonfield, Patrick Thomas and Langdon Winner. "The Rolling Stones Disaster at Altamont: Let It Bleed." *Rolling Stone*, January 21, 1970.

Bell, Daniel. *The Cultural Contradictions of Capitalism*. New York: Basic, 1976.

Bellah, Robert, et al. *Habits of the Heart: Individualism and Commitment in American Life*. New York: Harper Perennial, 1985.

Bloom, Allan. *The Closing of the American Mind*. New York: Simon & Schuster, 1987.

Bond, Paul. "David Crosby on Trump, New Songs, and a Possible Crosby, Stills, Nash and Young Reunion." *Hollywood Reporter*, February 2, 2018.

Booth, Stanley. *Dance with the Devil: The Rolling Stones and Their Times*. New York: Random House, 1984.

Bothmer, Bernard von. *Framing the Sixties: The Uses and Abuses of a Decade from Ronald Reagan to George W. Bush*. Amherst and Boston: University of Massachusetts Press, 2010.

Bibliography

Bream, Jon. "Graham Nash Dishes Ahead of Minneapolis Show: I'm Not Talking to David Crosby and Don't Want to." *Minneapolis Star Tribune*, March 19, 2018.

_____. "Without Crosby and Stills, Nash Sparks Wonderful Nostalgia," *Minneapolis Star Tribune*, March 19, 2018.

Brennan, Mary. *Turning Right in the Sixties: The Conservative Capture of the GOP.* 1995. Reprint, Chapel Hill: University of North Carolina Press, 2007.

Brillenberg Wurth, Kiene. *Musically Sublime: Indeterminacy, Infinity, Irresolvability.* New York: Fordham University Press, 2012; Oxford: Oxford University Press, 2012.

Brown, Donald. *Bob Dylan.* Lanham, MD: Tempo/Scarecrow, 2014.

Browne, David. "CSNY 1974." *Rolling Stone*, July 8, 2014.

_____. "Election 2016: A Musical Guide." *Rolling Stone* 1257 (March 24, 2016).

_____. *Fire and Rain: The Beatles, Simon and Garfunkel, James Taylor, CSNY and the Lost Story of 1970.* New York: Da Capo, 2011.

_____. "Graham Nash Talks Life After Divorce, CSNY's Future." *Rolling Stone*, August 30, 2016.

Burke, Edmund. *Enquiry into the Origins of the Sublime and Beautiful,* section XVII, 7–76. London: Dodsley, 1767. London: Routledge Kegan Paul, and New York: Columbia University Press, 1958.

Burks, John. "Rock and Roll's Worst Day." *Rolling Stone* 51 (February 7, 1970).

Buskin, Richard. "Crosby, Stills, and Nash, Suite: Judy Blue Eyes, Classic Tracks." Sound on Sound, www.soundonsound.com/people/crosby-stills-nash, August 2010.

Castillo, Piper. "What's David Crosby Reading?" *Tampa Bay Times*, November 24, 2017.

Caulfield, Keith. "CSN&Y, Oh, My," *Billboard* 126, no. 23 (July 26, 2014):73.

Cavallo, Dominick. *A Fiction of the Past: The Sixties in American History.* New York: St. Martin's, 1989.

Christgau, Robert. "The Rolling Stones." In *The Rolling Stone History of Rock and Roll.* New York: Random House, 1980.

_____. "The Rolling Stones: Can't Get No Satisfaction." *Newsday*, July 23, 1972. Reprinted in Robert Christgau, *Any Old Way You Choose It: Rock and Other Pop Music, 1967–1973.* New York: Penguin, 1973; rpt. New York: Cooper Square Press, 2000. Also at https://www.robertchristgau.com/xg/bk-aow/altamont.php.

Coates, Norma. "If Anything, Blame Woodstock: The Rolling Stones, Altamont-December 6, 1969." In *Performance and Popular Music,* ed. Ian Inglis. Aldershot: Ashgate, 2006.

Cotrell, Robert C. *Sex, Drugs, and Rock 'n' Roll: The Rise of America's 1960s Counterculture.* Lanham, MD: Rowman and Littlefield, 2015.

Cristafulli, Chris, and Hendrickson, Matt. "Déjà vu All Over Again: By the Time They Get to Woodstock in 1994." *Los Angeles Times*, July 24, 1994.

Crosby, David, and Carl Gottlieb. *Long Time Gone: The Autobiography of David Crosby.* Garden City, NY: Doubleday, 1988.

_____. *Since Then: How I Survived Everything and Lived to Tell About It.* New York: Berkeley/Penguin, 2006.

Crosby, David, and David Bender. *Stand and Be Counted: Making Music, Making History.* San Francisco: Harper, 2000.

Bibliography

Curry, David. "Deadly Day for the Rolling Stones." *The Canberry Times*, December 5, 2009.

Dalton, David. "Altamont: An Eyewitness Account." In *The Sound and the Fury: A Rock's Back Pages Reader, 40 Years of Classic Journalism,* ed. Barney Hoskins and Mark Pringle, 271–288. London and New York: Bloomsbury, 1999.

Damasio, Antonio. *The Feeling of What Happens: Body and Emotion in the Making of Consciousness.* New York: Harcourt, 1999.

_____. *Looking for Spinoza: Joy, Sorrow, and the Feeling Brain.* New York: Harcourt, 2003.

Denisoff, R. Serge. "Protest Songs: Those of the Top Forty and Those of the Streets." *American Quarterly* 22, no. 4 (Winter 1970): 807–823.

Denisoff, R. Serge, and Jans Lund. "The Folksong Revival and the Counterculture." *Journal of American Folklore* 84, no. 334 (October-December 1971): 344–405.

Denisoff, R. Serge, and Mark H. Levine. "Generations and Counter-Culture." *Youth and Society* 2, no. 1 (September 1, 1970).

Deriso, Nick. "David Crosby Discusses the Origin of His Feud with Graham Nash.[qm] ultimateclassicrock.com/david-crosby-graham-nash-origins-feud.

Dolan, Jon, Patrick Doyle, et al. "Greatest Stoner Albums." *Rolling Stone*, June 7, 2013.

Durkheim, Emile. *Division of Labor and Society.* 1893. New York: Free, 1997.

Dylan, Bob. *Chronicles,* Volume 1. New York: Simon & Schuster, 2004.

Echols, Alice. *Scars of Sweet Paradise: The Life and Times of Janis Joplin.* New York: Henry Holt/Metropolitan, 2000.

Eder, Bruce. "Crosby, Stills, Nash, and Young." In *Music in American Life: An Encyclopedia of the Songs, Styles, Stars and Stories That Shaped Our Culture,* ed. Jacqueline Edmonson. Santa Barbara, CA: Greenwood, 2013.

Einarson, John, and Richie Furay. *For What It's Worth.* Lanham, MD: Taylor Trade, 2016.

Epstein, Jonathon S., ed. *Adolescents and Their Music: If It's Too Loud, You're Too Old.* New York: Garland, 1994.

Farber, David. *The Age of Great Dreams: America and the 1960s.* Farrar, Straus, Giroux, 1994.

_____. "Building the Counterculture." *The Sixties,* vol. 6, 2013.

_____. *Chicago '68.* Chicago: University of Chicago Press, 1994.

_____. *The Sixties: From Memory to History.* 1994. Reprint, Chapel Hill: University of North Carolina Press, 2012.

Farrell, John. *Richard Nixon: A Life.* Garden City, NY: Doubleday, 2017.

Fitzpatrick, Eileen. "Crosby Stills Nash and Young Sued by Former Drummer." *Billboard* vol. 108 (May 18, 1996).

Fornatale, Pete. *Back to the Garden.* New York: Touchstone, 2009.

Frank, Thomas. *The Conquest of Cool: Business Culture, Counterculture, and the Rise of Hip.* Chicago: University of Chicago Press, 1997.

Fricke, David. "Crosby, Stills, Nash and Young." *Rolling Stone* no. 838 (April 13, 2000): 92.

Frith, Simon. *Sound Effects: Youth, Leisure and the Politics of Rock and Roll.* New York: Pantheon, 1987.

Bibliography

Gallo, Phil. "5 Things Graham Nash Wants You to Know About CSN&Y's New Live Album." *Billboard*, July 2, 2014, 15.

Gehr, Richard. "David Crosby, a Late Career Marvel, Embraces His Steely Dan Side." *Rolling Stone*, October 27, 2017.

Genzlinger, Neil. "The Politics of Song." *The New York Times*, July 25, 2008.

Gimme Shelter. Dir. Albert Maysles and David Maysles. Maysles Films, December 1970.

Gitlin, Todd. *Media Unlimited: How the Torrent of Images and Sounds Overwhelms Our Lives.* New York: Henry Holt/Metropolitan, 2002.

_____. *The Sixties: Days of Hope, Days of Rage.* New York: Henry Holt, 2013.

Gleason, Ralph J. "Aquarius Wept." *Esquire*, August 1970.

Glenn, Peter. "10 Political Notes." *Calgary Herald*, January 18, 2014.

Goldberg, M., and R. Duke. "Ticket Rip-Off." *Rolling Stone*, November 1, 1990.

Goodman, Fred. *Rolling Stone* no. 888 (January 31, 2002): 22.

Gray, Patrick. "Rock as a Chaos Ritual Model." *Popular Music and Society* 2, no. 7 (1980): 75–83.

Greene, Andy. "CSN&Y." *Rolling Stone* no. 1115 (October 14, 2010): 99.

_____. "David Crosby Carries On at 72." *Rolling Stone*, September 12, 2013, 26.

_____. "Inside CSN&Y's Doom Tour." *Rolling Stone*, July 3, 2014, 26–28.

_____. "Track by Track: Crosby, Stills and Nash on Their Self-Titled Debut." The Beat, *Rolling Stone*, August 18, 2008.

Guarino, Mark. "David Crosby: America Is No Longer a Democracy." *The Guardian*. October 2016.

Harrison, Hank. *The Dead: A Social History of the Haight-Ashbury Experience.* San Francisco: Archives, 1990.

Hebdige, Dick. *Subculture: The Meaning and Style.* London: Methuen, 1978.

Hunter, James Davison. *Culture Wars: The Struggle to Define America.* New York: Basic, 1991.

Interrobang Staff. "Graham Nash Talks About Crosby's Inappropriate Neil Young Comment and the Possibility of a CSN&Y Reunion." www.interrobang.com, October 30, 2014.

Kaye, Lenny. Review of Graham Nash, *Song for Beginners. Rolling Stone*, July 22, 1971.

Kaye, Sean. *How the Rock Revolution Changed America and the World.* Lanham, MD: Rowman and Littlefield, 2017.

Kershaw, Tom. "The Religious and Political Views of Neil Young." The Hollowverse, www.hollowverse.com, September 2, 2012.

Kirkpatrick, Rob. "Altamont." *Huffington Post*, December 6, 2009.

Kitts, Thomas M. *John Fogerty: An American Son.* New York and London: Routledge, 2016.

Knopper, Steve. "Rock's New Protest Era." *Rolling Stone*, February 23, 2017.

Kruse, Holly. "Subcultural Identity in Alternative Music Culture." *Popular Music* 12, no. 1 (1993): 34–41.

La Capra, Dominick. *Rethinking Intellectual History: Text, Context, Language.* Ithaca: Cornell University Press, 1983.

_____. *Writing History, Writing Trauma.* Baltimore: Johns Hopkins University Press, 1994.

Bibliography

Lang, Michael, with Holly George-Warren. *The Road to Woodstock.* New York: Harper-Collins, 2009.

Marcuse, Herbert. *An Essay on Liberation.* Boston: Beacon, 1971.

_____. *One Dimensional Man.* London: Routledge, Kegan Paul, 1968. Reprint, Boston: Beacon, 1991.

Marsh, Dave. *Glory Days: Bruce Springsteen in the 1980s.* New York: Pantheon, 1987.

Matusow, Allen. *The Unraveling of America: A History of Liberalism in the 1960s.* New York: Harper, 1987.

McDonough, Jimmy. *Shakey: Neil Young's Biography.* New York: Anchor, 2003.

McGirr, Lisa. *Suburban Warrior: The Origins of the New American Right.* Princeton: Princeton University Press, 2001.

Mead, George Herbert. *The Social Psychology of George Herbert Mead.* Chicago: University of Chicago Press, 1956.

Mendelsohn, John. Review of *Harvest. Rolling Stone.* March 30, 1972.

Michaels, Sean. "Recent Feud Leaves the Future of Crosby, Stills, Nash and Young Uncertain." *The Guardian,* October 14, 2014.

Miller, James. *Democracy in the Streets: From Port Huron to the Siege of Chicago.* Cambridge: Harvard University Press, 1987.

Moraski, Lauren. "Neil Young Chimes in on a Crosby, Stills, Nash and Young Reunion: Could Trump Bring Crosby, Stills, Nash and Young Back Together?" *Huffington Post,* April 3, 2018.

Nash, Graham. *Wild Tales: A Rock and Roll Life.* New York: Crown, 2013.

Newman, Melissa. "Crosby Stills and Nash Exercise Their Freedom." *Billboard* 118, no. 22 (June 3, 2006): 57.

Nora, Pierre, and Lawrence D. Kritzman. *Realms of Memory.* Trans. Arthur Goldhammer. New York: Columbia University Press, 1997.

Norman, Phillip. *Sympathy for the Devil: The Rolling Stones Story.* New York: Simon & Schuster, 1984.

O'Donnell, Lawrence. *Playing with Fire: The 1968 Election and the Transformation of American Politics.* New York: Penguin/Random House, 2018.

Palmer, Robert. *Rock 'n' Roll: An Unruly History.* New York: Harmony, 1998.

"Past, Present and Future: Graham Nash on Making Music." PBS, *Chicago Tonight,* July 27, 2017.

Pattison, Robert. *The Triumph of Vulgarity: Rock Music in the Mirror of Romanticism.* New York and Oxford: Oxford University Press, 1987.

Peck, M. Scott. *The Different Drum: Community Making and Peace.* New York: Simon & Schuster, 1987.

Peddie, Ian. *The Resisting Muse: Popular Music and Social Protest.* Aldershot: Ashgate, 2006.

Perrone, James. "Ohio," 217–220. In *Smash Hits: The 100 Songs That Defined America.* Santa Barbara, CA: Greenwood, 2006.

Plato, *Dialogues.* Book III. 398–403. Trans. Benjamin Jowett. London: Sphere, 1970, 165–171.

Platon, Adelle, and Dan Rys. "Trump Will Force Artists to Stay Woke by Default." *Billboard* 129, no. 1, January 14, 2017.

Bibliography

Powers, Ann. "Carrying on as Stardust Permeates the Garden." *New York Times*, April 5, 2000, E3.

Putnam, Robert D. *Bowling Alone: The Collapse and Revival of American Community*. New York: Simon & Schuster, 2000.

Reich, Charles. *The Greening of America*. New York: Random House, 1970.

Rogan, Taylor. *The Death and Resurrection Show: From Shaman to Superstar*. London: A. Blond, 1985.

Rolling Stones. *Beggar's Banquet*. Decca Records and London Records, 1968.

_____. *Hot Rocks, 1964–1971*. Decca Records and London Records, December 20, 1971.

_____. *Let It Bleed*. Decca Records and London Records, 1969.

_____. *Sticky Fingers*. Decca Records and London Records, 1971.

_____. *Their Satanic Majesties Request*. Decca Records and London Records, 1967.

Rose, Steven. *The Future of the Brain: The Promise and Perils of Tomorrow's Neuroscience*. Oxford and New York: Oxford University Press, 2005.

Ross, Andrew, and Tricia Rose, eds. *Microphone Fiends: Youth Music and Youth Culture*. New York: Routledge, 1994.

Ross, Jane. "Rocker Neil Young, a Canadian, Talks U.S. Presidential Politics." Reuters, May 24, 2016.

Roszak, Theodore. *The Cult of Information: The Folklore of Computers and the True Art of Thinking*. Cambridge: Lutterworth, 1986.

_____. *The Making of the Counterculture: Reflections on the Technocratic Society and Its Youthful Opposition*. 1970. Reprint, Berkeley: University of California, 1995.

_____. *Where the Wasteland Ends*. New York: Bantam-Doubleday, 1972.

Rovira, James, ed. *Rock and Romanticism: Blake, Wordsworth and Rock from Bob Dylan to U2*. Lanham, MD: Lexington, 2015.

Rowland, Marijke. "Graham Nash Rethinks 'Never' for Crosby, Stills, and Nash, Thanks to New Political Climate." www.grahamnash.com.

Sardiello, Robert. "Secular Rituals in Popular Culture: A Case for Grateful Dead Concerts and Deadhead Identity." In *Adolescents and Their Music: If It's Too Loud You're Too Old*, ed. Jonathon S. Epstein, 122–128. New York: Garland, 1994.

Sarlin, Bob. *Turn It Up! (I Can't Hear the Words): The Best of the New Singer-Songwriters*. New York: Simon & Schuster, 1975.

Scaduto, Anthony. *Mick Jagger: Everybody's Lucifer*. New York: Berkeley, 1975.

Scoppa, Bud. "Crosby, Stills and Nash." *Rolling Stone*, May 25, 1972.

_____. "Stills Manassas." *Rolling Stone*, May 25, 1972.

Shaffer, Paul. Interview with Graham Nash. "Graham Nash Wants to Fix His Relationship with David Crosby." Sirius XM, March 31, 2018.

Shelley, Percy Bysshe. "Adonais," in *Romanticism: An Anthology*, ed. Duncan Wu. Hoboken: John Wiley/Blackwell, 2005.

The Sixties: The Years That Shaped a Generation. Dir. David Davis and Stephen Talbot. Herzog Company and Playtone, 2014.

Skanse, Richard. "Crosby, Stills, and Nash and Perfectionist: Neil Young Sends Crosby, Stills, and Nash Back into the Studio." *Rolling Stone* no. 819 (August 19, 1999): 36.

Slate, Jeff. "David Crosby Thinks America Can't Be Wiped Out by One Bad President." *Quartzy Newsletter*, November 22, 2017.

Bibliography

Smart, Ninian. *Dimensions of the Sacred: An Anatomy of the World's Beliefs.* Berkeley: University of California Press, 1996.

Smith, Patti. "Jag-aar of the Jungle." *Creem*, January 1973.

_____. *Just Kids.* New York: Ecco, 2010.

Sophocles, *Antigone. Greek Tragedies*, ed. and trans. David Grene and Richard Lattimer. Chicago: University of Chicago Press, 1987.

Stern, Marlow. "Neil Young Fires Back at His Biggest Troll, Dana Loesch, 'I'm Glad I Got Under Her Skin.'" *The Daily Beast*, March 15, 2018.

Straw, Will. "Systems of Articulation, Logics of Change: Communities and Scenes in Popular Music." *Cultural Studies* 5, no. 3 (October 1991): 368–88.

Thompson, Dave. *Hearts of Darkness: James Taylor, Jackson Browne, Cat Stevens and the Unlikely Rise of the Singer-Songwriter.* Montclair, NJ: Backbeat, 2012.

Troper, Morgan. "*Sky Trails* Review." *Paste*, September 29, 2017.

Turner, Victor. *The Forest of Symbols.* Ithaca: Cornell University Press, 1967.

_____. *The Ritual Process: Structure and Anti-Structure.* Chicago: University of Chicago Press, 1960.

Turner, Victor, and Edith Turner. *Image and Pilgrimage in Christian Culture.* New York: Columbia University Press, 1978.

Tyragiel, Josh. "Old Masters, New Income." *Time* 173, no. 16 (April 27, 2009): 53.

Unger, Irwin, with the assistance of Debi Unger. *The Movement: A History of the American New Left, 1959–1972.* New York: Dodd, Mead, 1974.

USA Today. "Review: Neil Young Is as Political as Ever on Peace Trail." December 8, 2016.

Varias, Chris. "Donald Trump Could Inspire Crosby, Stills, Nash and Young Reunion." *Cincinnati Enquirer*, March 9, 2018.

Varon, Jeremy, M.S. Foley, and J. McMillan. "Time Is an Ocean: The Past and Future of the Sixties." *The Sixties* 1 (2008).

Wadell, Ray. "Stoned Math." *Billboard*, January 26, 2013.

Wagner, Richard. *The Art-Work of the Future and Other Works.* Lincoln: University of Nebraska Press, 1995.

Wasserman, Harvey. "Politics and Transcendence with Crosby Stills and Nash." www.commondreams.org, August 1, 2012.

Weinstein, Deena. *Rock'n America: A Social and Cultural History.* Toronto: University of Toronto Press, 2015.

Wenner, Jann, et al. Interview with Bill Clinton. *Rolling Stone* 639 (September 17, 1992).

Whitesell, Lloyd. *The Music of Joni Mitchell.* New York: Oxford University Press, 2008.

Will, George F. *Newsweek.* August 21, 1995.

Wolfe, Alan. "A Most Violent Year." *The New Republic* 249, no. 6 (June 2018): 46–52.

_____. *One Nation After All.* New York: Viking, 1998.

Yaffe, David. *Reckless Daughter: A Portrait of Joni Mitchell.* New York: Sarah Crichton/Farrar, Straus and Giroux, 2017.

Young, Alex. "David Crosby Mocks Neil Young Over His Donald Trump Comments: Everybody Makes Mistakes." COS News, May 25, 2016.

Young, Neil. *Special Deluxe: A Memoir of Life and Cars.* New York: Blue Rider, 2014.

_____. *Waging Heavy Peace: A Hippie Dream.* New York: Plume, 2013.

Zollo, Paul. *Songwriters on Songwriting.* New York: Da Capo, 2003.

Index

Index

Index

Index

Index